Manufacturing in transition

The manufacturing sector within the global economy is undergoing tremendous change and many industrialized nations have experienced 'deindustrialization'. This edited collection contains contributions by renowned scholars from economics, business, management, organization theory and economic geography in order to address the following questions:

- Does manufacturing matter in the mature economies of the twenty-first century?
- What is the current status of Britain's manufacturing sector within the global economy and what are the chances of manufacturing renewal?
- What impact has foreign direct investment had in the UK?
- What are the key developments in the management and organization of manufacturing operations and supply chains?
- What is the financial impact of adopting Japanese manufacturing methods?

This book provides a timely assessment of the UK's industrial development and makes a major contribution to debates over the UK's industrial strategy and the position of manufacturing within mature industrialized economies.

Manufacturing in transition

Edited by Rick Delbridge and James Lowe

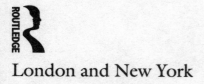

London and New York

First published 1998
by Routledge
11 New Fetter Lane, London EC4P 4EE

Simultaneously published in the USA and Canada
by Routledge
29 West 35th Street, New York, NY 10001

© 1998 Selection and editorial matter Rick Delbridge and James Lowe.
Individual chapters © their authors

Typeset in Galliard by RefineCatch Limited, Bungay, Suffolk
Printed in England by Clays Ltd, St Ives plc

British Library Cataloguing in Publication Data
A catalogue record for this book is available from the British Library

Library of Congress Cataloguing in Publication Data
Manufacturing in transition / edited by Rick Delbridge and James Lowe.
    p.   cm.
    Includes bibliographical references and index.
    1. Manufacturing industries – Great Britain.   I. Delbridge, Rick.
II. Lowe, James.
    HD9731.5.M358   1998
    338.4'767'0941 – dc21   97–51636
                                                            CIP

ISBN 0–415–18271–9 (hbk)
ISBN 0–415–18272–7 (pbk)

For Susan and for Georgina

Contents

Figures

Tables

Contributors

Stephen Ackroyd is interested in studying organizations as institutions that mediate social and economic power, and has applied his analysis to a range of organizations in both the public and private sectors. He is Professor of Organizational Analysis in Cardiff Business School and an organizational consultant.

Mike Bresnen is a Senior Lecturer in Organizational Behaviour at Warwick Business School. He has published extensively on the construction industry and his research interests and recent publications also include work on buyer–supplier relations, leadership and managers and professionals.

Wendy Currie is Professor of Management in the University of Sheffield's School of Management. Her research interests are the management of innovation and technology. She has recently completed a book on IT outsourcing in the United States and Europe.

Rick Delbridge is a Research Fellow at Cardiff Business School. He is the author of *Life on the Line in Contemporary Manufacturing* (Oxford University Press, 1998), an ethnographic account of workplace relations under lean production. His current research interests include high performance manufacturing and the learning factory, and trade union responses to new management techniques.

Carolyn Fowler is a Lecturer in Human Resource Management at Cardiff Business School. Her research interests and recent publications have been in the areas of professionals, interorganizational relations in manufacturing and institutional analysis of industrial sectors in Finland and Britain.

Ian Glover is in the Department of Management and Organization at the University of Stirling. His research interests are management-level work and occupations in the United Kingdom and elsewhere. In the 1970s his work was associated with the Finniston Committee of Inquiry into the Engineering Profession.

Gillian Hunter graduated with an MEng from the University of Cambridge in 1994. She worked briefly as a researcher at the Judge Institute of Management Studies in late 1994 before taking up a career in the Civil Service. She is currently in the Automotive Directorate of the Department of Trade and Industry.

Oswald Jones lectures in Technology Management in the Strategic Management Group at Aston Business School. He has researched and published on the topic of

R&D reputation in the UK pharmaceutical industry. Current research interests include the outsourcing of R&D, technological links between SMEs in mature sectors and HEIs, innovation networks and contemporary developments in labour process theory.

Martin Kenney is a Professor in the Department of Human and Community Development at the University of California, Davis. Most recently, he is the author of *Beyond Mass Production* (1993), a study of the Japanese production system and its transfer to the United States. His research interests include Japanese industry, high technology and the changing nature of work organization in knowledge-based industries.

Michael Kitson is a Fellow in Economics at St Catharine's College, University of Cambridge and the ESRC Centre for Business Research, Cambridge. He has published widely on issues of economic policy.

John Lovering is a Professor in the City and Regional Planning Department at University of Wales, Cardiff. His research interests include regional economic development and the international defence industry.

James Lowe was, until his recent tragic death, an ESRC Management Research Fellow at Cardiff Business School. His research interests included the roles of supervisors and front-line management, organizational learning in the manufacturing sector and different conceptions of business performance.

Jonathan Michie is Professor of Management at Birkbeck College, University of London. He directed the ESRC's 'Contracts and Competition' Programme (1992–7). He has held Visiting Professorships at Queen's University, Belfast and the University of the Witwatersrand, South Africa, and has written or edited seventeen books, mostly on economic policy issues.

Max Munday is a Lecturer in Economics at Cardiff Business School and a member of the Welsh Economy Research Unit. He has research interests in the economics of multinational enterprise, particularly the role of multinational firms in promoting economic development, and the history and development of the Japanese transplant manufacturing sector in the United Kingdom.

Nick Oliver is a Reader in Management Studies at the Judge Institute, University of Cambridge. He is co-author (with Barry Wilkinson) of *The Japanization of British Industry* (1992). His research interests cover the characteristics of high-performing manufacturing facilities, particularly in the automotive industry, and more recently, new product development in the international audio products sector.

Ivor Parry is a Senior Researcher at the Change Management Research Centre at Sheffield Hallam University. Previously, he was a human resource manager in the public sector. His main research interest lies in first-line supervision and leadership in manufacturing.

Michael J. Peel LLB (hons), MBA, CDipAF, Solicitor is currently a Distinguished Senior Research Fellow at Cardiff Business School. His current research focuses on corporate performance evaluation with particular reference to foreign-owned firms and transfer pricing. His previous research, *inter alia*, was concerned with investigating the impact of corporate restructuring and the liquidation/merger alternative.

Andy Pike is a Lecturer and Researcher at the Centre for Urban and Regional Development Studies (CURDS), at the University of Newcastle upon Tyne.

Stephen Procter is a Lecturer in the School of Management and Finance at the University of Nottingham. His research interests include flexibility in manufacturing and the nature of team working.

Nelson Tang lectures in Operations and Information Management at Leicester University Management Centre. His main research interests are concerned with the adoption and implementation of advanced manufacturing technologies as well as the use of operations management techniques for performance improvement.

John Tomaney works in the Centre for Urban and Regional Development Studies at Newcastle University. His main research interest is the development problems of Europe's declining industrial regions. He is co-editor, with Ash Amin, of *Beyond the Myth of European Union* (Routledge, 1995).

Paul Tracey is a doctoral student in the Department of Management and Organization at the University of Stirling where he gained his first degree. His research is concerned with the roles and abilities of engineers and their management-level colleagues in manufacturing and construction.

David Tranfield is Professor of Management and Organization and Director of the Change Management Research Centre at Sheffield Hallam University. His research interests are focused on the development and implementation of strategic change management for performance improvement.

Preface

The contributions to this volume are in large part drawn from the 11th Employment Research Unit Conference on 'Manufacturing matters: organization and employee relations in modern manufacturing', which was held at Cardiff Business School in September 1996. The conference was fortunate in attracting high-quality contributions from researchers from different backgrounds and research traditions. Following the conference a number of further chapters were commissioned and this book thus draws together contributors from a variety of disciplines who share our concern that manufacturing matters and that developments in the UK manufacturing sector should be at the centre of the UK policy debate.

We would like to thank Julie Roberts for her assistance in organizing the conference and the Welsh Development Agency, particularly Penny Mitchell, for their contribution to its success. We would also like to acknowledge the help and support of Stuart Hay at Routledge. In particular, we thank Wendy Brown who converted the various chapters into Routledge house style and generally made problems go away.

Rick Delbridge and James Lowe
Cardiff Business School
October 1997

Readers should be aware of the tragic death of Dr James (Jim) Lowe during the production of this volume. Jim undoubtedly had a bright academic future ahead of him and his research publications were already making an impact on the field to which he had dedicated much of the latter part of his working life. He was a valued colleague who contributed a great deal to the development of Cardiff Business School where he began his career as an undergraduate. Jim was highly respected and well liked by staff and students alike and will be remembered for his diligence, sensitivity, energy and warm good humour.

Roger Mansfield
Director, Cardiff Business School
May 1998

Abbreviations

ACAS	Advisory, Conciliation and Arbitration Service
AMT	advanced manufacturing technology
BAM	British Association of Management
BPR	Business Process Re-engineering
CAAT	Campaign Against Arms Trade
CAD	computer-aided design
CAM	computer-aided manufacturing
CAPM	computer-aided production management
CBI	Confederation of British Industry
CEC	Commission of the European Communities
CIB	computer-integrated business
CIM	Chartered Institute of Marketing
CIM	computer-integrated manufacturing
CIMA	Chartered Institute of Management Accountants
CIM-E	computer-integrated manufacturing-enterprise
CNC	computer numerically controlled
CSEU	Confederation of Shipbuilding and Engineering Unions
CURDS	Centre for Urban and Regional Development Studies
DERA	Defence Evaluation and Research Agency
DESO	Defence Export Services Organization
DNC	direct numerical computer
DTI	Department of Trade and Industry
EEF	Engineering Employers' Federation
EMU	economic and monetary union
ERM	Exchange Rate Mechanism
ESRC	Economic and Social Research Council
EU	European Union
FDI	foreign direct investment
FEER	Fundamental Equilibrium Exchange Rate
FMS	flexible manufacturing system
FOM	foreign-owned manufacturing
GDP	gross domestic product
GNP	gross national product

HRM	Human Resource Management
IEA	Institute of Economic Affairs
IM	Institute of Management
IOD	Institute of Directors
IPD	Institute of Personnel and Development
IPMS	Institution of Professionals, Managers and Specialists
IPPR	Institute of Public Policy Research
JETRO	Japanese External Trade Organization
JIT	just-in-time
JSF	Joint Strike Fighter
LFS	Labour Force Survey
MBA	Master of Business Administration degree
MNC	multinational corporation
MoD	Ministry of Defence
MSF	Manufacturing, Science, Finance (trades union)
NAO	National Audit Office
NC	numerically controlled
NDC	Northern Development Company
NEDO	National Economic Development Office
NTBF	new technology-based firm
OECD	Organization for Economic Cooperation and Development
OST	Office of Science and Technology
PEST	political, economic, social and technological factors
R&D	research and development
RDA	Regional Development Agency
RTC	Regional Technology Centre
SGA	small group activity
SME	small or medium-sized enterprise
SMT	Surface Mount Technology
SPC	statistical process control
SWOT	strengths, weaknesses, opportunities and threats
TFP	total factory productivity
TGWU	Transport and General Workers Union
TUC	Trades Union Congress
WDA	Welsh Development Agency
WDM	World Development Movement
WIRS	Workplace Industrial Relations Survey

Part I

An appraisal of UK manufacturing

1 British manufacturing in perspective[1]

Rick Delbridge and James Lowe

> I do not believe it is possible for Britain to trade its way into the future primarily as a service dominated economy. . . . A robust manufacturing base is a crucial element in a modern competitive economy.
>
> (Tony Blair, quoted in *The Economist*, 15 June 1996)

INTRODUCTION

The premise of this book is that manufacturing matters and that the UK needs a manufacturing sector that is internationally competitive for its long-term economic well-being. There are many who argue that a 'modern economy' will inevitably be services dominated and that deindustrialization is a signal of economic success. On this basis the eighteen years of Conservative government of the UK were extremely successful, presiding as they did over the collapse of manufacturing employment and the disintegration of traditional industries. Our rejoinder is straightforward: the dominant economies have a strong and dynamic manufacturing centre as their basis. The United States, Japan and Germany have manufacturing at the very heart of their economies and newly industrializing economies are enjoying rapid growth founded on their ability to produce and trade manufactured goods. A strong and internationally competitive economy cannot be based upon services alone.

In this book we present a series of empirically grounded accounts of aspects of the UK's manufacturing sector. In Part I, authors provide an overview of the current state of UK manufacturing with regard to the impact of deindustrialization, its causes and effects (Kitson and Michie), the nature of flexibility in British manufacturers (Ackroyd and Procter), and the comparative performance of UK, US and Japanese companies in the UK electronics sector (Munday and Peel). Part II covers recent developments in the management of manufacturing organizations and explores changes with regard to buyer–supplier relations (Bresnen and Fowler), the strategic choices of 'mid-corporate' firms (Jones and Tang), shop-floor reorganization and the introduction of team working (Parry *et al.*), and the impact of adoption of 'Japanese' manufacturing techniques on financial performance (Oliver and Hunter). In Part III, we reflect upon some of the implications current developments may have for manufacturing in the UK in the future. In working towards an outline agenda for renewal, these chapters deal with issues of regional policy development to support economic growth (Pike and Tomaney), the professionalization and wider role of engineers and managers in developing the manufacturing sector (Glover *et al.*), the UK defence industry's relationship with the state and development prospects in the wider European and North American context (Lovering), and the prospects for encouraging and sustaining high-value-added manufacturing activities and the associated research and design investment that will be the defining characteristic of successful manufacturers and economies in the twenty-first century (Delbridge *et al.*).

In this introductory chapter we establish the argument for the central importance of manufacturing, briefly review the debates over the reasons for the UK's long-standing relative decline in manufacturing performance, and establish the themes upon which our various contributors reflect in more depth. Certain issues – such as the role of the state and macroeconomic policy; skill formation, training and education; the local implementation of management tools and techniques; investment in (and management of) innovation – recur and appear fundamental in understanding both our current situation and our future prospects. These imply that some significant reform of the UK's central institutions will be necessary as a precursor to future economic growth and enhanced manufacturing performance. An agenda for these reforms is outlined in a final chapter.

WHY MANUFACTURING MATTERS

That manufacturing matters would now appear to be conventional wisdom in politics, yet the debate about the importance of the manufacturing sector and its influence on the UK's economic performance continues. Some point out that Britain already has a service-dominated economy and that the percentage contribution of manufacturing to the UK's GDP dropped from 35 per cent in 1960 to just 21 per cent in 1995 (*The Economist*, 1996). More generally, the share of manufacturing in total employment has also fallen across all OECD economies as service-sector employment has risen in its place. Thus it has been argued that Mr Blair, and others who share his view, have a misplaced nostalgia for Britain's manufacturing past and that the big opportunity, and challenge for government, lies in improving the efficiency of the non-traded sectors, many of which are services (*The Economist*, 1996).

While the relative decline of manufacturing has been seen as part of a somewhat inevitable historical process, we would argue that this sector remains fundamental to the continuing growth of mature economies. The foundation of global trade is in manufactures and the basis of much service provision is manufactured products; as Kaldor (1972) put it, the manufacturing sector is the 'flywheel of growth' underpinning economic development, international trade and improving living standards. Indeed, 80 per cent of world trade is in manufacturing and, as the head of one of Britain's largest retailers himself confirmed, 'Any serious analysis has to conclude that, to achieve sustained growth, we need a growing and dynamic manufacturing sector as much as a successful services sector' (Sainsbury 1996: 116).

Greenhalgh and Gregory (1997) recently outlined the case for the importance of manufacturing to the continuing prosperity of an advanced economy through the identification of four separate contributions made by the sector: productivity, jobs, technology and trade. In short, their position may be summarized as follows:

1 *Productivity* – The rate of productivity growth is consistently higher in manufacturing than services, and consequently, manufacturing makes a disproportionate contribution to economic growth.
2 *Jobs* – The number of jobs sustained by industry is not reflected in the totals directly employed. Manufacturing requires goods and services provision, and production activity generates output and employment in related sectors; when output declines there are indirect effects as well as direct job losses.
3 *Technology* – The manufacturing sector is the dominant source of innovations. Greenhalgh and Gregory (1997: 104) comment: 'As the domestic manufacturing sector shrinks, the fountain of domestic technology dries up and the capacity to generate innovation dwindles.'
4 *Trade* – Services are much less tradable than manufactures, and Greenhalgh and Gregory conclude that the volume of trade in services that the UK can generate is insufficient to balance the demand for imported manufactured products.

Deindustrialization is not a uniquely British phenomenon, but it has been more severe in the UK than elsewhere and it may reflect negative factors such as a small or uncompetitive manufacturing base as well as positives such as rising incomes and industrial maturity. Analysing the cause and effects of deindustrialization builds on the paper by Greenhalgh and Gregory (1997). In a recent paper entitled 'Does manufacturing matter?', Kitson and Michie (1997) complement the analysis of deindustrialization they give in Chapter 2 of this volume. Their paper makes four points that are central to our concerns (ibid. 71–95):

1 deindustrialization can be a serious problem for advanced industrial economies (and not just for the industrial sector itself);
2 the UK in particular is suffering from the adverse impacts of deindustrialization;
3 the key reason for the relatively poor performance of the UK economy has been underinvestment in manufacturing; and
4 this underinvestment and deindustrialization have been allowed to persist due to the lack of any strong modernizing force within British society, with government policy having been at best ineffectual and at worst positively harmful.

In Chapter 2, Kitson and Michie explain how the service sector is partly dependent upon the size and rate of growth in the manufacturing sector. Deindustrialization can create a spiral of decline which may spread from manufacturing and depress the social and economic environment more generally, and particularly with respect to training and investment. As discussed above, manufacturing is highly integrated in terms of international trade. Manufactured goods represent over 60 per cent of Britain's total exports (Greenhalgh and Gregory 1997), so a deteriorating position in manufacturing trade creates major balance of payments problems and this, in turn, may result in damaging deflationary macroeconomic policies. Such is the experience of the UK during the 1980s.

As Smith (1997: 30) has noted, manufacturing's influence over the rest of the UK economy is such that industry's plight during 1980–1 was big enough to produce the deepest recession since the Second World War:

> The problems of manufacturing ripple out to the rest of the economy in myriad ways: through the threat of declining turnover of service-sector suppliers to Britain's manufacturers; through the knock-on effects on demand of industrial redundancies; through the wealth effects of a weaker stock-market performance as corporate profits take a hit; and through the pressure on policymakers to take further action to slow the economy if falling exports produce a widening of the trade deficit. Compartmentalising the economy, neat though this would be, doesn't usually work.

Debates over the causes of Britain's relative economic decline have been wide-ranging and extensive. In the following section we reflect upon some of the key issues by way of introduction to the rest of the book. In particular, we draw attention to: the issues of finance, investment and the role of the state; the education and skills of Britain's workforce; and the adoption and implementation of new techniques.

EMERGENT THEMES IN BRITAIN'S RELATIVE ECONOMIC DECLINE

Finance, investment and the role of the state

A central theme in discussion of Britain's industrial decline is a historic failure to invest in sufficient quantities and over the long term (Hutton 1995; see also Kennedy 1990; Pollard 1982). The UK's record of investment is certainly relatively poor in comparison to other industrialized countries. Treasury figures show that overall UK investment as a percentage of GDP in the period from 1960 to 1995 was 18 per cent, compared with an OECD average of 21 per cent and the Japanese level of 32 per cent over the same period (*Management Today* 1997). While whether inadequate investment is a cause or a symptom of decline may be a somewhat circular argument, it is clear that basic problems include rigidities in UK capital markets, the policies of postwar government (the so-called crowding out effects of large public sector deficits and stop-go economic policies which caused greater economic volatility and uncertainty) and the misuse of investment funds by private enterprises, which brings correspondingly low returns (Dintenfass 1992; Hutton 1995).

It is increasingly evident that the role of the state is crucial, not directly in corporate decision making, but in providing the context for competitive manufacturing performance. Government is thus central, even if it may not play a 'starring role' in international competition (Porter 1980). Will Hutton (1995) is among those who have identified the state itself as an institutional weakness of the UK. Alford (1997: 330) comments that

> The nature and effectiveness of the relationship between government and industry in Western European countries and Japan is a subject of very active debate, but the evidence still points to the inferior performance of Britain in this regard . . . Government, no less than private enterprise, is open to the charge that it could do better.

In their analysis in Chapter 2, Kitson and Michie conclude that new government policies are required to promote economic stability, particularly in order to reverse the chronic underinvestment in British industry. Currently, they argue, the high levels and volatility of interest rates have discouraged investment and undermined business confidence. This confidence can only be provided by a switch in emphasis in government policy away from deflationary policies, which have led to the increasing severity of recessions and damage the long-run growth potential of the economy, and towards expansionary policies that seek to provide stability. Recent figures from Cambridge Econometrics demonstrate that manufacturing, particularly the major sectors of electronics, motor vehicles and chemicals, are especially vulnerable to recession primarily because of their high sensitivity to the value of sterling (*Management Today* 1997).

Recessionary pressures and macroeconomic instability are fundamentally damaging to investment, and UK government has been widely criticized for failing to establish greater economic stability. Nonetheless, the nature of Britain's financial markets has also been frequently cited as a contributory cause in the UK's poor investment record and relative industrial decline. In a recent analysis, Lee (1996) argues that UK firms are surrounded by financial institutions that have offered capital to industry at prohibitively high cost and demanded unrealistically short payback targets.

Lee extends his critique of the UK financial sector through systematic reference to the alternatives found in more successful economies. Drawing on the work of Albert (1993), Lee recognizes the advantages of the 'Rhine model of capitalism' as practised in Germany in comparison to the 'neo-American model'. The Rhine model is deemed superior since it demonstrates a higher degree of integration between finance and industry and provides a more stable and long-term financial outlook and a better supply of investment capital. Dore (1992) makes some similar points in his comparison of 'Anglo-Saxon' and 'Japanese' forms of capitalism. Handy (1996: 28) has followed this comparison and argues that 'the British can learn something from the German and Japanese models of capitalism where the financiers take second place to the employees and the continuity of the company'.

Along with the relatively low levels of investment, there is concern over the quality of investment decisions and their outcomes in the UK. Output per capital employed was a third higher in Germany than Britain in 1964, more than 50 per cent higher in 1973, and 75 per cent larger in 1979 (Crafts 1988). Over a similar period, the productive return in France and Italy was more than 50 per cent greater than in Britain, and in Canada and the US it was 60 per cent greater (*Midland Bank Review* 1976: 15). This inadequate or uncompetitive return may be explained in a number of ways: through excessive and damaging cost cutting; insufficient investment in new technology and research and development; and via a disproportionate concentration of investment in sectors such as defence, nuclear energy, space and aeronautics which have had limited commercial returns compared with newer and growing industries like computers and electronics (Dintenfass 1992: 47).

As Alford (1997) and Lee (1996) have reflected, analysis inexorably draws attention to the role of the state alongside the purported failings of Britain's managers, workers and financiers. Lee advocates the adoption of structures similar to those in Germany, but recognizes the problems in implementation due to the significant differences with regard to the relative decentralization of political, governance and financial institutions in Germany when compared to the highly centralized state and dominant role of the City of London in the UK. These issues are also discussed by Pike and Tomaney in Chapter 10 where they argue for a greater regional emphasis in government policy.

The contribution of Pike and Tomaney is important as they link macro-economic policy, foreign direct investment (FDI) and manufacturing development with a specific focus at regional level. Their chapter reflects the disparity in economic growth between north and south in Britain, and notes intra-regional differences between rural and urban locales. Pike and Tomaney draw unfavourable comparisons between the UK's mid-corporate sector and Germany's *Mittelstand*, which makes a relatively far greater contribution to value added and employment creation. Moreover, Pike and Tomaney recognize that the availability of finance, crucial in developing the mid-corporate sector, is highly skewed to the south-east. They follow Lee (1996) in calling for greater decentralization of finance and recognizing the need for institutional reform – in this case, the establishment of accountable regional institutions within a framework of national and Europe-wide relations.

The Labour government of Tony Blair has explicitly stated that its goal is to increase the level of investment. For instance Gordon Brown's July 1997 Budget reported that Britain's poor economic performance over the past twenty-five years was, to a large extent, 'a reflection of inadequate levels of investment in the UK economy. The Government wants to increase the quantity of long-term investment' (quoted in *Management Today* 1997). However, it is evident that close attention must be paid to the type and location of investment and that improvements in this will require close scrutiny of various institutions, particularly the role of regional development agencies. Kitson and Michie make it clear that unless the UK can effect an investment strategy that closes the capital stock gap with other major industrialized countries, then our fate will be to compete against newly industrialized countries for low-wage, low-technology production. Their conclusion is that the UK must combine effective investment in education and training with interventionist industrial policies and expansionary macro-economic policies.

This is very much in line with our own conclusions following our research of the nature of Japanese transplant operations in the electronics sector in the UK as reported in Chapter 12. While Japanese plants in Japan are lauded as exemplars of best practice in contemporary manufacturing (Womack *et al.* 1990; Fruin 1997) our evidence shows that their transplants are characterized by relatively lower value-added activities conducted by lower-skilled workers with comparatively poor terms and conditions of employment. Indeed, in electronics the UK transplants are rather more similar to those found in Mexico than their parent plants in Japan. This has led to discussion of 'branch' or 'screwdriver' factories (Williams *et al.* 1992), and Delbridge (1998) has described the UK as 'the *maquiladora* region of Europe'. Our conclusions are that the UK government and its development agencies – who have claimed much credit for attracting foreign investment – must take far greater note of the sort of investment that is attracted and of the necessary manufacturing infrastructure that will be required to support high-value-added, high-technology manufacturing facilities. Without that provision, the UK will not attract the requisite *quality* of investment.

Successive Conservative governments have been marked by attempts to market the UK as the preferred location for overseas investors. Firms have been enticed in part by the relatively low wages and flexible labour available in the UK. Foreign direct investment has been seen not only as a means of creating employment, incomes and trading opportunities, but also as a means of improving the UK's domestic manufacturing performance through technology transfer and increased competitive pressures (Eltis and Fraser 1992). However, the research presented by Munday and Peel in Chapter 4 underscores our case evidence on the UK-based electronics sector with regard to the performance of Japanese investors. While the evidence suggests that Japanese subsidiaries are more productive in terms of sales per employee, on five other measures of performance and profitability they fare worse than UK- and US-owned firms. Most notably, two-fifths of Japanese subsidiaries reported that they were loss-making during the financial year reported. The Japanese electrical and electronic engineering firms in the study were also troubled by relatively poor returns on capital and lower liquidity, and were typically rated as higher credit risks than their UK or US counterparts. Given these findings, Munday and Peel question how far the Japanese transplants may be considered a role model for domestically owned electronics companies.

The attraction of high-quality investment that brings the UK high-value-added activities, promotes growth and development in the supply chain, and provides good, secure, skilled employment, is largely dependent upon the ability of the UK to provide good-quality suppliers, infrastructure and skilled labour. In other words, there is an element of the chicken-and-egg conundrum about the attraction and support of high-quality investment. As we make clear in Chapter 12, the UK will not attract the type of investment that leads to the establishment of high-technology, high-value-added 'learning factories' from which indigenous industry may benefit unless it can provide a workforce educated and trained to the standards expected of workers in that production environment. Britain's failure to address this could lead to UK manufacturing becoming trapped in a 'low skill/ low quality' equilibrium (Finegold and Soskice 1988). Certainly, the breadth and quality of the UK's education and training provision has been a long-standing concern.

Education, training and skill

At no time in the history of capitalism has the education and training of the workforce assumed such widespread importance as at the present conjuncture . . . Rarely if ever has the education of the large majority of the workforce been seen as the central lever of economic growth. Now . . . a consensus is emerging . . . [that] the salience of a nation's education and training system is becoming the key item in the struggle for competitive superiority.

(Ashton and Green 1996: 1)

A particular aspect of the necessary environment for competitive manufacturing is the availability of a skilled and well-educated workforce. The inadequacy of British education and training, however, remains clearly and historically apparent. Hobsbawm (1975: 30) writes of the time of the Industrial Revolution in the eighteenth century that 'English education was a joke in poor taste', while noting that the Germans and French were more advanced 'scientifically' and with regard to technical training. Between 1899–1950, Crafts and Thomas (1986: 641–3) have demonstrated 'Britain's comparative advantage lay in unskilled-labour-intensive, capital neutral, and human-capital-scarce commodities'. Thus, judged by the comparisons with the industrial economies of continental Europe, North America and Japan, the 'British workforce appears to have been short of skill, and not well endowed with it since at least the late nineteenth century' (Dintenfass 1992: 33). Even in 1868, Lyon Playfair, the head of the science section of Britain's Department of Science and Art, was insisting that 'the crying want of this country is a higher class of education for the foremen and managers of industry'. A year later, J. Russell, in his *Systematic Technical Education for the English People*, commented that 'the English people do not believe in the value of technical training and education' (Wrigley 1986: 169).

While the informality of the British education and training system has had the virtue of flexibility, and thus adaptation and expansion over time, it has singularly failed to provide adequate levels of education and training right across the skill spectrum when compared to overseas competitors. This has been an historical failing.

For instance, in 1910–11 the proportion of the appropriate five-year cohort in higher education in Germany was a third larger than in Britain, and in 1914 there were six times as many university and polytechnic students in Germany than in Britain (Pollard 1989: 196); in 1958–9, just 4–5 per cent of the relevant age group went to college or university in Britain compared to 5 per cent in Soviet Russia, 7 per cent in France, 10 per cent in Sweden and 20 per cent in the US

(Sanderson 1972: 276–7). At the intermediate skill levels there are also weaknesses, and the breadth and quality of vocational training has come under close scrutiny (Greenhalgh and Gregory 1997). In 1976 just 5.7 per cent of all British 18 year olds obtained a non-higher technical or vocational education. The proportion educated to this level was nine times greater in Germany and Switzerland, almost six times higher in Denmark, three times higher in Norway and twice as great in Greece (Sanderson 1988: 43–5). In addition, Steedman and Wagner (1987) show that the gap in qualified mechanical, electrical and electronic engineers between Britain, France and Germany has widened significantly between 1975 and 1987, with Britain now having just a third the number of France and a quarter of the number in Germany.

While the history of UK training and education may seem irrelevant to the present, Ashton and Green's (1996) study of education and training in the global economy concludes that the education and training system set up at the time of a country's industrialization 'sets the tone for the subsequent character of the system' (ibid. 6). Specifically, they conclude that the UK's need for a national education system was not based primarily on the demands of the economy at the time of industrialization, since the first phase in the development in the productive system was completed before the state introduced a national system of education. This, in turn, they argue has resulted in a training and education system which is only producing a relatively low level of skill formation, termed the 'low-skills route'. Looking forward, Ashton and Green (ibid. 135) warn that both the US and UK share certain problems because of their low-skills route and that these do not bode well for the future living standards of their citizens; moreover, 'In neither country is there evidence of a commitment, on the part of the ruling political elites or of the major fractions of capital, to a system of high-skill formation'.

There are clear institutional differences in the way in which countries organize their education and training systems. In the 'dual' model of Germany, school leavers enrol on apprenticeships that involve continued general and vocational education, and in the 'schooling' model of Japan, vocational education is provided in schools up to age 18, but in the UK's 'mixed' model, vocational education is provided 'in a non-formal sector' (Ashton and Green 1996: 13). While education is rather like investment – it is quantity *and* quality that count – more recent OECD (1993) figures on rates of participation continue to show that the UK lags its competitors. For example, the UK is one of only three countries (along with Turkey and the Czech and Slovak Federal Republic) where less than 50 per cent of 17 years olds are in secondary education programmes. Of that relatively smaller proportion of students, just 20 per cent are enrolled in vocational or apprenticeship secondary education in the UK compared to 80 per cent in Germany under the 'dual' model (OECD 1993: 119). Furthermore, the UK has a 28 per cent entry ratio of 18 year olds to tertiary education (both university and non-university) compared to 45 per cent in Germany and 53 per cent in Japan (ibid. 126).

As Greenhalgh and Gregory (1997) reflect, there has been considerable debate and discussion regarding policy on vocational training but the outcomes to date have been unimpressive. The training targets put forward by the government during the early 1990s were below that already achieved in South Korea, and the level of government funding for all types of vocational training has been falling in real terms since 1987 (ibid. 106). Employers in the UK have exacerbated this training deficit with investment in training by industry amounting to 0.15 per cent of turnover in Britain in 1980 compared against 2 per cent in Germany and 3 per cent in Japan (Porter 1990: 498).

The skills deficit is reflected in management levels also, with, in the 1980s, some 85 per cent of senior managers in the US and Japan holding degrees, while barely a quarter of British managers were as well qualified (Ackrill 1988: 7). There is a large literature reflecting upon the relative lack of qualifications found in British management although, as Locke (1989: chapter 6) notes, such comparisons are often partial and essentially meaningless. Nonetheless, Locke reflects that the separation of higher education from industry (and its close association with elements in the City of London) has compounded the lack of integration between manufacturing and finance discussed above. Moreover, Locke notes Lawrence's (1980) comparison of German and British managers in which he states that British managers have a far narrower conception of the production function and that production managers and leaders often do not possess the necessary skills and knowledge to move between management functions (unlike their German counterparts). This, argues Locke (1989: 240), must result in 'a poorer coordination of efforts in the English factory and between the factory and the customers'. Indeed, our concern is less with attempting to compare the education of managements in different countries than to consider their relative capabilities and success in their functions.

Adoption and implementation of new techniques

Throughout most of the twentieth century, debate over the cause of Britain's comparatively poor productivity record has centred around the failings of Britain's workers and the problem of British trades unions rather than considering the failings of the UK's management and institutions. The capability and willingness of Britain's workers to meet international standards and the impact of British industrial relations has long been debated by sociologists and economists, most frequently under the label 'The British Worker Problem' (Nichols 1986). However, a number of studies have begun to indicate that a good deal of the cause of the 'problem' with British workers has been their managers (see Nichols 1986; Williams *et al.* 1992; and for an overview see Blyton and Turnbull 1992: chapter 3). Blyton and Turnbull (1992: 39) quote Batstone's (1986) conclusions regarding the 'British disease' of poor industrial relations and its relation with low productivity:

> the lack of sophistication in management organisation both in relation to labour relations and the more technical aspects of production . . . not only led directly to low productivity, but also exacerbated industrial relations prob-

lems . . . To a significant degree, therefore, rather than poor labour relations leading to production problems, production problems lead to poor labour relations and low productivity.

The failings of British management are now increasingly well documented. For instance, it has been widely suggested that British managers have systematically failed to replace and update their manufacturing tools and techniques in line with international competitors (Dintenfass 1992). This failure is frequently invoked as an explanation for Britain's languishing manufacturing performance, and there is plenty of anecdotal and analytical evidence to suggest that this has been a persistent problem. This lack of investment in tools and techniques has been offered as explanation of, for example, the evidence that labour productivity (gross domestic product per hour worked) increased more slowly in Britain than was the case in Japan, Sweden, France, Italy, Germany, Belgium, the Netherlands and the US over the period 1870–1984 (Feinstein 1988: 5).

This failure to upgrade tools and management techniques is clearly linked to the issue of investment discussed above. Appelbaum and Berg (1996) emphasize that the introduction of manufacturing strategies such as flexible specialization, lean production and total quality management may require significant levels of investment, particularly if the changes involve the introduction of new technology and/or the provision of training. The outcomes of internal reorganizations are often uncertain and diffuse with long-term pay-offs. Thus they do not fit well with the short-term payback expected by many sources of finance. These pressures, argue Appelbaum and Berg, often result in firms failing to make the necessary long-term innovations based on investment in training and technology, and also restrict their scope in incorporating the interests of stakeholders other than the financiers. These problems are likely to be felt by small and medium-sized manufacturers in particular.

Notwithstanding the constraints of the financial system and the failings in the UK's education and training provision, the relatively poor performance of British manufacturers must also be linked to the decisions and capabilities of British managers. There is growing evidence that UK firms have failed to successfully implement new manufacturing techniques despite the increasing availability of advice on what constitutes 'best practice'. In Chapter 5 in this volume, Oliver and Hunter report that those UK firms claiming to have adopted 'Japanese' manufacturing techniques do not demonstrate significantly better financial performance than their counterparts reporting little use of these techniques. The authors offer a number of possible explanations for their findings, including that Japanese methods are inherently 'fragile' and do not easily transfer outside the specific economic context of their origin. A further possible explanation would be the failure of British managers to successfully implement these techniques, or to introduce them in such a way that they have significant bottom-line effects.

Our research into the relative manufacturing performance of UK automotive component suppliers gives some further support to this explanation. In a survey of seventy-one suppliers of seats, brakes and exhausts we found that, on average, the twelve UK plants in the study performed relatively poorly on measures of labour productivity and delivered quality, particularly when compared to the average performance of the nine Japanese plants researched (Oliver *et al.* 1996). This was despite the fact that these UK plants had shown considerable enthusiasm for the adoption of the 'lean production' approach associated with Japan. Our conclusions were that UK managers were failing to implement the technical process-oriented techniques most closely linked to performance, and instead were concentrating on the easier options for change which had relatively little impact on operating efficiency – what an American manager of a Japanese transplant graphically described as 'picking the low hanging fruit'. A further conclusion, emphasizing the debates above over industrial infrastructure and the role of the state, is that we are pessimistic regarding the prospects for 'building world-class manufacturing facilities in what may be basically a non-world-class economy' (Oliver *et al.* 1996: S43).

In many respects this picture of UK manufacturing is reiterated by Ackroyd and Procter in Chapter 3 in this volume. Their concern is to assess the form and type of flexible manufacturing systems that British firms have adopted. Their examination of the 'flexibility' in UK manufacturing yields a consistent picture. They report that British manufacturers, outside a small number of large firms, utilize a low-technology approach where flexibility is centred on the number of workers and not on the *role* of labour or on flexible technology. According to Ackroyd and Procter, firms have adopted low-investment strategies in resiting and rearranging existing technology and are operationally reliant on small groups of semi-skilled workers that are numerically, but not functionally, flexible. Thus, as discussed above, the firm avoids the expense of training and new technology (see Appelbaum and Berg 1996). It is this observation that leads the authors to argue that British manufacturers are 'bad' at flexible manufacturing when compared to foreign modes of high-tech flexibility.

Ackroyd and Procter reiterate concerns over the quality of decisions taken by British management and their ability to implement 'best practice'. However, it should be noted that this particular form of flexible manufacturing, which relies on a low-tech, low-training strategy combined with low levels of technical flexibility on the shop floor, may constitute an appropriate response within the current constraints faced by UK manufacturing. It is possible to trace the adoption of this form of British 'flexible' manufacturing to the very factors discussed above, including restrictions in the supply of capital, stringent accounting for profitability and very short payback periods, and therefore it may be seen as symptomatic of Britain's wider industrial malaise. In fact, Ackroyd and Procter take a fairly pessimistic view themselves in concluding that, while the fact that manufacturing survives in this form provides prima facie evidence that it is productive, their findings demonstrate that in the current British financial context this low-tech, low-training strategy represents one of the few ways in which manufacturing can be organized in the UK and have some likelihood of success.

Weaknesses in the management of production appear to have been compounded by a more general management malaise. In a series of historical analyses of the commercial weakness of key British industries, Dintenfass (1992: 52) concludes that since the 1870s British businessmen in a disturbingly wide variety of industries have been less successful than their competitors in various facets of sales and marketing, including matching their products to available markets, cultivating potential customers, meeting orders promptly and reliably, and in providing financing and after-sales service. Britain's uncompetitive behaviour is underlined by several econometric studies which control for cyclical factors and show that while Britain's cost competitiveness improved between 1960 and the 1970s, Britain's share of world exports fell such that non-price factors alone – for example, product quality and customer service – account for the decline (Posner and Steer 1979: 159). However, Glover and colleagues find reason to be increasingly optimistic with regard to the future competence of management in Chapter 11 in this volume.

Managing innovation

Closely linked to the issues of finance, investment and management capability is the question of innovation in British manufacturing. As we note in Chapter 12, innovation is widely held to be the leitmotif of the large manufacturers that will lead the manufacturing sector of the twenty-first century (Cooke and Morgan 1998; Fruin 1997). However, a recurring feature in a number of chapters in this collection is the failure of UK manufacturing to manage change and development positively and successfully.

As Bresnen and Fowler's review of research into buyer–supplier relations in UK industry shows in Chapter 8, many studies have reflected upon a lack of development towards 'partnership'-based approaches that are proposed as more advanced and successful in sustaining long-term economic growth across industry. Bresnen and Fowler report that the majority of studies conclude that shifts in the nature of buyer–supplier relations have typically been characterized by the exploitation and control of small dependent firms by larger and more economically powerful customers. This suggests that, despite considerable evidence that the successful management of supply chains will require closer integration and a sense of mutual obligation and responsibility between firms, UK manufacturers have continued to adopt opportunistic and adversarial behaviour which is counterproductive. Certainly such an approach is counter to that reported as successful by Powell *et al.* (1996) in their exploration of 'networks of innovation' in the US biotechnology industry. They report a host of supportive alliances and agreements between different organizations across both public and private sector and including research institutions, financiers, universities and manufacturers. This network provides a framework within which there is a high degree of innovation and, particularly, product development. Of course, the biotechnology industry is unusual in a number of respects, but the extent of collaboration reported there by Powell *et al.* (1996) has also been revealed in studies of other industries (Sako 1992; Kaufman *et al.* 1996). Indeed, Lovering's discussion of the defence industry in the UK in this volume reveals that it is not impossible for the state, financial institutions and business to combine and collaborate.

In the cases presented by Bresnen and Fowler, the two mid-size UK manufacturers have limited product differentiation and have sought to avoid customer demands impinging on their internal operations. The two firms have very much attempted to retain an 'arm's length' approach to relations with their customers. Bresnen and Fowler report that both the firms have basically sought to cut costs and introduce flexibility in manning levels, while avoiding interaction with other members of the supply chain as far as possible. Cost-cutting and numerical labour flexibility are, of course, the characteristics of UK manufacturing in general that Ackroyd and Procter outline in Chapter 3. As Bresnen and Fowler underline, this defensive approach by the two firms demonstrates that buyer–supplier relations may continue to be marked by a lack of trust, with a consequent reluctance to adopt a greater customer orientation and a concomitant lack of collaboration across the supply chain.

As the Bresnen and Fowler study goes on to show, these firms have demonstrated innovation in their internal management practices, based around 'coping strategies' to avoid customer interference. However, the creativity and innovation shown in this case is defensive and negative, and there is little to suggest that this will lead to an improved likelihood of long-term growth for the firms involved or for the sector of which they are a part. It is a zero-sum orientation.

The problems of two mid-size manufacturers also form part of Chapter 7 by Jones and Tang in their discussion of the employment creation prospects and innovation strategies of UK mid-corporate firms. Here again we see UK manufacturing forced onto the back foot and adopting defensive, introspective and cost-cutting-based approaches to survival. While both case studies discussed by Jones and Tang have made investment in internal process improvements, and one of the companies appears to have benefited from learning from a Japanese customer, their essential story brings us full circle. Through a combination of lack of investment, a paucity of business confidence and management vision, and a restricted level of support from outside institutions, the two companies have failed to develop new products or new market opportunities and are consequently forced to adopt defensive cost-cutting strategies. One case, in which the company abandoned two ventures with university partners into new product development due to a lack of management confidence and restricted resources, is particularly instructive. The lack of viable partners with the commercial capability, financial backing and/or entrepreneurial spirit, along with the lack of confidence and faith needed for long-term thinking and investment, meant that these projects were abandoned, twenty engineers were sacked, R&D expenditure was slashed, and the company drew back from new markets and adopted an introspective and defensive approach, with innovation based on internal process improvements with a view to further cost-cutting. This is not the basis for growth at a firm, sector or national economic level.

SUMMARY

In this introduction we have touched upon what we see as the key issues facing UK manufacturing. By way of introducing the individual contributions to this collection we have reflected upon aspects of finance, government, education and management that are central to understanding where we are and how we could improve. It should be clear from this chapter that we see the various facets of the UK's manufacturing infrastructure and context as interwoven. And we look to the government to act as a catalyst for this period of transition and renewal.

Thus we share with others a desire to see a reform of the financial systems of the UK and an active and effectual industrial policy from the government. Our concern is that the UK should develop a national industrial strategy which will provide the basis for the proactive support and renewal of the country's manu- facturing sector – a strategy that will provide the environment conducive for the high-value-added, high-technology 'learning factories' that will be leading manufacturing into the twenty-first century (Fruin 1997). This is vital if the UK is to break out of a de facto spiral of relative decline in wages, skills and technology. It is our hope that the contributions in this edited collection will provide some substance within this agenda for manufacturing renewal.

NOTE

1 We are particularly grateful to our colleague Derek Matthews for his comments on an earlier draft of this chapter.

REFERENCES

Ackrill, M. (1988) 'Britain's managers and the British economy, 1870s to the 1980s', *Oxford Review of Economic Policy*, **4**, 59–73.

Albert, M. (1993) *Capitalism Against Capitalism*, London: Whurr.

Alford, B.W.E. (1997) *Britain in the World Economy since 1880*, London: Longman.

Appelbaum, E. and Berg, P. (1996) *Financial Market Constraints and Business Strategy in the USA*, Oxford: Oxford University Press.

Ashton, D. and Green, F. (1996) *Education, Training and the Global Economy*, Cheltenham: Edward Elgar.

Batstone, E. (1986) 'Labour and productivity', *Oxford Review of Economic Policy*, **2** (3), 32–43.

Blyton, P. and Turnbull, P. (1992) *The Dynamics of Employee Relations*, Basingstoke: Macmillan.

Cooke, P. and Morgan, K. (1998) *The Associational Economy: Firms, Regions, and Innovation*, Oxford: Oxford University Press.

Crafts, N. (1988) 'The assessment: British economic growth over the long run', *Oxford Review of Economic Policy*, **4** (1), i–xxi.

Crafts, N. and Thomas, M. (1986) 'Comparative advantage in UK manufacturing trade, 1910–1935', *Economic Journal*, **96**, September, 629–45.

Delbridge, R. (1998) *Life on the Line in Contemporary Manufacturing*, Oxford: Oxford University Press.

Dintenfass, M. (1992) *The Decline of Industrial Britain 1870–1980*, London: Routledge.

Dore, R. (1992) 'Japanese capitalism, Anglo-Saxon capitalism: how will the

Darwinian contest turn out?', Centre for Economic Performance, Occasional Paper no. 4, London School of Economics and Political Science.

Eltis, W. and Fraser, D. (1992) 'The contribution of Japanese industrial success to Britain and Europe', *National Westminster Quarterly Review*, November, 2–19.

Feinstein, C. (1988) 'Economic growth since 1870: Britain's performance in international perspective', *Oxford Review of Economic Policy*, 4, spring, 1–13.

Finegold, D. and Soskice, D. (1988) 'The failure of training in Britain: analysis and prescription', *Oxford Review of Economic Policy*, 4 (3), 21–53.

Fruin, M. (1997) *Knowledge Works: Managing Intellectual Capital at Toshiba*, Oxford: Oxford University Press.

Greenhalgh, C. and Gregory, M. (1997) 'Why manufacturing still matters: working with structural change', in J. Philpot (ed.), *Working for Full Employment*, London: Routledge.

Handy, C. (1996) 'People and change', in G. Radice (ed.), *What Needs to Change? New Visions for Britain*, London: HarperCollins.

Hobsbawm, E. (1975) *The Age of Revolution: 1789–1848*, London: Weidenfeld & Nicolson.

Hutton, W. (1995) *The State We're In*, London: Jonathan Cape.

Kaldor, N. (1972) 'The irrelevance of equilibrium economics', *Economic Journal*, 82, December.

Kaufman, A., Merenda, M. and Wood, C. (1996) 'Corporate downsizing and the rise of "problem-solving" suppliers: the case of Hadco Corporation', *Industrial and Corporate Change*, 5, 723–59.

Kennedy, W.P. (1990) 'Capital markets and industrial structure in the Victorian economy', in J.J. van Helten and Y. Cassis (eds), *Capitalism in a Mature Economy*, Aldershot: Edward Elgar, 23–51.

Kitson, M. and Michie, J. (1997) 'Does manufacturing matter?', *International Journal of the Economics of Business*, 4 (1), 71–95.

Lawrence, P. (1980) *Managers and Management in West Germany*, London: Croom Helm.

Lee, S. (1996) 'Finance for industry', in J. Michie and J. Grieve Smith (eds), *Creating Industrial Capacity Towards Full Employment*, Oxford: Oxford University Press, 113–40.

Locke, R. (1989) *Management and Higher Education since 1940*, Cambridge: Cambridge University Press.

Midland Bank Review (1976) 'Capital requirements and finance', February, 10–17.

Nichols, T. (1986) *The British Worker Question: A New Look at Workers and Productivity in Manufacturing*, London: Routledge & Kegan Paul.

OECD (1993) 'Education at a glance: OECD indicators', Centre for Educational Research and Innovation, Paris: OECD.

Oliver, N., Delbridge, R. and Lowe, J. (1996) 'Lean production practices: international comparisons in the auto components industry', *British Journal of Management*, 7, S29–S44.

Pollard, S. (1982) *The Wasting of the British Economy*, London: Croom Helm.

—— (1989) *Britain's Prime and Britain's Decline*, New York: Edward Arnold.

Porter, M. (1980) *Competitive Strategies: Techniques for Analyzing Industries and Firms*, New York: Free Press.

—— (1990) *The Competitive Advantage of Nations*, New York: Macmillan.

Posner, M.V. and Steer, A. (1979) 'Price competitiveness and performance of manufacturing industry', in F. Blackaby (ed.), *Deindustrialisation*, London: Heinemann, 141–65.

Powell, W., Koput, K. and Smith-Doerr, L. (1996) 'Interorganizational collaboration and the locus of innovation: networks of learning in biotechnology', *Administrative Science Quarterly*, 41 (1), 116–45.

Sainsbury, D. (1996) 'A competitive economy', in G. Radice (ed.), *What Needs to Change? New Visions for Britain*, London: HarperCollins.

Sako, M. (1992) *Prices, Quality and Trust: Inter-Firm Relations in Britain and Japan*, Cambridge: Cambridge University Press.

Sanderson, M. (1972) *The Universities and British Industry 1850–1970*, London: Routledge & Kegan Paul.

—— (1988) 'Technical education and economic decline: 1890–1980s', *Oxford Review of Economic Policy*, 4, spring, 38–50.

Smith, D. (1997) 'What goes up must come down', *Management Today*, September, 26–30.

Steedman, H. and Wagner, K. (1987) 'A second look at productivity, machinery and skills in Britain and Germany', *National Institute Economic Review*, November.

Williams, K., Haslam, C., Williams, J., Adcroft, A. and Johal, S. (1992) 'Factories or warehouses? Japanese manufacturing foreign direct investment in Britain and the US', Occasional Papers on Business, Economy and Society no. 6, University of East London.

Womack, J., Jones, D. and Roos, D. (1990) *The Machine that Changed the World*, New York: Rawson.

Wrigley, J. (1986) 'Technical education and industry in the nineteenth century', in B. Elbaum and W. Lazonick (eds), *The Decline of the British Economy*, Oxford: Clarendon Press, 162–88.

2 Deindustrialization may be bad for your wealth

Michael Kitson and Jonathan Michie

INTRODUCTION

There has been considerable debate over the causes of 'deindustrialization' (e.g. Singh 1977, 1987; Rowthorn and Wells 1987). The relative decline of manufacturing, and particularly manufacturing employment, and the corresponding relative growth of services, is prevalent in both slow- and fast-growing countries (see Petit 1986). Since 1960 the share of manufacturing in total employment and GDP has fallen in the major OECD countries (with a concomitant rise in the share of services). This relative decline of manufacturing has led some to see the process as being some sort of an inevitable historical evolution; the argument that there are definable stages of economic development as advanced by Fisher (1935), Rostow (1960), Kuznets (1966) and Chenery (1960) have as a common feature that the final stages are characterized by a modern tertiary sector with growing preferences for service products.

A first explanation of this phenomenon is based on the proposition that there is a faster relative growth of labour productivity in manufacturing than in services. This will result in the costs of manufactures falling relative to services. Assuming that the demand for manufactures and services is relatively price inelastic, the share of manufacturing employment in total employment will decrease. Many studies including those by Fuchs (1968), Baumol (1967) and Summers (1985) have presented evidence that productivity differences are the main source of the decline in manufacturing employment, although others such as Marquand (1979) dispute that services have low productivity.

Like much of the analysis of the service sector, the lagging productivity thesis is hampered by the data problems. In particular, there are substantial difficulties in measuring productivity in services, as in most cases no physical output is produced. In the UK, however, the evidence on relative price movements (assuming similar wage rates in manufacturing and services for the same occupation), and the suggestion that non-marketed service output may be overestimated (as such output is measured, in part, simply via wage bills) – service productivity may thus actually be lower than the official figures would suggest – does add support to the idea that differential productivity growth between the two sectors plays an important role (Gershuny and Miles 1983).

A second explanation for the relative decline of manufacturing and the relative growth of services stems from the changing structure of demand as incomes increase. This explanation is relevant to the growth of personal or consumer services as opposed to intermediate or producer services, although the distinction is often arbitrary. It has been argued that, as their income elasticity of demand is greater than one, the growth in demand for services will exceed the growth of income. Gershuny (1978), for example, pointed out that in Britain, wealthier households spent a greater proportion of their income on services; such relationships, however, seem to be unstable over time and suffer from definitional problems, as much of this service expenditure is on associated goods. Fuchs (1968) argued that the income elasticity of demand for services was only slightly greater than that for other products and was not a major explanation of the growth of the service sector. Similarly, Baumol *et al.* (1989) reject the demand explanation for the US, as during the past few decades manufacturing output has risen as fast as the output of services, and Rowthorn and Wells (1987) have argued that demand for manufactures and services tend to increase at the same rate as economies reach industrial maturity. Additionally, superior productivity growth in manufacturing will create a widening price advantage which will help maintain the share of demand as income rises.

A third explanation for the relative 'decline' of manufacturing is the changing source of service provision, with activities which were previously undertaken by firms becoming increasingly contracted out (to the service sector). Fuchs (1968) found that changes in intermediate service production in the US accounted for 10 per cent of the total expansion of service sector employment.

Contracting out can also take place with consumer services, such as the increased use of restaurants and housekeepers, with such service-sector activity replacing work that was previously done within the household but which did not appear in the national accounts. The evidence here, however, is mixed. Rising incomes may encourage the replacement of domestic activities with commercial equivalents, but, conversely, the opposite may happen due to increased leisure time and the relatively high cost of services. Also, manufactured products may replace or reduce the need for some services (the television replaces the theatre). Such a substitution effect led Gershuny and Miles (1983) to argue that we are moving towards a 'self-service' economy.

The impact of 'contracting out' is complicated not just by the usual measurement problems, but also because observing the net changes for the sector may reveal little about the significant changes within the sector. Some services may be internalized within firms and households while other services are contracted out. What is required is an understanding of both processes. The mode of service provision needs also to be considered in the context of changing economic, technological and institutional conditions. The recessionary and uncertain environment in the UK since 1979 led many firms in the UK to concentrate on 'core' or central activities, contracting out peripheral activities ranging from catering and cleaning to design. The impetus for this change, however, seems to differ between firms. Some responded to the contraction of markets by attempting to restructure their production processes in order to become more competitive in the long term; others by attempting simply to cut costs in the short term.

As income rises and economies approach industrial maturity it can be expected that manufacturing employment shares fall and manufacturing (current price) output shares rise and then fall (Cosh *et al.* 1994). It is, however, important to recognize that the process of deindustrialization may not just reflect positive factors, such as rising income and industrial maturity, but may also reflect negative factors such as an uncompetitive or small manufacturing sector. In this regard, negative deindustrialization will not only be reflected in falling output and employment shares (although these shares may fall more rapidly in countries suffering negative as opposed to positive deindustrialization), but also in low growth (of manufacturing and total output) and an inability to maintain external trading equilibrium. Furthermore, it may be possible for positive deindustrialization to lead to negative deindustrialization, since shifting sectoral shares may result in the domestic manufacturing sector being unable to reap the benefits of rapid productivity growth.

The notion that the manufacturing sector is a dynamic engine of growth can be traced to the work of Lewis (1954), Kaldor (1966), Cornwall (1977) and others. The extension of the market for manufactured products would lead through the benefits of economies of scale to increased competitive advantage and hence to increased economic growth. The implication of this argument is that the service sector may expand in terms of both output and employment, but if full employment is to be achieved there must be sufficient demand for manufactured products. And as noted by Godley (1986), Britain was the only advanced industrial nation since 1960 where the growth of manufacturing output was less than the growth of output of other goods and services – thus the relative decline in manufacturing output was a unique British phenomenon.

In neoclassical economics, divergences from 'equilibrium' are thought to be rectified through price adjustment and/or the correction of market failures. In reality, economies do not behave like this. First, history is important (as recognized in recent path-dependent models) such that the quantity and quality of factors of production accumulated from the past determine what can be produced in the immediate future. This is inconsistent with conventional equilibrium theory, which asserts that an economy is constrained by exogenous variables that remain stable over time (Kaldor 1985). Additionally, it implies that it is difficult and expensive to reverse many economic decisions. If a factory is closed or if a market is lost it is difficult to regain the status quo ante. Secondly, the impact of economic shocks may not only have a once-and-for-all impact on long-run capacity but may lead to cumulative changes. Thus, as Allyn Young stated, forces of economic change are endogenous:

> They are engendered from within the economic system. No analysis, of the forces making for economic equilibrium, forces that we might say are tangential at any moment of time, will serve to illumine this field, for movements

away from equilibrium, departures from previous trends are characteristic of it.

(quoted in Kaldor 1985: 64)

The factor generating economic change for Young (1928) was increasing returns.[1] This led to Myrdal (1957), Kaldor (1972) and others identifying the twin processes of virtuous cycles of growth and vicious cycles of decline. For Kaldor, manufacturing acts as an engine of growth as it exhibits increasing returns, while services are characterized by constant returns. As noted above, this proposition may be too simplistic, as increasing returns are likely to exist in services (despite problems of measurement). This does not, however, diminish the importance of the cumulative causation analysis for understanding the diverging economic performance and prospects of different countries. First, divergences in countries' growth paths can develop as a result of differences – due to the size of the market – in the ability of competing countries to exploit increasing returns in their *tradable* output sectors; and the tradable goods sector remains dominated by manufacturing. Secondly, the cumulative processes will not only lead to differences in cost competitiveness, but also to other non-price factors, such as product quality, customer service and technological development.

Growing economies, for instance, will be able to invest in capital and skills enabling them to improve processes and products. Conversely, in economies suffering relative decline, a lack of investment and a dwindling skill base are likely to constrain future growth. For the latter this may take the form of a reduction of in-house training and/or a decline in support for external provision by training agencies, so that the local infrastructure for skill generation is weakened. This, and the migration from the trade of workers in a position to do so, creates a skill shortage. The response to this, in the face of the decline in formal training, is the substitution of on-the-job instruction with a focus on a narrow range of specific skills to meet the firms' immediate needs, often accompanied by the exclusion of worker representatives from the training design and implementation processes. Consequently, the skill content of jobs is diluted, and this interacts with the deterioration of the terms and conditions of employment and the increasing pessimism about future prospects of the industry to discourage new entrants from traditional areas of recruitment. Any subsequent relaxation of hiring standards to meet the labour shortage then serves to further reinforce the social downgrading of the job, the dissipation of skills, the loss of competitiveness and industrial decline.[2]

MANUFACTURING IN THE UK

As the House of Lords Select Committee on Science and Technology reported, 'Manufacturing industry is vital to the prosperity of the United Kingdom. . . .Our manufacturing base is dangerously small; to achieve adequate growth from such a small base will be difficult' (House of Lords 1991: 3). The relative decline of manufacturing in the UK has been greater than the norm for the OECD countries. In terms of percentage shares of value added, the UK manufacturing sector contributed 13.3 percentage points less in 1993 than it did in 1960, compared to an average fall across the OECD of 9.3 percentage points. In terms of employment shares, the manufacturing sector's contribution fell by 19.9 per cent across the same period, compared to an average fall across the OECD of 7.3 per cent.

The extent of the UK's decline is prima facie evidence that the UK is suffering from negative deindustrialization. Manufacturing output in the UK is barely higher today than it was twenty-five years ago. The picture is one of rising output up to 1973, followed by a sharp fall to 1975 and subsequent recovery in the second half of the 1970s (generally taken as peaking again in 1979, although the annual index averages to a lower overall figure over 1979 than for 1978). The deep recession of the early 1980s was followed by a weak recovery, leading straight into the Lawson boom, which took manufacturing output to a new peak in 1989 before falling again in the early 1990s' recession. Despite the recovery from the recession of the early 1990s, and even talk of an overheating economy in 1997, manufacturing output in the second quarter of 1997 was only 3.7 per cent higher than in the second quarter of 1990, just before the recession began. And at the time of writing (August 1997), UK manufacturing is facing the threat of an overvalued currency as a result of the interest rate rises imposed by the newly independent Bank of England.

Meanwhile, manufacturing productivity grew in every year apart from 1975 and 1980, even when output fell. There has therefore been an almost continual decline in manufacturing employment from its peak level in 1966. Table 2.1 compares, in summary form, the UK's manufacturing performance with its main competitors. The UK is the only one of the six with a lower average level of manufacturing output over the years 1979–89 than over the years 1973–9, and was also the only country to experience a fall in output between the years 1973 and 1979 (between 1979 and 1989 this average growth returned to a positive figure, albeit lower than in any of the other countries apart from France). A similar picture emerges for manufacturing employment, with the UK being the only one to experience a fall between 1964 and 1973; others saw employment fall between 1979 and 1989, but none did so at the rate experienced in the UK, while during 1973–9 only Germany and Japan experienced a faster rate of job losses and, as indicated above, in both cases this was due to strong productivity growth rather than simply output loss as was the case for the UK. Looking at the three peak-to-peak periods, Britain was at the bottom of the league table of the six countries in two of the periods, and second bottom in the third.[3] This poor record on manufacturing output resulted in declining manufacturing employment.

Table 2.2 gives the average annual growth of manufacturing output for the six countries between the peak years 1964 and 1989, with the UK firmly at the foot of the performance league. Table 2.2 also reports the overall growth between 1964 and 1989, as well as for the more recent period of 1973 and 1989. Taking the overall growth figure to 1992 it can be seen that while the level of manufacturing output was more than 30 per cent higher by the end of the twenty-year period in Germany, and almost 70 per cent higher in Japan, in Britain the overall growth was barely 1 per cent: that is, the absolute level of manufacturing output in 1992

Table 2.1 Manufacturing output and employment: international comparisons

		1964–73	1973–9	1979–89
UK	Output (1985 = 100)	95.1	105.3	101.2
	Average annual growth	3.1%	−1.0%	1.4%
	Employment (millions)	8.254	7.481	5.759
	Average annual growth	−0.8%	−1.3%	−3.4%
Italy	Output (1985 = 100)	66.4	88.7	103.4
	Average annual growth	6.1%	2.6%	1.8%
	Employment (millions)	6.203	6.525	6.606
	Average annual growth	4.3%	0.2%	−1.5%
France	Output (1985 = 100)	72.4	97.8	103.7
	Average annual growth	5.9%	1.5%	0.7%
	Employment (millions)	5.670	5.825	5.140
	Average annual growth	2.1%	−0.9%	−1.7%
Germany	Output (1985 = 100)	73.4	90.2	99.5
	Average annual growth	4.8%	1.2%	1.5%
	Employment (millions)	8.060	7.684	6.972
	Average annual growth	0.8%	−2.2%	−0.5%
USA	Output (1985 = 100)	61.1	77.5	98.0
	Average annual growth	5.2%	2.7%	3.0%
	Employment (millions)	19.123	19.824	19.465
	Average annual growth	1.7%	0.7%	−0.8%
Japan	Output (1985 = 100)	45.7	70.3	95.8
	Average annual growth	11.9%	2.0%	4.1%
	Employment (1985 = 100)	97.3	96.8	97.3
	Average annual growth	1.8%	−1.9%	1.0%

Source: OECD, *Main Economic Indicators*, and own calculations.
Note: The figures indicate the average output and employment over each period, and the average annual percentage growth during each period. For employment, the figures for Italy include construction; there are definition changes in the data for West Germany from 1970; the first period average for France is for 1968–73 (with the average annual growth also calculated between these years); and the figures for Japan are index numbers with 1985 = 100.

Table 2.2 Growth of manufacturing output between 1964 and 1992

	Annual average % growth 1964–89	Total overall % growth		
		1964–89	1973–89	1973–92
UK	1.5	41.8	8.2	1.3
Italy	3.7	138.3	39.7	68.6
France	2.9	97.2	17.5	16.5
Germany	2.7	89.4	24.0	32.1
USA	3.9	150.3	58.1	55.2
Japan	6.6	363.7	69.2	68.9

Source: OECD, *Main Economic Indicators*, and own calculations.

was hardly different from that achieved in 1973. Between the peak years of 1964 and 1989, the average annual growth of manufacturing output was 6.6 per cent in Japan, 3.9 per cent in the US, 3.7 per cent in Italy, 2.9 per cent in France, 2.7 per cent in Germany, and only 1.5 per cent in the UK. Over the ten-year peak-to-peak period 1979–89, manufacturing output grew by a total of only 15 per cent, an average cumulative growth rate of barely 1 per cent a year (before dropping back in 1992 to around the same level as it had been in 1973).

An assessment of the UK's relatively poor growth rate performance must be tempered by consideration of different levels of income. It may be expected that growth rates will differ as countries have different per capita income levels. Countries with relatively low income levels may have relatively higher growth rates as they have the potential to appropriate technologies and organizational techniques from the leading countries. This process, even allowing for the fact that it may be both erratic and confined to countries at broadly similar stages of industrialization, cannot explain Britain's inferior growth performance. The UK's poor growth rate has not just been associated with other industrialized countries catching up with the UK GDP level, but with those countries overtaking that level. In 1950 the UK was the second richest European economy, by 1973 it was seventh, and by 1992 it was eleventh. During the period, 1950–73, the UK had the lowest growth rate of the sixteen European economies. During the period 1973–92, when all growth rates slowed, its growth rate ranked joint twelfth, with only two countries having an inferior growth performance.

Three important points are clear. First, the decline in manufacturing employment in the UK can *not* be explained solely by shifts in consumption patterns, nor by other sectors' requirements for labour. The loss of manufacturing jobs has been accompanied by a deteriorating performance in manufacturing trade and by a rise in unemployment. Second, manufacturing has experienced, not a rapidly rising output as a result of productivity growth, but, on the contrary, a stagnant trend in output, with the productivity growth translating not into output growth but instead into job losses. Third, the poor performance of the manufacturing sector has led to slow growth in the economy as a whole.

CAUSES OF UK DEINDUSTRIALIZATION

Two alternative approaches have been adopted in analysing the deindustrialization of the UK economy. First, the free market approach suggests that deindustrialization reflects excessive government intervention in the economy combined with other 'market imperfections' – most prominently, trade unions – that prevent the efficient allocation of resources. Alternatively, deindustrialization is seen as reflecting a lack of, or inappropriate forms of, intervention in the economy – most importantly, the lack of a coherent industrial policy, an unstable macroeconomic policy, and the failure to deal with the problem of chronic underinvestment.

Prominent aspects of the free market approach have been the arguments that the public sector (or more specifically, the non-marketable sector) crowds out jobs from the private sector (or more specifically, the marketable sector) (see Bacon and Eltis 1976), and that the increase of the wage share, due to the impact of corporatism, full employment and strong trade unions, has squeezed profits and thus investment (see Eltis 1996). In the spirit of this approach, some have argued that the Thatcher years transformed the supply side of the British economy, creating conditions for future prosperity. Crafts, for example, has argued that Thatcher's 'get tough' approach to trade unions had yielded significant benefits for the economy and that these might endure 'if the bargaining power of workers over manning levels remains weak' (Crafts 1991).[4] The 'Unions were the main reason . . .' thesis often forms part of a wider view, that unemployment is at heart a labour-market problem. This includes the more recent line of argument, that the key to the problem lies in education and training.

The key evidence presented in support of the Thatcher Shock is the improvement in productivity – see Crafts (1996) and Eltis (1996), and for an opposing view, Kitson and Michie (1996). Yet, we would argue, there was no productivity miracle during the 1980s – any such picture is a mirage. Certainly labour productivity in manufacturing grew in the 1980s, but this was due largely to job cuts rather than increased output, and these jobs were not being lost in a period of full employment when the labour would be taken up productively elsewhere.

Additionally, the official productivity figures are constructed using a single price deflator for both output and input prices; Stoneman and Francis (1992) have shown that when the appropriate deflators are used, productivity growth is lower, at only a 34 per cent rise between 1979 and 1989 rather than the 51 per cent increase shown in the official figures. The figures for total factor productivity (TFP), which is intended to capture the increase in output above that resulting from increased quantities of capital and labour, are also questionable. First, the growth-accounting approach which forms the basis for the construction of TFP measures usually assumes that factors of production are homogenous, that markets are perfectly competitive (ensuring marginal productivity factor pricing), and that there are constant returns to scale. Second, there are significant differences in TFP measures depending on the approach adopted and the data used.

Furthermore, the productivity record must be considered in the context of the increased intensification of labour.[5] Nolan (1989) and Nolan and Marginson (1990) have argued that an increase in output per head as a result of increased labour input through the intensification of labour should not be defined as an increase in productivity unless the growth of output is greater than the increased input; but Nolan (1989) and Nolan and O'Donnell (1998) have also gone on to argue, in our view persuasively, that far from paving the way for genuine productivity improvements, the Government's policies of deregulation and anti-trade union legislation impaired effective labour utilization and competitiveness in product markets.[6]

Lastly, the productivity gains that have been made went disproportionately into increased profits rather than reduced output prices (which would have allowed increased market share, with higher output and employment than was in fact experienced, along with a healthier balance of payments and lower inflation), and the increased profits went disproportionately into dividend payments rather than investment.[7,8]

So while labour productivity growth in the 1980s returned perhaps to the rates experienced in the 1960s, these rates of growth were never satisfactory; UK productivity levels still lag behind the other leading industrialized countries; and in the 1980s the benefits of this productivity growth went overwhelmingly into cutting costs and employment rather than into developing new products and expanding output.

Our interpretation of this performance by UK manufacturing is, first, that it is one of relative failure, and secondly, that such failure has been caused, at least in part, by underinvestment, which reflects a failure to manage and regulate the economy efficiently. Manufacturing net investment in the UK (as a share of manufacturing output) has been declining since the early 1960s, with negative figures for the early 1980s and 1990s (Table 2.3). It might be thought that there has been no problem of underinvestment in UK manufacturing as the ratio of gross manufacturing investment to output has remained stable. This stable ratio, however, is the result of inadequate investment matched only by stagnant output. The impact of the poor and erratic investment record has been to leave UK manufacturing with an inadequate capital stock.

During all three peak-to-peak periods since the mid-1960s the growth of the UK's manufacturing gross capital stock has been inferior to that of the other major industrial nations.[9] This is most evident during the 1979–89 period when, although there was a worldwide slowdown in the growth of manufacturing investment, the UK was the only country of the five not to experience any growth in the manufacturing capital stock (see Table 2.4). This has left a legacy of a relatively low level of capital in UK manufacturing.[10] Capital per worker in the UK is significantly below that of the US and Germany; the gap with these two countries (and France) has been widening since the mid-1960s.

In addition to a lack of investment, much of that which has taken place has been cost-cutting rather than capacity enhancing. Thus, while for the vast majority of OECD countries the growth rates of both total and industrial R&D were much higher in the 1980s than in the 1970s, the most notable exception to this was the UK (see Archibugi and Michie 1995: table 2.1). The dismal investment record of the UK economy since the 1960s has been a major cause of Britain's indifferent growth performance.[11] The lack of investment has constrained technological progress and the expansion of demand.[12] Furthermore, the cumulative effect of this record has resulted in British workers lacking the volume of capital equipment used by their main competitors. This capital stock gap is likely to widen as, through cumulative causation processes, the expectations that the manufacturing sector is not investing become self-fulfilling. Additionally, the process of de-industrialization will lead to further weaknesses in terms of skills deficiencies and continuing balance of payments problems.

The importance of education and training has recently been emphasized by endogenous growth models where the growth rate of productivity is associated with the level of education. An educated and motivated workforce is able to

Table 2.3 UK manufacturing net investment 1960–93

	£ million (1990 prices)	Expressed as a share of manufacturing output (%)
1960	4,000	5.5
1961	5,451	7.5
1962	4,446	6.1
1963	2,846	3.8
1964	3,729	4.5
1965	3,896	4.6
1966	3,931	4.6
1967	3,430	4.0
1968	3,936	4.2
1969	4,378	4.5
1970	4,967	5.1
1971	3,817	4.0
1972	1,947	2.0
1973	2,106	2.0
1974	2,985	2.8
1975	1,790	1.8
1976	1,004	1.0
1977	1,216	1.2
1978	2,747	2.7
1979	3,174	3.1
1980	1,671	1.8
1981	−993	−1.1
1982	−1,561	−1.8
1983	−1,746	−1.9
1984	−279	−0.3
1985	1,317	1.4
1986	531	0.5
1987	888	0.9
1988	1,881	1.7
1989	2,749	2.4
1990	1,712	1.5
1991	89	0.1
1992	−1,229	−1.2
1993	−1,881	−1.7

Averages for the three peak-to-peak periods

1964–73	3,614	4.0
1973–9	2,146	2.1
1979–89	694	0.6

Sources: CSO, *Economic Trends Annual Supplement* (1994); CSO, *United Kingdom National Accounts* (various editions); CSO, *National Income and Expenditure* (various editions); and CSO, *Economic Trends* (1994), November.

Note: The net investment series has been calculated by subtracting capital consumption from gross investment. The capital consumption series was constructed by linking the various series published in *United Kingdom National Accounts* and *National Income and Expenditure*. These series vary in their coverage as they use different definitions of manufacturing due to changes in the SIC classification system. The linked series adjusts for this by using the ratio between new and old definitions in overlapping years. This constructed series was preferred to that published in *United Kingdom National Accounts*, as the latter is deficient due to the variable inclusion of leased items and some other apparent anomalies in the series.

Table 2.4 Growth of the manufacturing gross capital stock: international comparisons

	Annual % growth rates		
	1964–73	*1973–9*	*1979–89*
United Kingdom			
Equipment	4.6	2.6	0.2
Structures	2.5	0.8	−0.5
Total assets	3.9	2.1	0.0
USA			
Equipment	4.2	5.0	2.4
Structures	4.9	2.6	1.4
Total assets	4.4	4.1	2.0
Germany			
Equipment	7.6	2.9	1.7
Structures	4.1	1.8	0.4
Total assets	6.1	2.5	1.2
France			
Equipment	7.8	3.5	1.7
Structures	8.4	6.6	3.4
Total assets	8.0	4.2	2.1
Japan			
Equipment	14.0	5.5	5.0
Structures	13.9	7.3	5.7
Total assets	14.0	6.0	5.2

Source: Authors' calculations from data in O'Mahony (1993).
Note: 'Equipment' includes all types of machinery, furniture, fixtures and vehicles. 'Structures' includes all types of buildings and other forms of infrastructure.

facilitate the development of, adapt more easily to, and exploit more fully, new processes and techniques of production. In the models of Romer (1986, 1990) increased education generates new technologies, whereas for Lucas (1988) there will be positive externalities from education, as a high level of human capital will encourage increased learning from others. A number of studies have illustrated the inadequacies in the provision of education and training in the UK. For instance, the OECD (1994) reports the relatively low rate of enrolment of 17 and 18 year olds in formal education and training programmes, and Marsden and Ryan (1991) and the Small Business Research Centre (1992) indicate significant dissatisfaction with the availability and quality of training provision. While lack of skills is therefore a problem for the UK economy, it must be stressed that training programmes alone are not enough; the lack of job opportunities itself stifles skill attainment and development. The stagnation of the manufacturing sector creates conditions for social deskilling which add to the spiral of decline, since a common response by firms to their declining fortunes is to cut back on training.

The historical legacy with which UK manufacturing has had to contend has included: a continued overseas orientation not only of the financial sector, but also of Britain's multinational corporations; a disproportionate burden of military spending and the distorting effect this has had on R&D; and the continued inability of successive UK governments to modernize the economy.[13] One manifestation of this legacy has been a failure to produce a sufficient volume of manufactured exports to pay for imports (at a reasonable level of economic growth). Despite assertions to the contrary by Chancellor Lawson (Lawson 1992) and others, the balance of payments does matter, and the loss of Britain's manufacturing trading surplus in 1983 and the subsequent annual trading deficit in manufactured goods does pose problems for the wider economy (on which, see Coutts and Godley 1992; McCombie and Thirlwall 1992; and Cosh *et al.* 1994). While Britain's balance of payments did benefit from the post-ERM devaluation, for the country's long-term trading position to be resolved, particularly at anything like full employment, will require a continual improvement in our industrial performance. The practically zero-trend growth over the past twenty years will not do it. Neither could the service sector do it alone, as has been demonstrated, for example, by Cosh *et al.* (1994); their modelling reveals that 'to offset the prospective manufacturing deficit would require a quite inconceivable increase in the exports of financial and miscellaneous services' (ibid. 29). Indeed, Crafts (1993) implicitly acknowledges that something is amiss, when he notes that the exchange rate needed to achieve full employment and trade balance at the same time has been falling since the early 1980s.[14]

POLICIES TO REVERSE UK DEINDUSTRIALIZATION

UK macroeconomic policy over the past thirty years has resulted repeatedly in an overvalued exchange rate and high interest rates, both of which are particularly damaging to manufacturing, while industrial policy has been ineffectual, with little attempt to use the public sector as a modernizing force.[15]

The most obvious cases of sterling being overvalued as a result of macro-economic policy were, first, the effects of the Thatcher Government's initial monetarist policies in 1979–80, and secondly, membership of the Exchange Rate Mechanism at an overvalued rate.[16] But the industrial policies of the 1964 Wilson Government were also sacrificed on the altar of defending the currency, as were those of the Callaghan Government in 1975; the former was a case of defending an existing parity, while the latter was a fear that the currency would float downwards (although whether our trading partners would have really allowed us to gain a significant competitive advantage which would have accrued to British industry from this is doubtful).

Additionally, the high levels and volatility of interest rates have discouraged investment and business confidence. This was particularly apparent during the early 1980s when high interest rates created cash flow problems for many companies, leading to bankruptcies and plant closures as well as contributing to the appreciation of sterling and the squeeze on exports. Interest rate policy during the 1980s has been identified as the main government policy which has impeded the growth of firms. The 1991 Cambridge survey (Small Business Research Centre 1992)[17] into business performance, the most extensive since the 1971 Bolton study, indicated that a third of all firms surveyed identified interest rate policy as the most important negative government policy, and half placed it in their top three policy concerns.[18]

The resulting instability to which the UK economy has been prone, particularly since 1979, has been worse than that experienced in other industrial nations, reflecting the UK Government's desire since 1979 to target nominal variables (inflation and interest rates) rather than real variables (jobs and output). Also, the long-term growth potential of the economy has been impaired. This is due to two factors. First, the depth of the recessions – they were much deeper than previous (at least pre-1974) postwar recessions – which led to large-scale scrapping of capital and the laying-off of workers. This contrasts with previous recessions where, as the long-term costs of abandonment were high (the cost of restoring capital equipment, severance payments and search and training costs), the moderate extent of the downturns encouraged firms to maintain capacity while waiting for the cyclical upturn. Conversely, during the post-1979 recessions, the depth of the recessions encouraged firms to reduce capacity in order to minimize short-term costs and maximize the possibility of survival.[19]

Secondly, as the domestic economy has, albeit falteringly, developed, the industrial structure has shifted to more segmented and niche product markets. These sectors require specialist capital equipment and sector-specific skills. The loss of such factors due to a recession may be more difficult to replace in a period of recovery. Furthermore, it is not possible to rely on future investment to make good the position; the existence of sunk costs means that restarting operations will be expensive, requiring a higher yield (in excess of the required or 'hurdle' rate) to encourage the replacement investment (Dixit 1992). This alone indicates that governments should adopt suitable expansionary policies to ameliorate the potential impact of external shocks, and certainly should not use severe contractionary policies to counter inflation. The long-term costs of recessions place an increasing premium on achieving stable economic growth.

We have stressed the negative impact of the economic shocks of the 1980s on the UK's long-run growth potential. Others have argued that the reduced bargaining power of workers and the creation of a more flexible labour market have had beneficial effects. This notion is based on a neoclassical view of the competitive process, where producers face a large number of competitors and price is the key indicator of competitiveness. In reality, many firms have few effective competitors, and the key factors which contribute to competitive advantage are product quality and the characteristics of the customer–client relationship.[20] Thus, in order to create and sustain a competitive economy, firms require stable economic growth to foster interfirm cooperation and encourage innovation, product development and the upgrading of the skill base of the economy.

NOTES

1 New models of economic growth also stress endogeneity due to externalities in the production of innovations. Endogenous technical progress, within a neo-classical framework, was developed by Romer (1986 and 1990) and Lucas (1988) among others. Unlike the traditional neoclassical model of growth (Solow 1970), the new models may allow for divergences in growth (as in Kaldorian models) depending on the extent to which there are international spillovers of knowledge and technology.

2 These points are argued in more detail in Wilkinson (1992) and Michie and Wilkinson (1995).

3 The reasons for France's particularly bad performance during 1979–89 are analysed in detail in Halimi *et al.* (1994).

4 Indeed, Crafts (1988) claims that the industrial missions organized by the Anglo-American Council on Productivity between 1948 and 1952 had identified restrictive labour practices as posing the major obstacle to the 'Americanization' of British industry, while in fact these reports pointed rather to the shortcomings of management (see Coates 1994; Nolan and O'Donnell 1997; Tiratsoo and Tomlinson 1994).

5 For a discussion of which, see Deakin *et al.* (1992).

6 See also the discussion of these issues by Deakin (1992) and Brown (1992), and by Nolan *et al.* (1997).

7 See Glyn (1992) and Cosh *et al.* (1993) where these last, distributional points are analysed in depth.

8 The following report is typical: 'Among appropriations, dividend payments rose by 17% in 1990, a lower growth rate than in the preceding two years (27% in 1989 and 33% in 1988), but one that was still surprisingly rapid. The dividend payout ratio, defined as the ratio of dividend payments to total income after deducting tax and interest payments, rose to 56% in the fourth quarter of 1990 and 64% in the first quarter of this year' (Bank of England, *Quarterly Bulletin*, August 1991, p. 364).

9 The gross capital stock series is from O'Mahony (1993) which constructs estimates using an internationally consistent methodology that employs standard US service lives.

10 The estimate of the UK capital stock level may be an overestimate as the collapse of manufacturing in the early 1980s led to substantial capital scrapping which was not incorporated into official figures (see Oulton and O'Mahony 1994).

11 Rowthorn (1995) shows that low investment over the past twenty years, especially in manufacturing, has been a significant factor in the rise of unemployment throughout Western Europe; as indicated above, this has been a particular problem in the UK.

12 Scott (1989 and 1992) emphasizes, in contrast to much of new growth theory, that all types of investment, not just certain kinds (R&D expenditure, investment in education, etc.), create and reveal new investment opportunities. Additionally, he stresses, in the spirit of Keynes, that investment responds to demand and the expectations of the growth of demand. The important two-way relationship between investment and demand is overlooked in many recent discussions of economic growth which ignore demand constraints on the level of economic activity. Investment can increase, as well as respond to, the level of demand, affecting the scale of production as well as its organization and technological efficiency. And through Verdoorn effects, increased scale can itself boost productivity.

13 On Britain's long-run relative economic decline, see Kitson and Michie (1995).

14 This point is made by Wells (1993: 56). Crafts (1993) cites the estimates of

Church (1992) which suggest that the Fundamental Equilibrium Exchange Rate (FEER) has been falling at a trend rate of 1.5 per cent per annum. This implies an annual terms-of-trade induced reduction of GDP growth of 0.4 per cent – a significant proportion of the UK trend growth rate.

15 As Postmaster General from October 1964 to August 1965, Tony Benn (1987: 264) concluded the following: 'This highlights in my mind one of the great difficulties of being a socialist in the sort of society in which we live. The real drive for improvement comes from those concerned to make private profit. If, therefore, you deny these people the right of extending private enterprise into new fields, you have to have some sort of alternative. You have to have some body which wants to develop public enterprise but our present Civil Service is not interested in growth. It is geared to care and maintenance.' (Diary entry for 28 May 1965.)

16 See, for example, the arguments of the Cambridge Economic Policy Group published in the *Observer* on 19 April 1992 and denounced the following week (26 October) by the *Observer*'s own Adam Raphael in a piece entitled, 'Beware the siren devaluers who lure us to ruin'; see also the reply from Coutts, Godley, Michie and Rowthorn in the *Observer* of 3 May 1992.

17 The Cambridge survey was undertaken during the spring and summer of 1991 and provides a national stocktake of approximately 2,000 enterprises. The sampling framework, and the respondents, was split equally between manufacturing and the rapidly expanding business service sector (for further details see Kitson 1994, and Small Business Research Centre 1992). For detail of subsequent survey work by the ESRC Centre for Business Research, which broadly reinforces the points being made here, see Kitson and Michie (1998).

18 In the Cambridge survey, firms were asked to identify which government policies hindered or helped their business in the previous ten years. Overall, firms believed that government policy had hindered their performance. What was noticeable was the high proportion of firms that considered that they had received no help from government policy during the past decade. Nearly a third of the firms surveyed did not identify any significant help from government policy during the past ten years.

19 The contrasting impacts of mild versus deep recession can also lead to contrasting productivity changes. With mild recessions we tend to observe 'Okun's Law', with a *short-term* productivity loss associated with a fall in output. With deep recession we observe a 'shock effect', with a short-term gain in productivity due to the shedding of labour and capacity.

20 The 1991 Cambridge survey (Small Business Research Centre 1992) indicated that 40 per cent of manufacturing firms had less than five competitors and 70 per cent had less than ten competitors. The survey also showed that personal attention to client needs, product quality and an established reputation were the most important factors which contributed to the competitiveness of manufacturing firms. Price was ranked sixth out of eleven identified factors. Again, see Kitson and Michie (1998) for additional survey results which reinforce these general findings.

REFERENCES

Archibugi, D. and Michie, J. (1995) 'The globalization of technology: a new taxonomy', *Cambridge Journal of Economics*, **19** (1), February, 121–40; reprinted (1997), in D. Archibugi and J. Michie (eds), *Technology, Globalization and Economic Performance*, Cambridge: Cambridge University Press.

Bacon, R. and Eltis, W. (1976) *Britain's Economic Problem: Too Few Producers*, London: Macmillan.

Baumol, W. (1967) 'Macroeconomics of unbalanced growth', *American Economic Review*, 57, 415–26.

Baumol, W., Blackman, S. and Wolff, E. (1989) *Productivity and American Leadership: The Long View*, Cambridge, Mass.: MIT Press.

Benn, T. (1987) *Out of the Wilderness: Diaries 1963–67*, London: Hutchinson.

Brown, W. (1992) 'Collective rights', in J. Michie (ed.), *The Economic Legacy, 1979–1992*, London: Academic Press.

Cambridge Economic Policy Group (1992) 'Hands-off economics equals stagnation', *The Observer*, 19 April.

Chenery, H.B. (1960) 'Patterns of industrial growth', *American Economic Review*.

Church, K. (1992) 'Properties of the fundamental equilibrium exchange rate in models of the UK economy', *National Institute Economic Review*, 141, 62–70.

Coates, D. (1994) *The Question of UK Decline: The Economy, State and Society*, Hemel Hempstead: Harvester Wheatsheaf.

Cornwall, J. (1977) *Modern Capitalism, Its Growth and Transformation*, Oxford: Martin Robertson.

Cosh, A.D., Hughes, A. and Rowthorn, R.E. (1993) 'The competitive role of UK manufacturing industry: 1979–2003', in K. Hughes (ed.), *The Future of UK Competitiveness and the Role of Industrial Policy*, London: Policies Studies Institute, ch. 2.

—— (1994) 'The competitive role of UK manufacturing industry, 1950–2003: a case analysis', mimeo, University of Cambridge.

Coutts, K. and Godley, W. (1992) 'Does Britain's balance of payments matter any more?', in J. Michie (ed.), *The Economic Legacy, 1979–1992*, London: Academic Press.

Coutts, K., Godley, W., Michie, J. and Rowthorn, B. (1992) 'Devaluation of sterling is no "quick fix"', *The Observer*, 3 May.

Crafts, N. (1988) 'The assessment: British economic growth over the long run', *Oxford Review of Economic Policy*, 4 (1), i–xxi.

—— (1991) 'Reversing relative economic decline? The 1980s in historical perspective', *Oxford Review of Economic Policy*, 7 (3), 81–98.

—— (1993) *Can Deindustrialization Seriously Damage your Wealth?*, London: Institute of Economic Affairs.

—— (1996) 'Deindustrialization and economic growth', *Economic Journal*, 106, January, 172–83.

Deakin, S. (1992) 'Labour law and industrial relations', in J. Michie (ed.), *The Economic Legacy, 1979–1992*, London: Academic Press.

Deakin, S., Michie, J. and Wilkinson, F. (1992) *Inflation, Employment, Wage-Bargaining and the Law*, London: The Institute of Employment Rights.

Dixit, A. (1992) 'Investment and hysteresis', *Journal of Economic Perspectives*, 6 (1), Winter, 107–32.

Eltis, W. (1996) 'How low profitability and weak innovativeness undermined UK industrial growth', *Economic Journal*, 106, January, 184–95.

Fisher, I. (1935) *The Clash of Progress and Security*, New York: Macmillan.

Fuchs, V. (1968) *The Service Economy*, New York: Columbia University Press.

Gershuny, J. (1978) *After Industrial Society*, London: Macmillan.

Gershuny, J. and Miles, I. (1983) *The New Service Economy*, London: Frances Pinter.

Glyn, A. (1992) 'The "productivity miracle", profits and investment', in J. Michie (ed.), *The Economic Legacy, 1979–1992*, London: Academic Press.

Godley, W (1986) 'Manufacturing and the future of the British economy', paper presented to Manufacturing or Services? A Conference on UK Industry and the Economy, Robinson College, Cambridge.

Halimi, S., Michie, J. and Milne, S. (1994) 'The Mitterrand experience', in J. Michie and J. Grieve Smith (eds), *Unemployment in Europe*, London: Academic Press, ch. 6.

House of Lords (1991) *Report from the Select Committee on Science and Technology*, London: HMSO.

Kaldor, N. (1966) *Causes of the Slow Rate of Growth in the United Kingdom*, Cambridge: Cambridge University Press.

—— (1972) 'The irrelevance of equilibrium economics', *Economic Journal*, December.

—— (1985) *Economics Without Equilibrium*, New York: M.E. Sharpe.

Kitson, M. (1994) 'Seedcorn or chaff? Unemployment and small firm performance', Small Business Research Centre, Working Paper no. 2, University of Cambridge.

Kitson, M. and Michie, J. (1995) 'Trade and growth: a historical perspective', in J. Michie and J. Grieve Smith (eds), *Managing the Global Economy*, Oxford: Oxford University Press, ch. 1.

—— (1996) 'Britain's industrial performance since 1960: underinvestment and relative decline', *Economic Journal*, **106**, January, 196–212.

—— (1998) 'Markets, competition, and innovation', in J. Michie and J. Grieve Smith (eds), *Globalization, Growth, and Governance*, Oxford: Oxford University Press.

Kuznets, S. (1966) *Modern Economic Growth: Rate, Structure and Spread*, New Haven: Yale University Press.

Lawson, N. (1992) *The View from No. 11*, London: Bantam Press.

Lewis, W. A. (1954) 'Economic development with unlimited supplies of labour', in *The Manchester School of Economic and Social Studies*, 139–91.

Lucas, R. (1988) 'On the mechanisms of economic development', *Journal of Monetary Economics*, **22**, July.

McCombie, J. and Thirlwall, T. (1992) 'The re-emergence of the balance of payments constraint', in J. Michie (ed.), *The Economic Legacy, 1979–1992*, London: Academic Press.

Marquand, J. (1979) 'The service sector and regional policy in the United Kingdom', Centre for Environmental Studies, London.

Marsden, D. and Ryan, P. (1991) 'Initial training, labour market structure and public policy: intermediate skills in British and German industry', in P. Ryan (ed.), *International Comparisons of Vocational Training for Intermediate Skills*, Lewes: Falmer Press.

Michie, J. and Wilkinson, F. (1995) 'Wages, government policy and unemployment', *Review of Political Economy*, 7 (2), April, 133–49.

Myrdal, G. (1957) *Economic Theory and Underdeveloped Regions*, London: Duckworth.

Nolan, P. (1989) 'Walking on water? Performance and industrial relations under Thatcher', *Industrial Relations Journal*, **20** (2), 81–92.

Nolan, P. and Marginson, P. (1990) 'Skating on thin ice? David Metcalf on trade unions and productivity', *British Journal of Industrial Relations*, **28** (2), 227–47.

Nolan, P. and O'Donnell, K. (1998) 'The political economy of productivity: Britain 1945–1994', mimeo.

Nolan, P., Saundry, R. and Sawyer, M. (1997) 'Choppy waves on air and sea', *New Economy*, **4** (3), Autumn, 167–72.

OECD (1994) *The OECD Jobs Study: Evidence and Explanations*, Part I and Part II, Paris: OECD.

O'Mahony, M. (1993) 'International measure of fixed capital stocks: a five-country study', National Institute of Economic and Social Research, Discussion Paper no. 51, September.

Oulton, N. and O'Mahony, M. (1994) *Productivity and Growth: A Disaggregated Study of British Industry, 1954–86*, Cambridge: Cambridge University Press.

Petit, P. (1986) *Slow Growth and the Service Economy*, London: Frances Pinter.

Raphael, A. (1992) 'Beware the siren devaluers who lure us to ruin', *The Observer*, 26 April.

Romer, P. (1986) 'Increasing returns and long-run growth', *Journal of Political Economy*, **94**, October, 1002–37.

—— (1990) 'Endogenous technical change', *Journal of Political Economy*, **98**, October, S71–S102.

Rostow, W.W. (1960) *The Stages of Economic Growth*, Cambridge: Cambridge University Press.

Rowthorn, R.E. (1995) 'Capital formation and unemployment', *Oxford Review of Economic Policy*, **11** (1), 26–39.

Rowthorn, R.E. and Wells, J. (1987) *Deindustrialization and Foreign Trade*, Cambridge: Cambridge University Press.

Scott, M.F.G. (1989) *A New View of Economic Growth*, Oxford: Clarendon Press.

—— (1992) 'Policy implications of "a new view of economic growth"', *Economic Journal*, **102**, 622–32.

Singh, A. (1977) 'UK industry and the world economy: a case of deindustrialization?', *Cambridge Journal of Economics*, **1** (2), June.

—— (1987) 'Deindustrialization', in J. Eatwell, M. Milgate and P. Newman (eds), *The New Palgrave Dictionary of Economics*, London: Macmillan.

Small Business Research Centre (1992) *The State of British Enterprise: Growth, Innovation and Competitive Advantage in Small and Medium Sized Enterprises*, Cambridge: Small Business Research Centre, University of Cambridge.

Solow, R.M. (1970) *Growth Theory: An Exposition*, Oxford: Oxford University Press.

Stoneman, P. and Francis, N. (1992) 'Double deflation and the measurement of output and productivity in UK manufacturing 1979–1989', Warwick Business School Discussion Paper.

Summers, R. (1985) 'Services in the international economy', in R.E. Inman (ed.), *Managing the Service Economy: Prospects and Problems*, Cambridge: Cambridge University Press.

Tiratsoo, N. and Tomlinson, J. (1994) 'Restrictive practices on the shopfloor in Britain, 1945–60: myth and reality', *Business History*, **36** (2), April, 65–82.

Wells, J. (1993) 'The trouble with Thatcher', *New Economy*, autumn, 52–6.

Wilkinson, F. (1992) *Why Britain Needs a Minimum Wage*, London: Institute for Public Policy Research.

Young, A. (1928) 'Increasing returns and economic progress', *Economic Journal*, December.

3 Are the British bad at flexible manufacturing?

Stephen Ackroyd and Stephen Procter

INTRODUCTION: WHY FLEXIBILITY?

In this chapter we consider the relevance of the idea of flexibility to manufacturing in contemporary Britain. This is not a new topic. The flexibility of manufacturing processes and systems has been considered frequently by writers from many different disciplinary backgrounds in recent years. Engineers, technologists and some social scientists have proposed flexible organizations and flexible manufacturing systems as providing some sort of answer to the problems of contemporary manufacturing. Almost equally as often, however, the idea of flexibility has been rejected as having little value. Social scientists, in particular, have been inclined to be dismissive. In an otherwise valuable recent book, for example, Sayer and Walker (1992) devoted considerable space to arguments about flexibility, but concluded that concern with it has been largely misplaced.

Against this, it has become an axiom of current thinking in many circles that manufacturing success depends on meeting the market with high-quality and differentiated products at competitive prices. Discussion amongst business pundits and academics has moved beyond the orthodox view of marketing strategy promoted by such as Michael Porter (1980, 1985), in which the object of production strategy is to adapt to pre-existing markets in optimal ways. It is now frequently assumed that it is possible and desirable to enact markets – an idea originated by the social psychologist, Karl Weick (1969). In this view, it is possible actively to lead the development of markets with a stream of innovative and differentiated products. Such an assessment, of course, coincides with the views of those who argue that we are currently encountering permanent changes in consumption patterns, in which novelty and variety are key features (Featherstone 1991, Lash 1991). Whatever we may make of such arguments it is also true that managers are interested in meeting markets promptly with a variety of goods. Slack (1987, 1990) found that the main types of flexibility seen as important by managers were concerned with output – product mix, product volume and product delivery.

There is no doubt that it is possible to exaggerate the likely rewards to be attached to flexibility in meeting markets with a variety of goods, and, more to the point, the ease with which production arrangements can be made more adaptive and flexible. No doubt, too, managers are likely to use the supposed imperatives of meeting the market as a reason for instituting policies with regard to labour that they see as generally advantageous, a point made to good effect by Pollert (1991a). But it is also the case that the ability to respond flexibly in meeting demand is taken to be important in current market conditions. Our point of view is that the debate about flexibility has been, for the most part, inadequately conducted. Building on earlier work (Procter *et al.* 1994; Procter and Ackroyd 1996), we argue here for a better understanding of the idea of flexibility and its nature and extent in British manufacturing operations.

TYPES, DIMENSIONS AND CONDITIONS OF FLEXIBILITY

The concept of flexibility

Distinctions between types of flexibility extant in the literature are by now numerous. Sayer and Walker (1992: 199), for example, offer a list of seven types of flexibility, and even this is far from being complete. In our account we began by considering flexibility as a matter of meeting the market for products in appropriate quantities, types and qualities – what we might call product or output flexibility. Indeed, it is reasonable to regard product flexibility as the primary type of flexibility, because the need for flexibility in output is the source of an interest in flexibility in production arrangements and systems.

In pursuit of product flexibility, it is, we suggest, useful to distinguish three dimensions of flexibility: flexibility of labour, technology and organization. Our view about the majority of the literature on flexibility is that it is partial and often damagingly so. Much of it takes as its main concern what we have identified here as a single dimension of flexibility, dealing very inadequately, if at all, with the others. Generally, there has been a failure to clarify the different sources of and limits to flexibility in manufacturing systems considered in total. Key issues, such as in what ways and to what extent British manufacturing could be considered flexible, have not been exposed or analysed. Some commentators have taken a broader view, but their aim has usually been that of making conjectures about general properties of productive systems. Since most of the ideas and prescriptions have been held not to apply to this country, they have not been helpful in clarifying the properties and qualities of the manufacturing arrangements found here.

It is our view that all manufacturing systems have degrees of flexibility in them, and the aim of analysis must be to arrive at an appraisal of the overall condition of flexibility built into a given system. It is appropriate to think of manufacturing systems as having various technical and organizational properties which enable them to operate in different and more or less effective ways. On systematic appraisal of the different dimensions of flexibility, it is clear that the sources of and limits to flexibility are quite different in different cases. Moreover, coming to a judgement about the capacity and nature of productive arrangements in terms of their flexibility is not only a question of considering the intrinsic qualities of what we have labelled here the dimensions of flexibility. It is also important to recognize and refer to the overall flexibility of a given system in its social, technical and organizational aspects taken together. Our main point is that the characteristic condition of the manufacturing system found in a country can be realistically established and the limits to its adaptiveness assessed.

The notion of flexibility is a useful metaphor precisely because it envisages specific pressures for change and limitations in the capacity for adaptation in production arrangements. The notion of flexibility is, in fact, a simple description of something (a suspension bridge, for example) that is a great deal more complex. When something flexes it makes some limited systemic changes to reflect changed pressures. Hence, in our terms, the value of the notion of flexible production is that it implies an account of the various sources of flexibility and the way these contribute to a production system with a particular capacity for adaptation. Considered in these terms, in even the most adequate writing on flexibility, analysis of the properties of manufacturing arrangements is limited. Not only are the kinds of flexibility inherent in systems not systematically explored, but the concern for the limits of these is often conspicuously absent.

In this chapter, then, we are concerned to review the writing about flexibility and flexible manufacturing in Britain. Although there is an embarrassingly large amount of this, much of it has limited usefulness. We analyse it in three groups. In the first and second of these there are those literatures which are limited by being focused on a narrow definition of flexibility – a technological definition in the first case, and one focused on considerations of labour in the second. Such writing can nonetheless be very revealing about the nature of British manufacturing systems because it can be shown that there are interesting variations in the extent to which the ideas and proposals of commentators have been taken up in practice. In the third group there is more general writing on the flexibility of manufacturing systems. This writing is also very partial and disappointing, since it typically considers the supposedly positive qualities of foreign systems of flexible manufacture. British manufacturing is not so much systematically described as characterized by a number of debilitating lapses and inadequacies by comparison with more successful models. However, we argue that it is possible to use the best of this writing as a source of evidence and argument from which to piece together an account of the actual qualities of British manufacturing. What we arrive at is an account of the flexibility in Britain which has some quite different emphases from currently authoritative models.

Flexibility and technology

For many commentators, the idea of flexibility is primarily associated with the capabilities of new forms of technology. In particular, flexibility is taken to be a feature of new technologies that are highly adaptable to different production sequences (Slack 1983). The idea of flexible manufacturing systems (FMS) is one of the most popular characterizations of advanced manufacturing technology

(AMT) (Boer 1994; Browne *et al.* 1984; Lim 1987; Gerwin 1987). An FMS is quite often thought of simply as the grouping of computer numerically controlled (CNC) machine tools, or other programmable appliances such as robots, linked by an automated system of control and material handling (Bennett *et al.* 1988). With some frequency, however, the term is used to cover more complex and technologically coordinated systems such as are found with computer-integrated manufacturing (CIM) (Boaden and Dale 1986). As the term FMS suggests, it is precisely in terms of flexibility – defined as the technical adaptability of machines to new fabrication processes – that the benefits of such systems are seen (Boer 1994; Jaikumar 1986; Parrish 1990).

FMS/CIM has in fact come to be thought of as the merely rudimentary forms of more complex systems which will potentially coordinate manufacturing systems and processes and so supplement or replace traditional management and organization. Very broadly, CIM shades into computer-integrated business (CIB), in which integration is extended to such functions as sales and purchasing (Harrison 1990), and, further, into CIM-enterprise (CIM-E), which extends integration to include links with customers and suppliers (Rowlinson *et al.* 1994). These ideas share with FMS the idea of technological coordination of the productive process and the proposition that flexibility can be programmed into the technical core of such systems. As in FMS, so with CIB and CIM-E, advantages in terms of flexibility are seen to proceed primarily from the acquisition of inherently adaptable computer technology.

Clearly, for writers on these subjects, there is the beginning of a concern for the broader organization of production; but, in almost all cases, there is little attempt to recognize the characteristics of existing arrangements. This writing is prescriptive and evinces little interest in socio-technical systems for manufacture as they currently exist. It is simply assumed that new technology will initiate the reshaping of managerial systems and processes as well as the manufacturing processes themselves. Where labour is referred to at all, it assumes a position of very minor importance. In Slack's 'flexibility hierarchy' (1987, 1990), for example, flexible labour can be found at the bottom, as part of the structural element of resource flexibility. Gerwin (1987) makes the most systematic attempt we have found to link flexible manufacturing with requirements for labour. Arguing that the design of manufacturing systems needs to take account of both technological and social factors, he says that 'the critical workforce characteristic is multi-skilling but its nature varies depending upon the type of flexibility' (1987: 47). In other words, even the best of these writers tend to assume the subordination of labour to the requirements of technology.

However, something of the actual importance of technology in contemporary British manufacturing systems can be retrieved from considering the extent of the adoption of different forms of flexible manufacturing systems. Considered in this way, there are real problems with the idea that manufacturing processes will be technologically driven. Although Ray (1984) estimated that, within Europe, Britain had the highest proportion of NC and CNC machines, Northcott and Rogers (1984) found them in less than a quarter of manufacturing establishments.

According to Jones (1988), assembly and automated welding robots were found in only 22 per cent of firms covered by a survey by *The Engineer* and in only 24 per cent of firms on a DTI list. Northcott *et al.* (1986) found robotics in 25 per cent of plants with more than 1,000 workers.

Sophisticated types of flexible manufacturing are very rare. In 1982, Jones (1988) reports, there were just two FMS in the UK. By 1987 this figure had increased to around thirty. In their review of the diffusion of AMT, Rush and Bessant (1992) show that between 1980 and 1989 the number of FMS in the world as a whole increased from 154 to 827. Of the latter figure Japan accounted for 25.8 per cent, the United States for 16.8 per cent and the EC for 37.5 per cent. Within Europe, the United Kingdom, with ninety-seven, had the greatest number of systems, this figure being 11.7 per cent of the total. However, what evidence there is suggests that FMS were introduced for the wrong reasons or have proved unsuccessful: 'flexibility-as-versatility, in switching between different product-types, was either not sought or proved difficult to achieve in practice' (Jones 1988: 458).

The diffusion of CIM is difficult to ascertain. However, Rush and Bessant (1992) draw on Edquist and Jacobsson (1988) to show that by 1982 over 10,000 computer-aided design (CAD) systems existed worldwide. Using a number of studies conducted between 1980 and 1984, Edquist and Jacobsson arrived at a total figure of over 88,000. The great majority of these were in the United States, the figure for the UK being around 9,000. McLoughlin (1990) reports a gradual diffusion of CAD, citing Northcott and Walling's (1988) prediction that, by 1989, 46 per cent of manufacturing establishments would have had CAD. However, Jones (1988) found even CAD/CAM to be quite rare. Of the DTI's 'demonstration' firms, while 66 per cent had CAD, only 36 per cent had CAD and CAM (computer-aided manufacturing) systems.

CIM in anything approaching its purest form is almost impossible to locate. In 1985, Ingersoll Engineers simply gave up in their attempt to study the diffusion of CIM, though examples do exist of companies who aspire to it (Clark 1994, Jones 1988, Rowlinson *et al.* 1994). The extreme rarity of fully integrated CIM systems is itself testament to the idea that great difficulties have been found in their operation. Evidence exists which shows how this applies to each of its potential constituent elements. McLoughlin (1990) draws on a variety of sources to argue that CAD has not on the whole fulfilled its potential and that many organizations have had negative experiences with the idea. Webster and Williams' (1993) report on the adoption of computer-aided production management (CAPM) claims that it has failed to provide the benefits expected from it.

On the other hand, it would seem that what are technologically very much more simple manufacturing systems are being rapidly introduced. The most compelling example here is cellular manufacture. The reduction of machine set-up times, allowing the production of smaller batches and a flexible response to changes in demand, is given as its primary justification. Considered as a technical system, however, it is fairly basic. It often involves simply the regrouping of machine tools in ways that will allow batches of similar or related products to be produced. In these versions of cell working the system leaves a great deal of the coordination of production between cells, as well as within them, to labour. Although in more sophisticated versions of cellular manufacture, production design and scheduling are planned within integrated information systems, the need for tight technical coordination is lessened by, among other things, flexible labour utilization. Some writers have also seen JIT, particularly as it is used in the UK, as operating in this sort of way, as facilitating the development of technical integration of productive processes. JIT delivery provides a buffer between elements in manufacturing processes which would otherwise have to be more adequately integrated through technology (Harrison 1990). Nonetheless, with JIT, assemblers can supply to the market a large variety of goods despite relatively low levels of dedicated plant and machinery, without the need to hold large stock of manufactured parts (Bennett and Forrester 1994).

By contrast with the more sophisticated and capital-intensive forms of technically led flexibility, with cellular manufacture and JIT there is much more evidence of widespread introduction. The former is particularly widely diffused in British industry. In 1990 the consultancy Ingersoll Engineers surveyed engineering companies with turnovers in excess of £10m (Ingersoll Engineers 1990). They found what they described as a 'quiet revolution': 51 per cent of their sample had introduced some form of cellular manufacturing, most of them in the previous few years. This finding was supported by Oliver and Wilkinson (1992), whose 1991 survey of the extent of a number of manufacturing practices showed that 50 per cent of their sample of large companies were using cellular manufacturing, nearly all of them having started doing so since 1983. A second survey conducted by Ingersoll Engineers in 1993 (Ingersoll Engineers 1994) found that the proportion of engineering companies using cellular manufacturing had increased to 73 per cent.

Survey evidence also exists on the extent to which JIT has been adopted in the UK. Voss and Robinson (1987) found that 57 per cent of their sample of manufacturing companies were either implementing or planning to implement some aspects of JIT. Oliver and Wilkinson (1992) based their findings on two surveys. Of companies involved in the first of these, undertaken in 1987, 34 per cent said that JIT was in use, and 30 per cent that it was planned or being implemented. Oliver and Wilkinson's second study, carried out in 1991, found that the percentage of companies using or planning to use JIT had increased from 64 per cent to 82 per cent. Of the total sample, 68 per cent said that JIT was actually in use, and of the thirty-nine companies that answered the question on the date of introduction, 31 per cent said that it had been introduced in the period 1983–7 and 63 per cent the period 1988–92.

Oliver and Wilkinson's two surveys asked respondents to evaluate the success of the practices they had implemented. In the 1987 analysis, 87 per cent of companies which had introduced JIT said that it had been 'quite' or 'very' successful, but only 6 per cent said it had been 'highly' successful. In the 1991 survey, JIT production was ranked eighth out of ten Japanese-style innovations in manufacturing practices, 16 per cent of those using it regarding it as 'highly' successful and 79 per cent as 'quite' or 'very' successful. Procter's (1995) examination of aggregate figures on firms' holdings of stocks, however, suggests that the introduction of JIT has not resulted in reduced levels of stocks. From this evidence it is at least arguable that JIT recommends itself in Britain for similar reasons that cellular manufacture is common. Although it depends on a certain degree of technical coordination, it is very dependent on labour flexibility to be effective.

Flexibility and labour

A good deal of the work of social scientists on flexibility is almost equally as one-sided as that of technical specialists. From this group of commentators, the most influential work is centred on the model of the 'flexible firm' put forward by Atkinson and others in the mid-1980s (Atkinson 1984; NEDO 1986). Counter-claims about forms of labour utilization have also been central to the responses of critics to this work (Pollert 1988, 1991b; Gilbert *et al.* 1992).

For Atkinson, the flexibility sought by management is of two main kinds: functional and numerical. In the terms used in this chapter, these forms of flexibility primarily involve the flexible use of labour. A central proposition of the Atkinson model involves the division of a firm's workforce between a 'core' of long-term employees and a 'periphery' of workers in a less continuous employment relationship. Core workers are expected to display a wide range of accomplishments and high task adaptability, capacities referred to as 'functional flexibility'. The periphery would have less skill, but would contribute to the flexibility of the firm by being quickly pulled into or pushed out of employment as demand for products fluctuates, a potentiality referred to as 'numerical flexibility'. Functional flexibility and numerical flexibility therefore refer primarily to different forms of adaptability in the utilization of labour. Clearly, what both these conceptualizations of flexibility do is propose (presumably, to management) a particular way of thinking about the flexible use of labour.

Atkinson and his co-workers' ideas about the flexible firm do, in a limited way, refer to other dimensions of manufacturing systems. This work supposedly proposes a model of the firm, and there is therefore some discussion of aspects of organization and management. However, it is worth noting how limited and partial this is. Although flexibility is to be achieved by management seeking functional and numerical flexibility, there is little reference to the ways in which the types of policy are to be achieved by management, or how they may contribute to an overall management strategy. There is also little reference to technology and to the way that technical and labour requirements might mesh together.

The question of the extent to which the forms of labour flexibility identified in the model actually exist has been extensively debated (see, for example, Pollert 1991b; Gilbert *et al.* 1992). The majority of the evidence has been from surveys and is concerned with the growth of numerical flexibility. In the original NEDO (1986) study of seventy-two companies drawn from four industrial sectors, sixty-four (89 per cent) had sought to increase numerical flexibility since 1980. Subsequent studies have each tended to concentrate on the question of the growth in a particular part of the 'peripheral' workforce. Hakim (1990), for example, used Labour Force Survey (LFS) data to show an increase in the size of the peripheral workforce in the period 1981–7. Casey (1991:180) saw a substantial growth in self-employment between 1979 and 1987, a 'substantial but more steady' growth in part-time employment over the same period, and almost no growth in temporary employment between 1983 and 1987.

A similar kind and volume of survey evidence does not exist on the question of the development of functional flexibility. However, the NEDO (1986) report found that 54 per cent of its sample had sought to increase functional flexibility since 1980. Perhaps the most systematic survey data on functional flexibility is provided by Daniel (1987). Using Workplace Industrial Relations Survey (WIRS) data he shows that between 1980 and 1984, 29 per cent of the firms surveyed had taken action to relax demarcations between crafts, 28 per cent had sought to create new categories of either multiskilled or enhanced craftsmen and 20 per cent had relaxed demarcations between production and maintenance functions. For the most part, however, as Elger (1991) points out, the surveys have been unrepresentative in nature and have had problems in defining and identifying functional flexibility.

With functional flexibility there is also the question of the nature of change. It has been argued that although widespread, the development of functional flexibility has not cut very deep (Elger 1991; Cross 1988). Similar points have been made by Ackroyd *et al.* (1988), when they suggest that employers tend to adopt those aspects of innovations that serve their pre-existing inclinations in regard to labour and to disregard aspects that are out of keeping with them. As O'Reilly (1992: 370) argues, a clearer distinction needs to be made between functional flexibility 'accompanied by an increase in training and upgrading' and functional flexibility 'used in an *ad hoc* manner to meet shortages and intensify work'.

What divides commentators in this area are such issues as whether the forms of flexibility identified by Atkinson are empirically or substantively significant or not. As we have seen, there has been substantial research relevant to the question of the existence of numerical flexibility, but very few connections have been made concerning other areas of debate about flexibility. The implications of the forms of labour-led or labour-centred flexibility for technology utilization make no appearance. There has been negligible discussion of the relevance of numerical and functional flexibility for firms utilizing different kinds of technology, for example. Because manufacturing necessarily involves the use of both physical technology and labour, it is questionable indeed to discuss one without considering the other.

General accounts of flexibility

Attempts to set out what is happening in the development of more flexible manufacturing systems in general terms are many (see, for example, Piore and Sabel 1984; Tolliday and Zeitlin 1991; Sayer and Walker 1992). However, these accounts of the general features of flexible manufacturing often take the form of developing idealized pictures of what is happening in other countries, most frequently Japan and Germany. It is widely suggested, for example, that the manufacturing systems of these countries successfully combine highly flexible technology and highly skilled and flexible labour. By comparison, British practice is characterized as being either indeterminate or featuring a whole series of failures to come close to the best practice overseas. In their eagerness to say what is evidently not happening, there is an inability or unwillingness to say what is.

There are several examples of this sort of thing. Sayer and Walker (1992), for one, offer an admirably extended discussion of flexibility. They are also aware of the diversity of institutional and organizational forms developed at different times and in different places. However, they reject the idea that it is possible to clarify general characteristics of manufacturing systems in terms of their particular flexibility. For much of their discussion they are so busy documenting the range of possible variations in the institutions of capitalism that little emerges about the distinctiveness of the available forms of organization for production. Only at the end of their discussion is there a sustained attempt to set out the structural features of the Japanese industrial system. What emerges is that they have a clearer view of the distinctive patterns of manufacture in America and Japan than they do about what is distinctive about Britain. Discussing the introduction of FMS, for example, they say that in the US such technology was 'used within a traditional Taylorist automation framework for cutting operating costs and not [as in Japan] for broadening the product range and raising the rate of product innovation' (1992: 202). By implication, the options are to choose between Japanese and American practices, but what there may be by way of distinctive patterns of organization for production in Britain is not specified.

There are some writers who have fared better in bringing British practices into focus. In a series of penetrating papers comparing organization and practices in the engineering industry in Japan, the US and Britain (Jones 1988, 1989, 1991), Bryn Jones has moved further than some other accounts to clarify some aspects of flexibility of the manufacturing system in Britain. In a valuable chapter in which he discusses the introduction of FMS in the three countries, Jones (1991) argues that there are distinct local limits to the emergence of a technologically determined common pattern for the arrangement of work. Although he recognizes important sectoral differences in British industry, in that large, monopolistic (usually defence-oriented) firms are developing different policies, he is clear that the introduction of FMS in Britain has led to some development of more flexible and responsible work roles. His view is that a more cost-driven policy is also possible, especially in the middle range of British engineering companies that have settled for mid-quality types of production. He does not expand on this suggestion or give details of the organization of such firms and the character of their managerial regimes. However, since Jones's main concern is relatively high-technology FMS, which it would seem are not used by many British manufacturing firms, this is perhaps excusable.

In a discussion of the development of flexible specialization in Britain and Germany, Christel Lane (1988; see also 1995) is also quite successful in sharpening appreciation of what is happening in British manufacturing to secure flexible production. Lane echoes Jones and others by suggesting that managers of British firms have been reluctant to invest in new technology. According to Lane, failure to deliver flexibility through technology has forced managements to focus on obtaining flexibility from labour. For its part, labour has also not been multiskilled nor able to insist on a policy of multiskilling. The organization of skilled labour has been much weakened, and is in any case only disposed to defend narrow and traditional skill demarcations. The combined effects of a secular decline of manufacturing capacity and the weakening of craft unionism has led to the decay of the apprenticeship system and the erosion of control of work by skilled labour. We might add that legislation hostile to trade unionism and structural unemployment has empowered new forms of labour utilization and limited effective trade unionism for skilled labour to a few isolated pockets.

Using language derived from the Atkinson model of the firm, Lane contrasts the development of manufacturing in Britain unfavourably with that found in Germany. Core members of the workforce in Britain, she says, may be formally designated as skilled but will not have a broad spectrum of transferable skills. Lane also argues that managerial power is routinely exerted through the use of numerical flexibility: that is, through hiring and firing, the extended use of part-time, and other kinds of limited employment contract. Although some functional flexibility and upskilling is in evidence in the UK, she argues, the tendency is to favour the pursuit of numerical flexibility. With much of this we can agree, but how it amounts to a viable package of practices is left obscure. There is a need for some qualifications and development of her argument in order to develop a clear picture of flexible manufacturing as a distinctive socio-technical system.

THE PATTERN OF FLEXIBLE MANUFACTURING IN BRITAIN

In some ways the three bodies of work we have so far examined reveal an impressive consistency. On this evidence it does not seem to be the case that in Britain there has been the widespread introduction of flexible manufacture that combines high levels of investment with the use of highly skilled 'polyvalent' workers. Such arrangements are alleged to be widespread if not predominant in Japan (Jones 1991) and in Germany (Lane 1988, 1995), but, for Britain, this pattern, if it exists at all, is restricted to a few very large companies. On the other hand, it is possible to read much of the existing evidence as revealing a quite different pattern of flexible manufacture. This involves some limited technological reconfiguration, but depends much more heavily on changes in labour utilization as well as on managerial and other organizational changes. It is not difficult to describe this system in general terms.

So far as technology is concerned, levels of investment remain relatively low, sometimes involving simply the resiting and rearrangement of existing technology. More commonly, however, existing capital is supplemented by limited investment in new machine tools – such as small numbers of CNC machines – and limited investment in information technology with associated information systems. Typically such automation falls well short of CIM, but does involve the introduction of company-wide stock inventory and cost analysis. The utilization of labour is also reconfigured, in that semi-skilled labour is used wherever possible. Hence, contemporary changes clearly have, as Lane suggests, accelerated the decay of the apprenticeship system. Labour also contributes flexibility to production by being deployed in small self-managed teams, which usually have some delegated autonomy. In cell working, which, as we have seen, is now a very commonly utilized arrangement, workers are paid on a group incentive basis to produce a mix of components or subassemblies in teams. Although work study has at some point been used to calculate the cost of the items produced, a high proportion of the total wage is paid as group bonuses for output in appropriate amounts and qualities. Using Friedman's (1977) concepts to describe this system, it appears to be closer to responsible autonomy than direct control. Teams and cells often have considerable autonomy in deciding the allocation of labour to jobs and the sequence of tasks. Although the range of tasks undertaken by cells is typically not very wide, production tasks often being very similar over periods of months, there is nonetheless scope for job rotation. Given a sharing of roles within groups, there is the possibility of on-the-job training and limited enskilling. From the point of view of the unskilled worker, opportunities for exposure to a range of tasks calling for the development of practical skills are often present. For these reasons, too, training for a broadening range of activities – if not skills – can be achieved on-the-job, a feature which recommends such systems to management.

There should be no doubting the contribution made by labour to flexible output in these arrangements. In these developments, perhaps the most remarkable change is the domestication of skilled labour. Although high proportions of workers classed as skilled are sometimes retained and paid as such, skilled labour is generally not as privileged as it was. Formally skilled workers are found working in teams with multiple tasks and with other grades of labour. Traditional job demarcations are, in practice, routinely ignored so far as general work allocation is concerned. This has been achieved through domestication of trade unions (assisted by legislation against unions and high structural unemployment), but also because of managerial willingness to pay premium wages to highly productive work groups.

Clearly the arrangement we are describing here departs quite widely from the Atkinson model of the flexible firm. It is difficult to see highly skilled workers forming the privileged core of firms. Consistent with this is that functional flexibility and numerical flexibility are not so easily differentiated as the Atkinson model implies. The expansion of firms does not take place on the basis of an increased volume of standardized activities, as provided by growth in the numbers of (relatively unskilled) employees. Rather, flexibility is secured by adding to (or dispensing with) whole areas of production utilizing teams of more or less similarly skilled operatives. In fact, every activity undertaken by a firm is recurrently costed in terms of its contribution to profitability. If it is known that a component or subassembly that cannot be made profitably will be automatically sub-contracted, it can be a potent source of work discipline. This is the Atkinson model, but with a core of varying size and a much reduced contribution from the periphery so far as routine production is concerned.

Capacity for internal reorganization along these lines also implies a good deal of flexibility at the level of the organization considered as a socio-technical system. Certainly, if the range of activities, and, through this, the scale of operations, is constantly adjusted, the organization must also constantly adjust its external relations as well. Transitions between making and buying, for example, imply good interfirm relations and the development of interorganizational networks. Such developments help make sense of secular trends in the size of organizations – which have been consistently smaller and smaller productive units – and the growth in the importance of interfirm networks and cooperative relationships (see Bresnen and Fowler, Chapter 8).

CONCLUSIONS: ARE THE BRITISH BAD AT FLEXIBLE MANUFACTURING?

The short answer to this question is a qualified yes. By comparison with foreign modes of high-tech flexible manufacturing, Britain is well out of the game. However, in this chapter we have appraised the available evidence and come to the conclusion that the British can do, and are doing, a particular kind of flexible manufacturing. There is a discernible low-tech, low-training strategy in the approach to flexibility adopted by the management of British companies. This strategy involves relatively low levels of technical flexibility and depends heavily on the adaptability and flexibility of labour. It does this, however, without very high levels of commitment to training. Numerous piecemeal and pragmatic adjustments in management and organization are also necessary to make this package work.

Analysing the contingencies surrounding the introduction of flexibility into manufacturing leads to the conclusion that numerous factors are tending to determine the choice of the low-tech, low-training strategy, but that this is unlikely to result in outcomes that will lead to sustained growth in the sector. In other words, the resulting strategy may not be effective in counteracting the effect of constraining contingencies such as restrictions in the supply of capital, stringent accounting for profitability, and very short payback periods. On the contrary, this low-tech, low-training strategy is perhaps best understood as being a symptom of the secular processes of decline in manufacturing documented elsewhere (Ackroyd and Whitaker 1990; Coates 1994).

We are inclined to conclude that the forms of flexibility being introduced in manufacture are neither disastrous nor particularly effective in themselves. They combine in distinctive ways some technical flexibility with changes in labour flexibility and in organization and management. That manufacturing survives in this form is prima facie evidence that it is productive. It is also worth saying that, given our historical preference for 'responsible autonomy' (Friedman 1977) in the management of labour, and the responsiveness of labour to such regimes (Ackroyd and Lawrenson 1995), there is some reason to think that the low-tech, low-training strategy has some likelihood of success for the time being. In view of recurrent difficulties with capital supply and the pressure for profitability that is endemic to British business, the low-tech, low-training strategy is, realistically considered, probably one of the few ways in which manufacturing can be organized in this country today.

REFERENCES

Ackroyd, S. and Lawrenson, D. (1995) 'Manufacturing decline and the managerial division of labour in Britain: the case of vehicles', in I. A. Glover and M. Hughes (eds), *The Professional-Managerial Class*, Aldershot: Avebury.

Ackroyd, S. and Whitaker, A. (1990) 'Manufacturing decline and the organization of manufacture in Britain', in P. Stewart, P. Crowther and P. Garrahan (eds), *Restructuring for Economic Flexibility*, Aldershot: Avebury.

Ackroyd, S., Burrell, G., Hughes, M. and Whitaker, A. (1988) 'The Japanization of British industry?', *Industrial Relations Journal*, **19** (1), 11–23.

Atkinson, J. (1984) 'Manpower strategies for flexible organizations', *Personnel Management*, August, 28–31.

Bennett, D. and Forrester, P. (1994) 'Product variety and just-in-time: conflict and challenge', *International Journal of Logistics Management*, **5** (1), 73–9.

Bennett, D., Lewis, C. and Oakley, M. (1988) *Operations Management*, London: Philip Allan.

Boaden, R. and Dale, B. (1986) 'What is computer-integrated manufacturing?', *International Journal of Operations and Production Management*, **6** (3), 30–7.

Boer, H. (1994) 'Flexible manufacturing systems', in J. Storey (ed.), *New Wave Manufacturing Strategies*, London: Paul Chapman.

Browne, J., Dubois, D., Rathmill, K., Sethi, S. and Stecke, K. (1984) 'Classification of flexible manufacturing systems', *The FMS Magazine*, April, 114–17.

Casey, B. (1991) 'Survey evidence on trends in "non-standard" employment', in A. Pollert (ed.), *Farewell to Flexibility?*, Oxford: Blackwell.

Clark, J. (1994) 'Computer integrated manufacturing, supervisory management, and human intervention in the production process', *International Journal of Production Economics*, **34** (3), 305–12.

Coates, D. (1994) *The Question of UK Decline: The Economy, State and Society*, London: Harvester Wheatsheaf.

Cross, M. (1988) 'Changes in working practices in UK manufacturing, 1981–88', *Industrial Relations Review and Report*, **415**, 2–10.

Daniel, W. (1987) *Workplace Industrial Relations and Technical Change*, London: Pinter.

Edquist, C. and Jacobsson, S. (1988) *Flexible Automation: The Global Diffusion of New Technology in the Engineering Industry*, Oxford: Blackwell.

Elger, T. (1991) 'Task flexibility and the intensification of labour in UK manufacturing in the 1980s', in A. Pollert (ed.), *Farewell to Flexibility?*, Oxford: Blackwell.

Featherstone, M. (1991) *Consumer Culture and Postmodernism*, London: Sage.

Friedman, A. (1977) *Industry and Labour*, London: Macmillan.

Gerwin, D. (1987) 'An agenda for research on the flexibility of manufacturing processes', *International Journal of Operations and Production Management*, **7** (1), 38–49.

Gilbert, N., Burrows, R. and Pollert, A. (eds) (1992) *Fordism and Flexibility: Divisions and Change*, Basingstoke: Macmillan.

Hakim, C. (1990) 'Core and periphery in employers' workplace strategies: evidence from the 1987 ELUS survey', *Work, Employment and Society*, 4 (2), 157–88.

Harrison, M. (1990) *Advanced Manufacturing Technology Management*, London: Pitman.

Ingersoll Engineers (1990) *Competitive Manufacturing: The Quiet Revolution*, Rugby: Ingersoll Engineers.

—— (1994) *The Quiet Revolution Continues*, Rugby: Ingersoll Engineers.

Jaikumar, R. (1986) 'Postindustrial manufacturing', *Harvard Business Review*, 64 (6), 69–76.

Jones, B. (1988) 'Work and flexible automation in Britain: a review of developments and possibilities', *Work, Employment and Society*, 2 (4), 451–86.

—— (1989) 'Flexible automation and factory politics: the United Kingdom in current perspective', in P. Hirst and J. Zeitlin (eds), *Reversing Industrial Decline?*, Oxford: Berg.

—— (1991) 'Technological convergence and limits to managerial control: flexible manufacturing systems in Britain, the USA and Japan', in S. Tolliday and J. Zeitlin (eds), *The Power to Manage?*, London: Routledge.

Kenney, M. and Florida, R (1988) 'Beyond mass production: production and labour process in Japan', *Politics and Society*, 16 (1), 121–58.

Lane, C. (1988) 'Industrial change in Europe: the pursuit of flexible specialization in Britain and West Germany', *Work, Employment and Society*, 2 (2), 141–68.

—— (1995) *Industry and Society in Europe: Stability and Change in Britain, Germany and France*, Aldershot: Edward Elgar.

Lash, S. (1991) *Sociology and Postmodernism*, London: Routledge.

Lim, S. (1987) 'Flexible manufacturing systems and manufacturing flexibility in the United Kingdom', *International Journal of Operations and Production Management*, 7 (6), 44–54.

McLoughlin, I. (1990) 'Management, work organization and CAD: towards flexible automation?', *Work, Employment and Society*, 4 (2), 217–37.

NEDO (National Economic Development Office) (1986) *Changing Working Patterns: How Companies Achieve Flexibility to Meet New Needs*, London: NEDO.

Northcott, J. and Rogers, P. (1984) *Microelectronics in British Industry: The Pattern of Change*, London: Policy Studies Institute.

Northcott, J. and Walling, A. (1988) *The Impact of Microelectronics: Diffusion, Benefits and Problems in British Industry*, London: Policy Studies Institute.

Northcott, J., Brown, C., Christie, I. and Sweenie, M. (1986) *Robots in British Industry: Expectations and Experience*, London: Policy Studies Institute.

Oliver, N. and Wilkinson, B. (1992) *The Japanization of British Industry: New Developments in the 1990s*, 2nd edn, Oxford: Blackwell.

O'Reilly, J. (1992) 'Where do you draw the line? Functional flexibility, training and skill in Britain and France', *Work, Employment and Society*, 6 (3), 369–96.

Parrish, D. (1990) *Flexible Manufacturing*, London: Butterworth-Heinemann.

Piore, M. and Sabel, C. (1984) *The Second Industrial Divide: Possibilities for Prosperity*, New York: Basic Books.

Pollert, A. (1988) 'The "flexible firm": fixation or fact?', *Work, Employment and Society*, 2 (3), 281–316.

—— (1991a) 'The orthodoxy of flexibility', in A. Pollert (ed.), *Farewell to Flexibility?*, Oxford: Blackwell.

—— (ed.) (1991b) *Farewell to Flexibility?*, Oxford: Blackwell.

Porter, M. (1980) *Competitive Strategy: Techniques for Analysing Industries and Competitors*, New York: Free Press.

—— (1985) *Competitive Advantage: Creating and Sustaining Superior Performance*, New York: Free Press.

Procter, S. (1995) 'The extent of just-in-time manufacturing in the UK: evidence from aggregate economic data', *Integrated Manufacturing Systems*, **6** (4), 16–25.

Procter, S. and Ackroyd, S. (1996) 'Managing advanced manufacturing technology: production-led and labour-led flexibility in UK manufacturing', in *Proceedings of the Second International Conference on Managing Integrated Manufacturing*, University of Leicester.

Procter, S., Rowlinson, M., McArdle, L., Hassard, J. and Forrester, P. (1994) 'Flexibility, politics and strategy: in defence of the model of the flexible firm', *Work, Employment and Society*, **8** (2), 221–42.

Ray, G. (1984) *The Diffusion of Mature Technologies*, Cambridge: Cambridge University Press.

Rowlinson, M., Procter, S. and Hassard, J. (1994) 'CIM and the process of innovation: integrating the organization of production', *International Journal of Production Economics*, **34** (3), 359–69.

Rush, H. and Bessant, J. (1992) 'Revolution in three-quarter time: lessons from the diffusion of advanced manufacturing technologies', *Technology Analysis and Strategic Management*, **4** (1), 3–19.

Sayer, A. and Walker, R. (1992) *The New Social Economy: Reworking the Division of Labour*, Oxford: Blackwell.

Slack, N. (1983) 'Flexibility as a manufacturing objective', in C. Voss (ed.), *Research in Production/Operations Management*, Aldershot: Gower.

—— (1987) 'The flexibility of manufacturing systems', *International Journal of Operations and Production Management*, 7 (4), 35–45.

—— (1990) 'Flexibility as managers see it', in M. Warner, W. Wobbe and P. Brodner (eds), *New Technology and Manufacturing Management: Strategic Choices for Flexible Production Systems*, Chichester: Wiley.

Tolliday, S. and Zeitlin, J. (eds) (1991) *The Power to Manage?*, London: Routledge.

Voss, C. and Robinson, S. (1987) 'Application of just-in-time manufacturing techniques in the United Kingdom', *International Journal of Operations and Production Management*, 7 (4), 46–52.

Webster, J. and Williams, R. (1993) 'The success and failure of computer-aided production management: the implications for corporate and public policy', PICT (Programme on Information and Communication Technologies) Report no. 2, University of Edinburgh.

Weick, K. (1969) *The Social Psychology of Organising*, Reading, Mass.: Addison-Wesley.

4 An analysis of the performance of Japanese, US and domestic manufacturing firms in the UK electronics/electrical sector

Max Munday and Michael J. Peel

INTRODUCTION

A combination of trade pressures and yen appreciation contributed to a surge of Japanese overseas investment during the 1980s. Prior to the collapse of the Japanese 'bubble economy' in 1989, Japanese outward direct investment had reached a record level of $67,540m. A significant proportion of this outward investment came to the European Union. Ando (1995) reports that between 1982 and 1992 Japanese manufacturing investment into the European Union increased from $137m to $2,055m. The UK was the chief European beneficiary of this surge in Japanese manufacturing investment, attracting an annual average of 40 per cent of Japanese direct investment into Europe in the period from 1982 to 1992.

In 1981, the Census of Production showed that seventeen Japanese manufacturing enterprises employed approximately 3,000 people in the UK. A survey (JETRO 1996) undertaken by the Japanese External Trade Organization in 1995 suggested that the total number of Japanese manufacturing plants in the UK had grown to 215, employing approximately 70,000 people (representing about 9 per cent of foreign manufacturing employment in the UK). Growth in the Japanese transplant manufacturing sector in the UK between 1985 and 1995 reflected not just new greenfield ventures, but also expansion projects among existing investors, and growth in joint ventures with domestic firms.

Electrical and electronic engineering companies dominate the Japanese transplant sector in the UK. Of the 215 Japanese enterprises surveyed in 1995 by JETRO, sixty-seven (31%) were producing electronic engineering equipment or related components (JETRO 1996). Japanese electronics equipment manufacturers are supported by a number of Japanese-owned electronics suppliers in the UK (see Munday 1995). In 1993, electrical engineering and related industries accounted for 35 per cent of the value of Japanese manufacturing assets in the UK (Business Monitor 1995a).

Other important constituents of the Japanese sector in the UK include transport equipment makers and components, which although comprising just 12 per cent of enterprises in 1995 (twenty-six companies), accounted for a third of the value of Japanese manufacturing assets (Business Monitor 1995a). This sector includes some of the largest Japanese investments in the UK, including car makers

Nissan (Sunderland), Honda (Swindon) and Toyota (Burnaston), between them employing over 8,000 people in 1995. This sector is also supported by a significant number of Japanese-owned suppliers, the largest of which include Calsonic (Llanelli), SP Tyres (Birmingham and Sunderland), Hashimoto Forming (Tyneside) and ND Marston (Leeds). Other sectors with significant Japanese involvement include chemicals and general machinery.

A number of studies have considered the economic impact of the growing number of Japanese manufacturing transplants in the UK. Taylor (1993) examined the determinants of the spatial distribution of Japanese investment in the UK. Morris *et al.* (1993) provided an extensive case study of the development of the Japanese manufacturing sector in the Welsh economy, focusing on the role of the Japanese sector in promoting regional economic growth. Another group of studies has considered the impact of increased competition from Japanese subsidiaries on domestic firms (Dunning 1986; Brech and Sharp 1984; Strange 1993).

Other research studies (reviewed below) have focused more explicitly on the performance and performance objectives of Japanese-owned firms in the UK. These studies include macro-level and regional studies, comparisons at the firm level and micro (plant level) studies using primary data drawn from questionnaires and/or case studies. Underlying many of these studies is a recognition that a relatively strong performing Japanese manufacturing sector in the UK could have considerable benefits for national and regional economic development. Foreign direct investment (particularly Japanese manufacturing investment) appears to be seen by the Department of Trade and Industry as not just a means of creating employment, incomes and trading opportunities, but also a possible means of improving UK domestic manufacturing performance through technology transfer and increased competitive pressure (see Eltis and Fraser 1992).

However, other commentators remain to be convinced that Japanese manufacturing in the UK is either performing at a satisfactory level, or that it can provide a fillip to national and regional economic development. For example, Haslam *et al.* (1995), and Williams *et al.* (1992), question whether UK enterprises necessarily benefit from the local presence of Japanese manufacturing capital. They argue that the strategic and political rationale underpinning Japanese FDI in the West, limits the scope of local subsidiary operations, and that Japanese manufacturing plants are largely constrained to production-only operations, which are characterized by comparatively low value added performance measures (see also Delbridge *et al.* in Chapter 12).

Clearly, these contributions feed into the wider debate on the role of foreign direct investment in regional and national development. Munday *et al.* (1995), in a study of the Japanese transplant sector in Wales, concluded that the Japanese subsidiaries contributed regional economic benefits comparable to those of North American and European Union firms, and that Japanese firms were characterized by higher labour productivity, and more efficient production practices, albeit with some reservations about earnings levels, profitability and the degree of local purchasing of goods and services. However, in a wider review, Young *et al.*

(1994) show that the extent to which concentrations of inward investment contributes towards the development of long-term and sustainable dynamic and competitive advantages for regions and nations is questioned by an increasing body of research evidence.

The extant research on the comparative performance of Japanese enterprises in the UK has covered a number of areas. One line of research has focused on the general productivity of plants in Japan relative to those in the UK (Dunning 1986; Strange 1993). However, such comparisons are made difficult because of problems in comparing firms operating in significantly different production environments. Furthermore, Dunning (1986) demonstrated that, while production methods in Japanese subsidiaries in the UK were mainly the same as those in the Japanese parent companies, they were scaled down to produce lower volumes. The different volumes produced in Japan and the UK clearly make accurate productivity comparisons difficult.

Other research has investigated the financial and marketing performance of Japanese subsidiaries located in the UK. For example, Doyle *et al.* (1992) examined the characteristics of matched samples of ninety US, Japanese and indigenous subsidiaries in the financial services, consumer and industrial goods sectors. The study, drawing on data obtained from interviews with senior managers, suggested that the managers of US and UK subsidiaries were, on average, more likely than Japanese managers to be 'short termist' in terms of preferences for 'quick profits' over 'consolidation' of market share. Market performance (market share) was also rated as being a significantly more important corporate objective by Japanese managers than by US and UK managers.

The increased commitment of Japanese firms to long-term performance objectives was thought to lead to greater support for, and confidence in, employees within their subsidiaries. Doyle *et al.* also reported that the managers of UK and US firms viewed cost-cutting as a means of improving productivity. On the other hand, Japanese managers placed more emphasis on increases in market share as a strategy to increase productivity and reduce costs. Bromwich and Inoue (1994) also provide evidence on the commitment of the Japanese-owned firms to long-term strategic objectives. Based on an interview survey of Japanese subsidiary managing/finance directors in 1991, they reported that the most important strategic objectives were return on sales and increasing market share. In terms of the achievement of stated objectives, the managers were least satisfied with earnings growth and return on investment, and most satisfied with sales growth.

At the macroeconomic and regional level, Census of Production data demonstrates that Japanese manufacturing subsidiaries outperform UK enterprises with reference to gross value added per employee, sales per employee and stock turnover. Relative to US subsidiaries, however, manual earnings in Japanese subsidiaries located in the UK are lower, but higher than the overall national average. For example, Figure 4.1 shows that in 1992 plant operative earnings in Japanese subsidiaries were around 5 per cent above those found in UK manufacturing firms, but nearly 30 per cent below those found in US-owned firms.

More recent research and commentary has drawn specific attention to the poor reported profit performance of Japanese subsidiaries in the UK (see, for example, Piper 1996; Haslam *et al.* 1995; Oyelere and Emmanuel 1996; Williams *et al.* 1992), with the evidence suggesting that transfer price manipulation artificially depresses Japanese profit returns in the UK. Buckley and Hughes (1997), however, while acknowledging that transfer pricing manipulation occurs among Japanese subsidiaries in the UK, suggest that the motive may not be deliberately to minimize UK tax payments, but that it is more likely to be the result of internal pricing structures which are designed to generate profit for the parent organization in Japan. In this context, the notion of an overseas Japanese subsidiary being viewed as a profit centre is seen as dysfunctional in the Japanese organizational context.

In a recent study, Munday and Peel (1997) examined the comparative performance of Japanese manufacturing subsidiaries with reference to a range of financial and performance indicators relating to profitability, labour and asset productivity, stock efficiency, liquidity, gearing, credit risk, employment and remuneration. Their research focused on matched samples of ninety-seven Japanese and domestic manufacturing subsidiaries drawn from the FAME CD-ROM accounts corporate database, and covered the company reporting periods 1993–4. Matching was undertaken on the basis of industry (three-digit standard industrial classification), size (in terms of sales) and year of data. The study found that in comparison to their matched domestic counterparts, Japanese manufacturing subsidiaries generated a relatively high level of sales per employee. However, UK-owned subsidiaries outperformed their Japanese counterparts in terms of the returns generated from a given set of assets. On average, Japanese subsidiaries had smaller workforces and a lower wage bill to sales ratio, but paid their employees more. Somewhat contrary to prior expectations, Japanese subsidiaries were found to hold relatively high levels of stock, and also performed comparatively badly on a number of liquidity indicators. Japanese subsidiaries were also characterized by significantly higher measures of credit and financial risk.

The research also confirmed earlier work (see Buckley and Hughes 1997) that has commented on the poor recorded profitability of Japanese subsidiaries. On the basis of reported accounts evidence, Munday and Peel noted that some 20 per cent of the Japanese subsidiaries were not in a position to continue trading without external support. The findings were confirmed when the population of Japanese, other foreign-owned and domestic manufacturing firms on the research database were examined. Over 40 per cent of Japanese subsidiaries were discovered to be loss-making in 1994–5, a significantly higher proportion than that found for other foreign-owned subsidiaries (26 per cent) and domestic firms (21 per cent). Interestingly, however, Japanese firms, despite their relatively high credit risk and relatively poor profitability, were not found to be more failure prone than domestic (or other foreign-owned) firms. The authors suggested that their findings provided prima facie evidence of transfer pricing manipulation, with parent companies appearing to support a significant number of Japanese subsidiaries in the UK which, under normal circumstances, may not have been able to continue trading.

Clearly, further analyses of the performance of the Japanese sector in UK manufacturing is still required to inform public policy. The earlier work of Munday and Peel was focused on a single time period (1993–4) during which a large proportion of the Japanese transplant sector was still subject to recessionary pressures. Furthermore, initial research did not compare the performance of the Japanese sector with other foreign-owned subsidiaries in the UK. Comparison with other foreign subsidiaries could be important in the context of performance analysis, with the Census of Production, for example, providing strong evidence of differences in the performance of subsidiaries with different national origins.

The research findings reported in this chapter seek to extend the earlier work of Munday and Peel (1997) through an examination of the performance of Japanese, US and domestically owned subsidiaries in the electrical and electronic engineering sector, a sector in which there has been substantial Japanese investment (see Table 4A.1 in appendix to chapter).

There is some prior expectation that both Japanese and US subsidiaries would outperform their domestic counterparts on financial performance ratios relating to employment, earnings, profits, productivity, stock efficiency, liquidity and financial risk. General expectations of superior performance in the foreign-owned sector are largely based on the theory pertaining to multinational corporations. Theory explaining the growth of multinational enterprises initially focused on the fact that such firms possessed 'ownership advantages' denominated in terms of specific income-generating assets which compensate for the additional costs of MNCs locating operations in host economies (Dunning 1993; Pitelis and Sugden 1991). Superior asset possession, often in the form of new technology or patents, may be associated with high levels of comparative efficiency (see, for example, Hymer 1976).

Existing empirical work on productivity and profitability comparisons between foreign subsidiaries and their domestic counterparts also suggests superior performance by foreign firms and tends to confirm theoretical perspectives. For example, Dunning (1993), in his review of comparative studies (matched pairs and intra-industry) which examined the performance of US-owned subsidiaries in the UK, Canada and Australia, reported that US firms significantly outperformed their domestic counterparts on both productivity and profit indices, although Dunning shows that the productivity gap between US, foreign firms and their domestic counterparts has tended to close through time.

Prior expectations on superior performance are also based on the results of UK Census of Production data. While the Census does not control for structural firm-specific differences (for example, relating to size and industry) between Japanese, US and UK manufacturing companies, it does highlight the relative characteristics of these manufacturing sectors at the national level. For example, Figure 4.1 shows how Japanese and US subsidiaries outperformed UK-owned manufacturing firms in 1992 with reference to sales per employee, gross value added per employee, net output per employee and stock turnover. The relatively high stock turnover ratios of foreign-owned subsidiaries is often attributed to the utilization of superior stock management techniques (see, for example, Oliver and Wilkinson

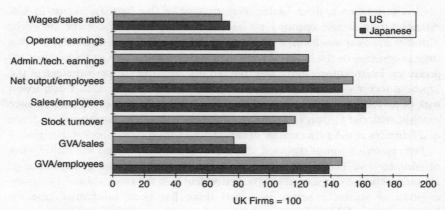

Figure 4.1 Relative performance of US and Japanese subsidiaries in 1992 (UK-owned manufacturing firms = 100)
Source: Business Monitor (1995b).

1992). However, Figure 4.1 reveals that the Japanese and US manufacturing sectors are characterized by lower gross value added to sales than their domestic counterparts. This may be partly explained by the relatively higher proportion of goods bought in by foreign-owned subsidiaries (Munday *et al.* 1995).

As is shown in Figure 4.1, the Japanese and US manufacturing enterprises pay their employees more than firms in the domestic sector. At the same time, the ratio of total remuneration to sales is higher in the domestic sector. Figure 4.1 also demonstrates that, on the majority of indicators, US subsidiaries outperform their Japanese counterparts, particularly on productivity measures. This (at least partially) reflects the fact that a higher proportion of US investment in the UK is in capital intensive sectors.

The remainder of this chapter is structured as follows. The next section considers the overall characteristics of foreign-owned and domestic manufacturing firms in the UK, before focusing on the electrical and electronic engineering sector. The analysis here is based on corporate profitability and failure rates. The third section contains an empirical examination of the comparative performance of Japanese, US and domestic firms in the electrical/electronics sector. It discusses the derivation of the subsamples, the analytical method and the sample characteristics. The analysis focuses on size characteristics (in terms of employment, assets and sales), earnings, profitability, productivity, stock efficiency and liquidity. The section also includes an appraisal of the relative credit risk of these manufacturing subsidiaries. The final section contains conclusions derived from the empirical evidence, and explores some public policy implications of the analysis.

POPULATION CHARACTERISTICS

In total, 29,653 companies with financial year-ends falling in the annual period April 1995 to March 1996 (hereafter referred to as 1995/6), and whose primary business activity was manufacturing (primary manufacturing SIC [1980] codes 2, 3 and 4), were contained in the FAME CD-ROM database[1] in 1997. Of these 29,653 manufacturing firms, 3,910 (13.2%) were foreign-owned (that is, where the controlling interest resides in a non-British company), with the remainder split between independent (that is, not held as a subsidiary) British firms (n = 20,643, 69.6%) and subsidiaries of British companies (n = 5,100, 17.2%). Of the 3,910 foreign-owned manufacturing firms, 174 (4.5%) are Japanese-owned subsidiaries and 1,312 (33.6%) are owned by US parent companies.

Table 4.1 reports failure rates for these various subsamples. It shows that none of the Japanese subsidiaries (n = 174) had failed in the annual period (1995/6) examined, compared to 0.73 per cent of US subsidiaries (n = 1,312). However, US subsidiaries exhibit lower failure rates than both independent British firms (1.07%, n = 20,643) and British-owned subsidiaries (0.88%, n = 5,100). In total, the table reveals that the 1995/6 failure rate for all domestic (British-owned) companies (1.03%, n = 25,743) is significantly higher than that for foreign-owned firms (0.64%, n = 3,910).

Table 4.2 reports the proportion of loss-making firms (that is, with negative profit before tax) for the subsamples described above. In total, 19,379 firms had disclosed profit figures in the annual period (1995/6) analysed, of which 21.6 per cent were loss-making. However, Table 4.2 reveals that a significantly higher proportion (33.3%, n = 162) of Japanese subsidiaries were loss-making than were US subsidiaries (22.7%, n = 1,107), British subsidiaries (18.6%, n = 4,347) and

Table 4.1 Manufacturing firms on FAME and failure rates (1995/6)

Manufacturing companies[1]	*Proportion (%) and number failing/closing*[2]
Japanese subsidiaries (n = 174)	0.0% (n = 0)
US subsidiaries (n = 1,312)	0.726% (n = 10)
All foreign-owned subsidiaries (n = 3,910)	0.639% (n = 25)
British-owned subsidiaries (n = 5,100)	0.882% (n = 45)
Independent British firms (n = 20,643)	1.066% (n = 220)
All British-owned firms (n = 25,743)	1.029% (n = 265)
All firms (n = 29,653)	0.978% (n = 290)

Notes:
[1] n = the total number of companies in each category (including failures/closures). The analysis is based on all the companies on the FAME database with a primary manufacturing SIC code and with annual accounts (year-ends) falling in the period 1.4.95 to 31.3.96.
[2] n = the total number of corporate deaths/failures (liquidation/insolvency/ceased trading/receivership and administration) in each category. Percentages refer to corporate deaths in each category.

Table 4.2 Loss-making manufacturing firms (1995/6)

Manufacturing companies[1]	Proportion (%) loss-making[2]
Japanese subsidiaries	33.3% (n = 162)
US subsidiaries	22.7% (n = 1,107)
All foreign-owned subsidiaries	26.0% (n = 3,312)
British-owned subsidiaries	18.6% (n = 4,347)
Independent British firms	21.5% (n = 11,720)
All British-owned firms	20.7% (n = 16,067)
All firms	21.6% (n = 19,379)

Notes:
[1] Analysis is based on all manufacturing companies on the FAME database with a primary manufacturing SIC code, with annual accounts (year-ends) falling in the period 1.4.95 to 31.3.96, and which disclosed net profit margin figures (net profit before tax/sales). All failed firms (Table 4.1) are excluded.
[2] Percentages refer to the proportion of all firms (shown in parentheses) in each category which were loss-making (negative net profit before tax).

independent British firms (21.5%, n = 11,720). The table also shows that a significantly higher number of foreign-owned subsidiaries were loss-making (26.0%, n = 3,312) than were British-owned firms (20.7%, n = 16,067).

Given that a higher proportion of foreign-owned (particularly Japanese) companies are loss-making, it might have been expected that this would be reflected in higher failure rates for foreign subsidiaries (see Peel 1990). However, the analysis in Tables 4.1 and 4.2 demonstrates that Japanese subsidiaries, despite being more prone to declare losses, have a zero failure rate. A similar pattern is repeated with respect to US subsidiaries and all foreign-owned firms – with British-owned firms suffering a higher failure rate, despite the relatively low proportion declaring losses.

These results are consistent with the findings of an earlier study (Peel and Munday 1997) which, inter alia, examined similar data for the annual period 1994/5. As noted in that study (ibid. 20): 'a possible explanation of these findings is that Japanese and other foreign owned subsidiaries are "objectively" more failure prone, but receive more support from their parent organizations. An alternative explanation ... is that transfer pricing strategies reduce the "objective" profitability ... of a number of foreign owned subsidiaries resulting in poor disclosed profitability ... '.

A total of 2,789 companies with primary manufacturing SIC codes in the electronics/electrical sector (SIC 34: electrical and electronic engineering), and with annual account year-ends falling in the annual period April 1995 to March

1996 (1995/6), were available for analysis on the FAME database – comprising 9.4 per cent of all (29,653) firms with a primary manufacturing SIC code on the FAME database in that period (see Table 4.1). Table 4.3 shows that, of the 2,789 firms recorded in the electronics/electrical sector (hereafter referred to as the electrical sector), 39 (1.4%) are Japanese subsidiaries,[2] 221 (7.9%) are US subsidiaries, 468 (16.8%) are British-owned subsidiaries and 1,786 (64%) are independent British companies. In total, 535 (19.2%) of the 2,789 firms analysed in the table are foreign-owned.

Table 4.3 also reports relative failure rates for the subsamples. Consistent with the results reported in Table 4.1 for all manufacturing companies, it shows that foreign-owned subsidiaries in the electrical sector display a lower failure rate (0.75%) than independent British firms (1.06%); but that British-owned subsidiaries have a lower failure rate (0.64%) than their foreign-owned counterparts. The remaining subsample failure rates are consistent with those analysed in Table 4.1. In addition, Tables 4.1 and 4.3 show that the failure rate for all manufacturing firms (0.98%) is similar to the failure rate in the electrical sector (0.93%).

Excluding failed firms, Table 4.4 shows that a total of 1,774 manufacturing firms in the electrical sector had disclosed annual net profit margin figures (profit before tax/sales) in 1995/6. It reveals that no less than 40% of Japanese subsidiaries (n = 35) were loss-making, which is substantially higher than for US

Table 4.3 Manufacturing firms and failure rates in electronics/electrical sector (1995/6)

Manufacturing firms in electronics/ electrical sector[1]	*Proportion (%) and number failing/closing*[2]
Japanese subsidiaries (n = 39)	0.0% (n = 0)
US subsidiaries (n = 221)	0.904% (n = 2)
All foreign-owned subsidiaries (n = 535)	0.748% (n = 4)
British-owned subsidiaries (n = 468)	0.641% (n = 3)
Independent British firms (n = 1,786)	1.064% (n = 19)
All British-owned firms (n = 2,254)	0.976% (n = 22)
All firms (n = 2,789)	0.932% (n = 26)

Notes:
[1] n = the total number of companies in each category (including failures/closures). The analysis is based on all the companies on the FAME database with a primary manufacturing SIC code in the electronics/electrical sector (SIC 3.4: electrical and electronic engineering), and with annual accounts (year-ends) falling in the period 1.4.95 to 31.3.96.
[2] n = the total number of corporate deaths/failures (liquidation/ceased trading/insolvency/ receivership and administration) in each category. Percentages refer to corporate deaths in each category.

Table 4.4 Loss-making manufacturing firms in electronics/electrical sector (1995/6)

Manufacturing firms in electronics/electrical sector[1]	Proportion (%) loss-making[2]
Japanese subsidiaries	40.0% (n = 35)
US subsidiaries	20.3% (n = 177)
All foreign-owned subsidiaries	28.2% (n = 426)
British-owned subsidiaries	18.6% (n = 365)
Independent British firms	21.9% (n = 983)
All British-owned firms	20.9% (n = 1,348)
All firms	22.7% (n = 1,774)

Notes:
[1] Analysis is based on all companies on the FAME database with a primary manufacturing SIC code in the electronics/electrical sector (SIC 3.4: electrical and electronic engineering), with annual accounts (year-ends) falling in the period 1.4.95 to 31.3.96, and which disclosed net profit margin figures (net profit before tax/sales). All failed firms (Table 4.3) are excluded.
[2] Percentages refer to the proportion of all firms (shown in parentheses) in each category which were loss-making (negative net profit before tax).

subsidiaries (20.3%, n = 177), British-owned subsidiaries (18.6%, n = 365) and independent British firms (21.9%, n = 983).

Overall, the proportion of loss-making foreign-owned manufacturing firms in the electrical sector (28.2%, n = 426) is significantly higher than the proportion of British-owned loss-making firms (20.9%, n = 1,348). In general, the proportion of loss-making firms in the subsamples in the electrical sector are similar to those reported for all manufacturing companies in Table 4.2. However, a higher proportion of Japanese-owned subsidiaries in the electrical sector are loss-making (40%) than in the Japanese manufacturing sector as a whole (33.3%) – with US-owned subsidiaries in the electrical sector having a lower proportion (20.3%) of loss-making firms than the US manufacturing sector as a whole (22.7%).

THE COMPARATIVE PERFORMANCE OF JAPANESE, US AND DOMESTIC FIRMS

This section presents a detailed analysis of the relative performance of Japanese, US and domestic manufacturing firms in the UK electrical sector with reference to a wide range of variables covering corporate profitability, labour and asset productivity, employment, remuneration, stock efficiency, liquidity and credit risk.

Data, variables and method

The initial sampling frame comprises the 1,774 manufacturing firms in the electrical sector on the FAME database (with account year-ends falling in 1995/6), which disclosed net profit margin figures[3] (see Table 4.4). The US subsample is comprised of a random sample of 100 (56.5%) of the 177 US-owned subsidiaries; whereas the Japanese subsample contains all (n = 35) of the available Japanese-owned subsidiaries. Data was also collected for a random sample of 203 British-owned firms – amounting to 15 per cent of all domestic manufacturing firms in the electrical sector (n = 1,348) on the database (see Table 4.4).

A wide range of performance variables, derived from the most recent annual report and accounts for each company (1995/6), were collected for the sample firms. The data therefore falls in a common annual time period (account year-ends falling in the period 1 April 1995 to 31 March 1996). A full list of the twenty variables used in this study, together with their definitions, is provided in Table 4.A2 (see appendix to chapter). The variables are standard ones used by both researchers and investment analysts to assess the relative characteristics and financial performance of companies (see Munday and Peel 1997; Van Horne 1987).

Variables 1 to 3 in Table 4A.2 cover corporate size attributes – that is, turnover (TURN), total assets (TASS) and number of employees (EMPL). Variables 4 and 5 are average employee pay (AREM) and whether or not companies are loss-making (LOSS), on the basis of profit before tax. Variables 6 to 10 are ratio variables which cover various aspects of corporate profitability: gross (trading) profit margin (GPMG), return on sales before (RESB) and after tax (RESA), and return on capital employed before (RCAPB) and after tax (RCAPA).

Five variables (11–15) focus on labour and asset (capital) productivity. These are: sales (turnover) per employee (SALEM), gross trading profit (sales minus manufacturing expenses) per employee (GPEM), profit before tax per employee (NPEM), the ratio of sales to total assets (SALTA) and the ratio of sales to fixed assets (SALFA). The latter ratios measure how efficiently a company uses its total (SALTA) and fixed (SALFA) assets to generate revenue (Van Horne 1987). Variable 16 in Table 4A.2 (REMS) is the ratio of employee remuneration to sales and therefore shows the percentage of revenue represented by the total wage bill expense.

Finally, variables 17–20 in Table 4A.2 cover stock efficiency, liquidity (solvency) and credit risk. Stock efficiency is measured with reference to the average days stock held (DAYST). Two ratios focus on corporate liquidity: the 'current' ratio (CURA), which is the ratio of current assets to current liabilities, and the 'quick' ratio (QRAT), which is the ratio of current assets less stock to current liabilities. As noted by Dixon (1989: 186):

> The current ratio shows how well the company is able to meet its immediate debts . . . as the ratio goes up the company's profitability and risk declines . . . [the quick] ratio is a rather better guide to a company's liquidity position because it does not include an inventory which the company may not be able

to realize easily. The ratio has been viewed as a measure of the firm's ability to meet its short term cash obligations.

The final variable (CRISK) is the credit rating assigned to each company on FAME (in 1995/6) by a credit risk assessment agency (Qui Credit Assessment Ltd) employed by the proprietor (Jordan). The credit rating is in the form of a credit score varying between zero (highest risk) and 100 (lowest risk). Credit scores are categorized (by Qui Credit) as follows: 'high risk' (scores 0–20), 'caution' (21–40), 'normal' (41–60), 'stable' (61–80) and 'secure' (81–100). With respect to firms assigned a high-risk score, the FAME manual advises that: 'Companies in the high risk sector are unlikely to be able to continue trading unless significant remedial action is undertaken, there is support from a parent company, or specific circumstances apply.'

In the analysis which follows, the three subsamples are compared with reference to the mean and median values of each variable. Significance tests for mean differences are conducted using separate variance estimates (Norusis 1988). However, because a number of financial ratios exhibit non-normal distributions (see, for example, Ezzamel and Mar-Molinero 1990), and because the corporate size variables (distributions) in this study are positively skewed by large outliers (see below), non-parametric Mann–Whitney tests were also conducted to test whether the variable distributions (medians) differ significantly across the three subsamples.[4]

In relation to the variables collected for this study, it should be noted that some companies on FAME had missing values – which arises largely because smaller UK companies may file modified annual reports and accounts at Companies House (see Munday and Peel 1997). In consequence, in the tables which follow, the number of observations available for each variable (across the three subsamples) is indicated.

Sample characteristics

Table 4.5 shows that the mean values of the corporate size variables (TURN, TASS and EMPL) do not differ significantly across the Japanese, US and domestic subsamples. However, the table reveals that the median values of TURN, TASS and EMPL are significantly larger for Japanese subsidiaries than for US ones, which, in turn, are significantly larger than the median size values of British firms. As noted above, the disparity between mean and median values may occur because of the presence of large outliers. This is certainly the case with the size variables used in this study, with Table 4.5 showing that, relative to the median values, the means for TURN, TASS and EMPL (for all subsamples) are positively skewed (that is, the distributions are positively skewed). This is particularly evident in respect of the domestic subsample.[5]

Table 4.6 therefore reports descriptive statistics for the three subsamples using natural log transformations of the size variables – LTURN, LTASS and LEMPL – a transformation which reduces the influence of outliers. It shows that, in

Table 4.5 Sample characteristics

Variables	Japanese [1] Mean [1] (median)	US [2] Mean [2] (median)	British [3] Mean [1] (median)	Significance tests [2] (probabilities)		
				IV.2	IV.3	2V.3
TURN	73,640 (32,167) n = 35	79,528 (10,266) n = 100	75,289 (4,524) n = 203	0.904 (0.002)***	0.975 (0.000)***	0.950 (0.000)***
TASS	45,816 (14,675) n = 35	46,910 (6,608) n = 100	67,301 (2,815) n = 203	0.968 (0.007)***	0.673 (0.000)***	0.710 (0.000)***
EMPL	515.2 (386.0) n = 34	455.9 (157.0) n = 99	1098.5 (86.0) n = 169	0.716 (0.033)**	0.441 (0.001)***	0.401 (0.001)***
AREM	18,884 (16,302) n = 34	20,895 (20,194) n = 99	18,603 (16,778) n = 169	0.188 (0.012)***	0.852 (0.979)	0.013††† (0.000)***
LOSS	40.0% (N/A) n = 35	23.0% (N/A) n = 100	20.7% (N/A) n = 203	N/A	N/A	N/A

Notes:
[1] Means are unbracketed, with medians shown in parentheses.
[2] Probabilities for Student's t-tests are unbracketed, with probabilities for Mann–Whitney U-tests shown in parentheses.
††† indicates sample means are significantly different at the 1% level (two-tailed Student's t-test).
***, ** indicate sample distributions are significantly different at the 1% and 5% levels respectively (two-tailed Mann–Whitney U-tests).

Table 4.6 Size variables (natural logs)

Variables	Japanese 1 Mean[1] (median)	US 2 Mean[1] (median)	British 3 Mean[1] (median)	Significance tests[2] (probabilities)		
				IV.2	IV.3	2V.3
LTURN	10.35 (10.38) n = 35	9.51 (9.24) n = 100	8.60 (8.42) n = 203	0.004††† (0.002)***	0.000††† (0.000)***	0.000††† (0.000)***
LTASS	9.85 (9.59) n = 35	9.12 (8.79) n = 100	8.11 (7.94) n = 203	0.011††† (0.007)***	0.000††† (0.000)***	0.007††† (0.000)***
LEMPL	5.56 (5.96) n = 34	5.03 (5.06) n = 99	4.54 (4.45) n = 169	0.054†† (0.033)**	0.000††† (0.000)***	0.007††† (0.001)***

Notes:

[1] Means are unbracketed, with medians shown in parentheses.

[2] Probabilities for Student's t-tests are unbracketed, with probabilities for Mann–Whitney U-tests shown in parentheses.

†††,†† indicate sample means are significantly different at the 1% and 5% levels respectively (two-tailed Student's t-tests).

***,** indicate sample distributions are significantly different at the 1% and 5% levels respectively (two-tailed Mann–Whitney U-tests).

common with the untransformed median size values, the means of LTURN, LTASS and LEMPL are all significantly higher for Japanese subsidiaries than for US subsidiaries, which in turn are significantly higher than for British firms – with a similar pattern evident in respect of median values for LTURN, LTASS and LEMPL.

Turning to remuneration levels, Table 4.5 reveals that the average pay of employees (AREM) in Japanese subsidiaries (£18,884) is similar to that (£18,603) of employees in domestic firms. However, the mean pay of employees in US subsidiaries (£20,895) is significantly higher – with statistically significant mean and median differences between the US and British subsamples, and the US and Japanese subsamples, respectively. This information is consistent with the aggregate data for the UK manufacturing sector as a whole (see Figure 4.1). However, it is important to recognize that the sample in the current study was not matched by age of subsidiary. Japanese subsidiaries in aggregate are relative new-comers to the UK (compared to US investment) and there is some expectation that older subsidiaries would have marginally higher wage bills. Furthermore, it is noteworthy that Japanese electronics subsidiaries have shown a preference for periphery areas of the UK where earnings levels are often lower than in the core south-east. Clearly, comparative pay levels in subsidiaries are one indicator of the nature of manufacturing operations being undertaken, with production-only facilities expected to have lower wage bills than those engaged in higher-order functions such as research, product development and engineering.

Finally, Table 4.5 shows that a significantly[6] higher proportion (40%) of Japanese subsidiaries were loss-making than both US subsidiaries (23%) and domestic firms (20.7%). These findings are similar to those reported in Table 4.4 (for the population of electronics/electrical manufacturing companies on the FAME database), a finding which was expected, given the firms in the US and domestic subsamples were selected randomly.

Profitability characteristics

Consistent with previous evidence (Munday and Peel 1997), Table 4.7 reveals that Japanese subsidiaries have a significantly lower mean gross trading profit margin (sales minus manufacturing expenses) than both US subsidiaries and domestic firms – with the mean gross profit margin (GPMG) of Japanese subsidiaries (14.8%) being less than half that of US subsidiaries (29.2%) and British firms (31.2%). The table also shows that, on average, GPMG does not differ significantly between domestic firms and US subsidiaries. An identical pattern is evident for differences between the median values of GPMG across the three subsamples.

With respect to the before (RESB) and after (RESA) tax return on sales variables, the table shows a similar pattern as above – with the mean returns of Japanese subsidiaries (RESB = 1.98%, RESA = 0.91%) being substantially lower than for both US subsidiaries (4.69%, 2.99%) and domestic firms (5.18%, 3.41%). However, only the median values of RESB and RESA differ significantly between

Table 4.7 Profitability characteristics

Variables	Japanese 1 Mean (median)	US 2 Mean (median)	British 3 Mean (median)	Significance tests[2] (probabilities)		
				IV.2	IV.3	2V.3
GPMG	14.76 (10.46) n = 34	29.26 (28.92) n = 93	31.21 (29.07) n = 174	0.000†† (0.000)***	0.000††† (0.000)***	0.255 (0.394)
RESB	1.98 (0.65) n = 35	4.69 (4.76) n = 100	5.18 (4.92) n = 203	0.406 (0.001)***	0.329 (0.001)***	0.704 (0.912)
RESA	0.91 (0.52) n = 35	2.99 (4.15) n = 100	3.41 (3.64) n = 203	0.471 (0.001)***	0.387 (0.000)***	0.700 (0.879)
RCAPB	1.14 (1.10) n = 35	8.13 (8.26) n = 100	9.14 (9.10) n = 203	0.089† (0.001)***	0.049†† (0.000)***	0.648 (0.635)
RCAPA	−0.07 (0.79) n = 35	5.34 (5.89) n = 100	6.18 (6.29) n = 203	0.157 (0.002)***	0.092† (0.000)***	0.647 (0.632)

Notes:
[1] Means are unbracketed, with medians shown in parentheses.
[2] Probabilities for Student's t-tests are unbracketed, with probabilities for Mann–Whitney U-tests shown in parentheses.
†††,††,† indicate sample means are significantly different at the 1%, 5% and 10% levels respectively (two-tailed Student's t-tests).
*** indicates sample distributions are significantly different at the 1% level (two-tailed Mann–Whitney U-tests).

the US and Japanese subsamples, and between the domestic and Japanese sub-samples. Also noteworthy, and consistent with the preceding analysis, is the fact that Table 4.7 demonstrates that, on average, a lower proportion (1.07%) of the turnover of the Japanese subsidiaries is represented by tax (RESB minus RESA), than for both US subsidiaries (1.70%) and domestic firms (1.77%).

A similar picture emerges when the subsamples are analysed with reference to the commonly used return on capital employed ratio. Table 4.7 reveals that, for both the before (RCAPB) and after (RCAPA) tax return on capital employed ratios, the mean returns of British companies (RCAPB = 9.14%, RCAPA = 6.18%) and US subsidiaries (8.13%, 5.34%) are significantly higher than the mean returns of the Japanese subsidiaries (1.14%, −0.07%). An identical pattern is again evident for the median values of RCAPB and RCAPA, but neither the mean nor median values differ significantly between the US and domestic subsamples. Also consist-ent with the preceding analysis, the table shows that the mean ratio of tax paid to capital employed (RCAPB minus RCAPA) for Japanese subsidiaries (1.21%), is less than half that of both US subsidiaries (2.79%) and domestic firms (2.96%).

Performance characteristics

Table 4.8 reports descriptive statistics for the six performance variables (SALEM to REMS) previously described. For the variables SALEM, GPEM and NPEM, the presence of outliers again positively skews the means for all three subsamples. This is particularly evident in respect of the domestic subsample (see Note 5),[7] where the means for these variables in the British subsample are all higher than in the US subsample, but with the reverse being the case for median values.

With reference to median values, however, the table reveals that Japanese sub-sidiaries exhibit significantly higher levels of turnover per employee (SALEM = £114,422) than US subsidiaries (£89,451), which, in turn, is significantly higher than the median value of SALEM (£63,396) for domestic firms. In addition, Table 4.8 shows that the mean level of sales per employee generated in the Japa-nese subsample (£166,334) is significantly higher than that in the US subsample (£109,396).

Although the mean values of the gross (GPEM) and net (NPEM) profit per employee ratios do not differ significantly across the three subsamples, Table 4.8 reveals that the median values of GPEM and NPEM in the domestic subsample (£19,754 and £3,368) are significantly higher than those in the Japanese subsam-ple (£10,398 and £901). Furthermore, the median value of GPEM in the US subsample (£22,966) is significantly higher than that of both the Japanese and domestic subsamples – with the median value of NPEM also being substantially (and significantly) larger in the US subsample (£4,333) than in the Japanese subsample (£901).

With reference to asset efficiency (SALTA, SALFA), the table reveals that domestic firms have higher mean and median total asset turnover ratios (SALTA) than both US and Japanese subsidiaries – with both the mean (1.83) and median (1.69) values of SALTA in the domestic subsample being significantly higher than

Table 4.8 Performance characteristics

Variables	Japanese [1] Mean[1] (median)	US [2] Mean[1] (median)	British [3] Mean[1] (median)	Significance tests[2] (probabilities)		
				IV.2	IV.3	2V.3
SALEM	166,334 (114,442) n = 34	109,396 (89,451) n = 99	157,953 (63,396) n = 169	0.025†† (0.003)***	0.907 (0.000)***	0.477 (0.001)***
GPEM	29,084 (10,398) n = 33	28,527 (22,966) n = 92	33,144 (19,754) n = 145	0.946 (0.011)***	0.720 (0.089)*	0.579 (0.051)**
NPEM	5,267 (901) n = 35	5,899 (4,333) n = 99	6,667 (3,368) n = 169	0.917 (0.007)***	0.826 (0.019)**	0.748 (0.342)
SALTA	1.76 (1.54) n = 35	1.62 (1.51) n = 100	1.83 (1.69) n = 203	0.284 (0.197)	0.585 (0.772)	0.031†† (0.008)***
SALFA	52.80 (7.19) n = 35	23.88 (7.01) n = 100	19.33 (7.80) n = 192	0.478 (0.617)	0.400 (0.807)	0.643 (0.155)
REMS	15.48 (13.07) n = 34	24.01 (24.16) n = 99	27.83 (28.18) n = 176	0.000††† (0.000)***	0.000††† (0.000)***	0.004††† (0.011)***

Notes:
[1] Means are unbracketed, with medians shown in parentheses.
[2] Probabilities for Student's t-tests are unbracketed, with probabilities for Mann–Whitney U-tests shown in parentheses.
†††,†† indicate sample means are significantly different at the 1% and 5% levels respectively (two-tailed Student's t-tests).
***, **, * indicate sample distributions are significantly different at the 1%, 5% and 10% levels respectively (two-tailed Mann–Whitney U-tests).

those (1.62 and 1.51 respectively) in the US subsample. However, the mean and median fixed asset turnover (SALFA) ratios do not differ significantly across the three subsamples.

Finally, Table 4.8 shows that, on average, the wage bill to sales ratio (REMS) of British firms (27.8%) is significantly higher than that of US subsidiaries (24.0%), which in turn is significantly higher than the mean value of REMS (15.5%) in the Japanese subsample, with an identical pattern repeated for the median value of REMS across the three subsamples. Hence, although British firms, on average, pay their employees less than those employed by US and Japanese subsidiaries (Table 4.5), the mean wage bill expense as a proportion of sales is significantly higher in the British subsample than in both the US and Japanese subsamples.

Stock efficiency, liquidity and credit risk

Table 4.9 reveals that, although domestic firms have the lowest stock holdings, there are no significant differences between the mean and median days stock held (DAYST) across the three subsamples. Despite the large volume of literature which suggests that Japanese firms (and their foreign transplants) are leaders in the field of stock management techniques (see, for example, Voss and Robinson 1987; Schonberger 1992), there is therefore no evidence (at least from this study) that Japanese subsidiaries operating in the UK electrical manufacturing sector are more efficient in managing stock than their US and domestic counterparts – with Table 4.9 showing the mean days stock held in 1995/6 was 54.4, 55.1 and 50.1 for the Japanese, US and British firms respectively. In this context, it is worth noting that in a previous UK study by the authors (Munday and Peel 1997) of matched samples (by size and industry) of ninety-seven Japanese and ninety-seven domestic manufacturing subsidiaries, the mean days stock held by Japanese-owned subsidiaries in 1993/4 (77 days) was significantly higher than for their matched domestic counterparts (51 days). In this context, reported results for 1993–4 still reflected the effects of a European recession which had hit Japanese subsidiaries in the UK particularly hard.

With reference to corporate liquidity, Table 4.9 reveals that both the current (CURA) and quick (QRAT) ratios are highest in the US subsample (means = 1.95 and 1.41 respectively) followed by the domestic subsample (1.55 and 1.10) and the Japanese subsample (1.22 and 0.81), with both the means and the medians of CURA and QRAT differing significantly across the three subsamples. Consistent with previous evidence (Munday and Peel 1997), these results demonstrate that Japanese subsidiaries have substantially lower liquidity (solvency) measures than both domestic firms and US subsidiaries, with the latter also exhibiting significantly higher liquidity ratios than their domestic counterparts.

Finally, Table 4.9 shows that Japanese subsidiaries have significantly higher mean credit risk assessments (i.e. lower credit scores) than both US subsidiaries and domestic firms – with mean CRISK scores of 39.2, 56.2 and 54.2 for the Japanese, US and domestic firms, respectively – but with CRISK, on average, not differing significantly between US and domestic firms. An identical pattern is also

Table 4.9 Stock efficiency, liquidity and credit risk

Variables	Japanese 1 Mean[1] (median)	US 2 Mean[1] (median)	British 3 Mean[1] (median)	Significance tests[2] (probabilities)		
				1V.2	1V.3	2V.3
DAYST	54.37 (54.94) n = 34	55.11 (49.99) n = 99	50.75 (43.75) n = 190	0.884 (0.865)	0.439 (0.204)	0.274 (0.164)
CURA	1.22 (1.03) n = 34	1.95 (1.56) n = 100	1.55 (1.30) n = 200	0.000††† (0.000)***	0.046†† (0.001)***	0.004††† (0.001)***
QRAT	0.81 (0.61) n = 34	1.41 (1.07) n = 99	1.10 (0.89) n = 189	0.000††† (0.000)***	0.036†† (0.001)***	0.008††† (0.000)***
CRISK	39.17 (39.00) n = 35	56.20 (53.00) n = 100	54.18 (54.00) n = 178	0.001††† (0.001)***	0.003††† (0.001)***	0.502 (0.533)

Notes:
[1] Means are unbracketed, with medians shown in parentheses.
[2] Probabilities for Student's t-tests are unbracketed, with probabilities for Mann–Whitney U-tests shown in parentheses.
†††,†† indicate sample means are significantly different at the 1% and 5% levels respectively (two-tailed Student's t-tests).
*** indicates sample distributions are significantly different at the 1% level (two-tailed Mann–Whitney U-tests).

evident with respect to the median CRISK scores. Furthermore, a significantly[8] higher proportion (20.0%) of Japanese subsidiaries were classified as 'high' credit risks (scores 0–20) than both US subsidiaries (9.0%) and British firms (7.9%). These results are consistent with the preceding analysis: that is, since Japanese firms exhibit lower liquidity and profitability measures (Table 4.7), they might be expected to have worse credit ratings (see also Munday and Peel 1997). However, this is not reflected in a higher failure rate for Japanese subsidiaries.

CONCLUSIONS

The performance appraisal of Japanese, US and UK-owned subsidiaries in the UK electrical and electronic engineering sector evidences several significant para-doxes. The findings showed that Japanese subsidiaries were generally larger than their US and UK counterparts on a range of size variables. Earnings in Japanese firms in the sector were comparable to those of UK firms, but significantly lower than those in US-owned subsidiaries, although it was noted that the latter finding could owe much to the location, age and the functions undertaken by Japanese subsidiaries in the UK. In spite of the differences in earnings, the proportion of Japanese sales represented by earnings was significantly lower than in the UK or US cases. Furthermore, in spite of their greater size in terms of employment, there was some evidence that labour productivity (sales per employee) in Japanese subsidiaries exceeded that of their UK and US counterparts. However, on other performance indicators, Japanese subsidiaries did not fare so well. There was no evidence to suggest that Japanese (or US) subsidiaries generated more sales on a given asset base, and there were also no significant differences in terms of days stock holdings, an important indicator of operational efficiency.

Perhaps most disappointing is the performance of Japanese subsidiaries with respect to profitability. On each of the five profitability indicators reported here, Japanese subsidiaries performed significantly worse than their US or UK counter-parts. Indeed, the performance of US subsidiaries in this respect was very similar to that of the domestic subsidiaries. Japanese electrical and electronic engineering firms were also characterized by poor liquidity, and relatively high credit risk. Im-portantly, high credit risk and poor performances on liquidity indicators were not reflected in higher failure rates for the population of Japanese firms on the FAME database. This may occur because parent companies are providing financial support for subsidiary operations, without which it is unlikely they could trade under normal terms. The study also confirms some of the prior expectations with regard to earn-ings, labour productivity and wage share. However, on other performance indica-tors there is little to positively differentiate the Japanese from the UK subsample.

Clearly, in the UK context, Japanese firms, particularly in the electrical/ electronic engineering sector, have been successful in creating employment (and incomes) in less favoured areas, and have created opportunities for domestic suppliers. However, UK policy towards inward investment promotion also pre-supposes that the attraction of foreign direct investment can have significant third-party (or knock-on) effects. For example, in the introduction to the chapter, it was noted that there is an expectation that foreign capital can improve the efficiency of domestic producers in allied and competing sectors, can develop an industry's human capital base, and can provide a conduit for the transfer of technology (see, for example, Haddad and Harrison 1993; Blomstrom 1989).

Empirical evidence has also suggested that foreign multinationals should improve the labour productivity of the industries they enter, and thus enhance international competitive advantage. While there is some case evidence of such favourable third-party effects in the Japanese electronics case (see, for example, Morris *et al.* 1993; Munday *et al.* 1995) the empirical evidence here questions how far the Japanese can be a role model for the domestically owned electronics sector. Of course, the results may also confirm that UK subsidiaries in the electronics sector have now established themselves as a more globally competitive entity, achieving a successful manufacturing transition. Only a more detailed longitudinal study would confirm this.

More disturbing were the results from the profitability comparisons. Here, there was a clear dividing line between US and UK subsidiaries, which disclosed similar reported returns, and the Japanese, where the before tax return on sales of the thirty-five firms analysed averaged just under 2 per cent. This confirms some of the research outlined earlier, which suggests that Japanese subsidiaries in the UK may be operating as cost centres to break even. Poor reported returns in the 1995/6 financial year are not isolated, and other reports have focused on a lengthy trend of low declared Japanese profits in the UK and Europe (see, for example, JETRO 1996). Poor returns in the subsidiaries would seem to be only marginally affected by factors in the Japanese parent economy, with poor profits a feature of all periods in the trade cycle. Apologists for the Japanese point to the fact that the lost tax revenues occurring as a result of transfer pricing are insignificant in terms of the movements of Japanese manufacturing resources that occurred in the 1980s. Furthermore, it has been highlighted that such practices may not amount to a deliberate attempt to avoid tax, but rather may reflect a different organizational context – partially evidenced by the fact that corporation tax rates are actually higher in Japan than in the UK. Clearly, Japanese firms are not alone in engaging in transfer pricing manipulation. However, this research, adding to existing evidence, shows that Japanese firms may be manipulating interfirm transfers more than firms of other origins. Recent pressure inside Japan for a reduction in already high corporate tax rates could add to problems here, and consideration needs to be given by the UK tax authorities to new methods by which Japanese (and other) subsidiaries are taxed efficiently (see, for example, Piper 1996).

In conclusion, while Japanese investment in the electrical/electronics sectors has provided benefits for the UK economy in a number of areas, this study has questioned how far these transplants have been able to maximize their returns on the possession of specific tangible and intangible assets. In these circumstances there may be limits to the extent to which UK enterprises can learn from the Japanese transplant sector.

APPENDIX

Table 4A.1 Japanese electrical and electronic engineering investment in the UK: selected investments 1995

Company	Products	Established	Number of employees
Aiwa	Hi-fi equipment, CD players	1980	877
AK Fans	Electric fans	1983	49
Alps	VCRs and CTV components	1985	810
Apricot	Computer hardware	1990	280
AVX	Electronic components	1990	2,659
Canon Audio	Audio equipment	1991	na
Clarion	Car audio equipment	1989	96
Elco	Electronic components	1962	242
Electronic Harnesses	Electronic components	1988	250
Fuji Electric	Semiconductors	1991	170
Fujikura	Electronic components	1988	12
Fujitsu	Semiconductors and integrated circuits	1991	508
Fujitsu Telecommunications	Telecommunications equipment	1991	655
Hitachi Home Electrical	CTVs, VCRs and microwave ovens	1978	699
Hosiden Besson	Mobile comms/telecomm products	1990	650
ICL PLC	Computers	1990	na
JVC	CTVs	1988	480
KME Information Systems	Telephone equipment	1989	180
Matsushita	CTVs and microwave ovens	1974	1,810
Matsushita Electrical Company	Electronic components	1988	191
Minebea Electronics	Switching power supplies	1991	170
Mitsubishi	CTVs and VCRs	1979	1,440
Mitsumi	Electronic components	1987	150
Murata	Ceramic capacitors	1989	190
NEC Semiconductors	Integrated circuits	1981	1,113
NEC Technologies	Monitors and car telephones	1987	490
Nittan UK	Fire alarms	1972	76
Omron	PCB assemblies, etc.	1987	85
Optec DD	Electronic components	1987	163
Orion Electric	CTVs and VCR	1986	536
Pioneer	Audio equipment	1990	1,000
Sanken Power	Electronic components	1989	250
Sanyo Electric	Microwave ovens	1988	415
Sanyo Industries	CTVs	1981	448
Sharp Manufacturing	CDs, VCRs, and microwave ovens, etc.	1985	1,420
SMK	Remote control units	1988	160
Sony Manufacturing	CTVs and components	1973	2,890
Surface Technology	Semiconductor equipment	1995	100
Tabuchi	Transformers	1985	230
Tamura Hinchley	Power supply units	1989	430
Terasaki	Circuit breakers	1972	140
Toshiba Consumer Products	CTVs and air conditioning equipment	1981	1,100
Yaskawa Electric	Power inverters	1991	80
Yuasa Battery	Lead acid batteries	1981	769

Source: Derived from JETRO (1996).

Table 4A.2 Variable definitions

Variable	Definition
1 TURN	Turnover (£000)
2 TASS	Total assets (£000)
3 EMPL	Number of employees
4 AREM	Average employee remuneration (£)
5 LOSS	Proportion (%) loss-making (negative net profit before tax)
6 GPMG	Gross profit margin = gross trading profit (sales – manufacturing expenses)/TURN (%)
7 RESB	Return on sales before tax = profit before tax/TURN (%)
8 RESA	Return on sales after tax = profit after tax/TURN (%)
9 RCAPB	Return on capital employed (TASS) before tax = profit before tax/total capital employed (%)
10 RCAPA	Return on capital employed after tax = profit after tax/total capital employed (%)
11 SALEM	Sales (TURN) per employee (£)
12 GPEM	Gross trading profit/EMPL (£)
13 NPEM	Profit before tax/EMPL (£)
14 SALTA	Sales (TURN)/TASS
15 SALFA	Sales (TURN)/fixed assets
16 REMS	Total wage bill (employee remuneration)/TURN (%)
17 DAYST	Days' stock = (stock/sales)* 365
18 CURA	Current assets/current liabilities
19 QRAT	(Current assets – stock)/current liabilities
20 CRISK	Credit risk rating (rating assigned by Qui Credit Assessment Ltd)

NOTES

1 The FAME CD-ROM database (produced by Jordan) contains financial and non-financial data, largely drawn from annual company reports and other returns filed at Companies House, on over 200,000 British registered (including foreign-owned) companies. Companies which meet one or more of the following criteria are included on the database: (i) pre-tax profits of £50,000 or more; (ii) shareholder funds of £250,000 or more; and (iii) turnover (sales) of £500,000 or more. The database does, however, include a substantial number of smaller firms which have been included in previous surveys conducted by Jordan. For example, Munday and Peel (1997) report that the database contained 25,061 companies with turnover below £500,000 in 1996.

2 The number of Japanese subsidiaries recorded on the FAME database is lower than that shown in Table 4A.1 (see chapter appendix). Japanese firms were selected from the FAME database on the basis of having a primary SIC code in electrical and electronic engineering. Some of the firms in Table 4A.1 undertake sales and distribution activities, as well as manufacturing, and are classified as having primary SIC codes relevant to distribution. Furthermore, FAME excludes some of the smallest Japanese subsidiaries which are included in the JETRO (1996) survey, carried out in 1995, from which Table 4A.1 is derived.

3 As well as being able to search against country of ownership (that is, where the controlling interest resides in a non-UK parent) and industrial classification, FAME allows searches against, inter alia, net profit margin figures.

4 As noted by Siegel and Castellan (1988: 129) hypothesis formulation for Mann–Whitney tests may be stated in terms of whether the sample medians differ

significantly. In this context, Norusis (1988: 40) states that: 'The arithmetic mean is greatly influenced by outlying observations while the median is not ... [I]f there are values far removed from the rest of the observations, the median may be a better measure of central tendency than the mean.'

5 For example, the largest company in the domestic subsample is BTR with sales of £9,778m, some 2,161 times larger than the sales of the median firm (£4.524m) in the domestic subsample. For the Japanese subsample, the largest firm is NEC, with sales of £331.231m, which is only 10.3 times larger than the median sales value (£32.167m) of the Japanese subsample. However, the sales (£4,594.9m) of the largest US firm (IBM) is 447.6 times larger than the sales of the median firm (£10.266m) in the US subsample. A similar pattern is evident in respect of TASS and EMPL.

6 Chi-square statistics for the difference between the proportion of loss-making companies in each subsample were as follows: Japanese versus US: chi-square = 3.77 (p = 0.052); British versus Japanese: chi-square = 6.19 (p = 0.013); US versus British: chi-square = 0.212 (p = 0.645).

7 See n. 5.

8 Chi-square statistics for the difference between the proportion of companies in each subsample receiving a 'high' credit risk rating were as follows: Japanese versus US: chi-square = 3.00 (p = 0.083); British versus Japanese: chi-square = 4.85 (p = 0.028); US versus British: chi-square = 0.109 (p = 0.742).

REFERENCES

Ando, K. (1995) 'Japanese and American direct investment into peripheral Europe', a paper presented at the conference on The Japanese and the Peripheral Regions of Europe, Queen's University, Belfast, March.

Blomstrom, M. (1989) *Foreign Investment and Spillovers: A Study of Technology Transfer to Mexico*, London: Routledge.

Brech, M. and Sharp, M. (1984) *Inward Investment: Policy Options for the UK*, Chatham House Papers no. 21, London: Routledge & Kegan Paul.

Bromwich, M. and Inoue, S. (1994) *Management Practices and Cost Management Problems in Japanese Affiliated Companies in the UK*, London: CIMA.

Buckley, P. and Hughes, J. (1997) 'Japanese transfer pricing policy: a note', *Applied Economic Letters*, 4, 13–17.

Business Monitor (1995a) *Overseas Transactions (1993)*, MA4, London: HMSO.

—— (1995b) *UK Census of Production Summary Tables (1992)*, London: HMSO.

Dixon, R. (1989) *Financial Management*, London: Longman.

Doyle, P., Saunders, J. and Wong, V. (1992) 'Competition in global markets: a case study of American and Japanese competition in the British market', *Journal of International Business Studies*, 3, 419–42.

Dunning, J. (1986) *Japanese Participation in British Industry*, London: Croom Helm.

—— (1993) *Multinational Enterprises and the Global Economy*, Harlow: Addison-Wesley.

Eltis, W. and Fraser, D. (1992) 'The contribution of Japanese industrial success to Britain and Europe', *National Westminster Quarterly Review*, November, 2–19.

Ezzamel, M. and Mar-Molinero, C. (1990) 'On the distribution and properties of financial ratios in UK manufacturing companies', *Journal of Business Finance and Accounting*, 17 (1), 1–27.

Haddad, M. and Harrison, A. (1993) 'Are there dynamic externalities for FDI? Evidence from Morocco', in R. Newfarmer and C. Frischtak (eds), *TNCs, Market*

Structure and Industrial Performance, UN Library on Transnational Corporations, London: Routledge.

Haslam, C., Williams, K., Adcroft, A., Johal, J. and Williams, J. (1995) *Learning from Japan*, a paper presented at the conference on The Japanese and the Peripheral Regions of Europe, Queen's University, Belfast, March.

Hymer, S. (1976) *The International Operations of National Firms: A Study of Direct Investment*, Cambridge, Mass.: MIT Press.

JETRO (1996) *The 12th Survey of European Operations of Japanese Companies in the Manufacturing Sector*, London: Japanese External Trade Organization.

Morris, J., Munday, M. and Wilkinson, B. (1993) *Working for the Japanese*, London: Athlone.

Munday, M. (1995) 'The regional consequences of the Japanese second wave: a case study', *Local Economy*, 10 (1), 4–20.

Munday, M. and Peel, M.J. (1997) 'The Japanese manufacturing sector in the UK: a performance appraisal', *Accounting and Business Research*, 28 (1), 19–39.

Munday, M., Morris, J. and Wilkinson, B. (1995) 'Factories or warehouses? A Welsh perspective on Japanese transplant manufacturing', *Regional Studies*, 29 (1), 1–17.

Norusis, M.J. (1988) *SPSS-X Introductory Statistical Guide*, Chicago: SPSS Inc.

Oliver, A. and Wilkinson, B. (1992) *The Japanization of British Industry*, Oxford: Blackwell.

Oyelere, P. and Emmanuel, C. (1996) 'Seeking evidence of international transfer pricing abuse', Working Paper no. 96/3, Department of Accounting and Finance, University of Glasgow.

Peel, M.J. (1990) *The Liquidation/Merger Alternative: Theory and Evidence*, Aldershot: Avebury.

Piper, A. (1996) 'Secret corporation tax', *Sunday Business*, special report, 9 June, 12–13.

Pitelis, C. and Sugden, R. (eds) (1991) *The Nature of the Transnational Firm*, London: Routledge.

Schonberger, R. (1992) *Japanese Manufacturing Techniques*, New York: Free Press.

Siegel, S. and Castellan, N. (1988) *Non-Parametric Statistics*, London: McGraw-Hill.

Strange, R. (1993) *Japanese Manufacturing Investment in Europe: Its Impact on the UK Economy*, London: Routledge.

Taylor, J. (1993) 'An analysis of the factors determining the geographical distribution of Japanese manufacturing investment in the UK 1984–1991', *Urban Studies*, 30 (7), 1209–24.

Van Horne, J. (1987) *Financial Management and Policy*, London: Prentice-Hall International.

Voss, C. and Robinson, S. (1987) 'The application of JIT techniques', *International Journal of Operations and Production Management*, 7 (4), 46–52.

Williams, K., Williams, J., Haslam, C., Adcroft, A. and Sukhdev, L. (1992) *Factories or Warehouses? Japanese Manufacturing FDI in Britain and the US*, Occasional Papers on Business Economy and Society, no.6, Polytechnic of East London.

Young, S., Hood, N. and Peters, E. (1994) 'Multinational enterprises and regional economic development', *Regional Studies*, 28 (7), 657–77.

Part II

Manufacturing management in transition

5 The financial impact of 'Japanese' manufacturing methods

Nick Oliver and Gillian Hunter

INTRODUCTION

During recent years the virtues of lean production and just-in-time methods have been forcefully extolled in the management literature. These expressions typically function as umbrella terms for a package of management practices found in their purest form amongst the major Japanese manufacturers. Interest in these methods has been fuelled by the large performance gaps which apparently exist between Japanese manufacturers and their western counterparts in terms of productivity, quality and other measures of manufacturing performance (Parnaby 1987; Womack *et al.* 1990; Andersen Consulting 1993).

Western perceptions of Japanese manufacturing superiority have led to the widespread pursuit of manufacturing reform in many western countries, including the UK, where many firms have attempted to introduce just-in-time manufacturing practices, total quality and their related practices (Voss and Robinson 1987; Oliver and Wilkinson 1992). Sometimes these implementations have been approached strategically and in conjunction with what many have argued are necessary supports to the system, such as high commitment human resource policies (MacDuffie 1989) and integrated supply chain management. As often as not the approach has been piecemeal, and, unsurprisingly, many programmes have failed to live up to their promises (Elger 1990).

In the car industry the performance superiority of the Japanese car makers (in particular, Toyota) has been ascribed to a distinct set of practices subsumed under the term *lean production* (Womack *et al.* 1990). The lean production model comprises a number of elements, including low inventories, systems of work organization focused around production teams to encourage ownership and foster problem solving, and 'high commitment' human resource policies. The lean model describes similar patterns in supply chain management, arguing that lean firms enjoy close, shared destiny relations with their suppliers, whose operations are closely integrated with their own.

Lean production is significant because it represents an attempt to take Japanese methods out of their Japanese context, and elevate them to the status of universal principles that, properly applied, can produce elsewhere in the world the same outcomes as occur in Japan. This point is made quite explicitly:

In presenting our work to a broad audience we have one great fear: that readers will praise it or condemn it as yet another 'Japan' book, concerned with how a sub-set of the population within a relatively small country produces manufactured goods in a unique way. Our intention is fundamentally different. We believe that the fundamental ideas of lean production are universal – applicable anywhere by anyone – and that many non-Japanese companies have already learned this.

(Womack *et al.* 1990: 9)

This view has not gone unchallenged. *The Machine that Changed the World* has attracted fierce criticism on a number of grounds. On the one hand, students of Japanese industry argue that the piece, in common with many western accounts of Japanese practice, skates over the diversity of approaches found within Japanese industry. Secondly, a number of commentators, particularly those on the left of the political spectrum, argue that too much emphasis is placed on the firm as the unit of analysis, to the neglect of the wider context, such as economic and market conditions (Williams and Haslam 1992). More recently, the critique has shifted towards the issue of the financial performance of the Japanese car makers in an attempt to challenge the usually taken-for-granted assumption that Japanese methods, with their apparently enormous superiority in terms of physical conversion, actually translate into superior financial performance (Williams *et al.* 1994).

Undoubtedly the literature on JIT, one of the most prominent elements of Japanese manufacturing methods, contains little empirical evidence concerning the financial outcomes of the methods. As Golhar and Stamm comment: 'Although benefits and costs have been discussed separately in the literature, no empirical studies have been undertaken to examine the cost effectiveness of JIT implementation' (Golhar and Stamm 1991).

The purpose of this chapter is to examine the issue of Japanese methods and their relationship to financial performance by measuring the use of these methods by individual UK manufacturers and comparing these measures to independent measures of financial performance drawn from company accounts.

RESEARCH METHODS

In 1991 a survey of UK manufacturing companies was carried out to gather information about the use of management practices, principally in the three areas of manufacturing practice, human resource policy and supplier relations. The survey data were used to construct the indices of management practice described in this chapter. Of the 350 questionnaires sent out, sixty-eight were returned completed, a response rate of approximately 20 per cent. The companies operated in several sectors of manufacturing.

Management practice measures

The questionnaire consisted of three main parts. The first part sought data on the *context* in which the companies were operating, and covered issues such as size of the enterprise, nature of markets, whether or not the plants were union-ized and so on. The second part of the questionnaire asked companies to indi-cate the status of several elements of the Japanese or lean manufacturing model. These elements were derived from a number of descriptions of Japanese manu-facturing methods (Schonberger 1982; Voss and Robinson 1987; Womack *et al.* 1990). From the companies' responses to the questionnaire three indices were calculated to indicate the level of usage of techniques in the three categories of manufacturing practice, human resource practice and buyer–supplier relations. The elements comprising each index are shown in Table 5.1.

All three indices were scored in the same direction and according to the same scale. A zero score indicated that the techniques were never used, and a score of five indicated extensive use of all the techniques. In calculating the indices no credit was given to firms still planning the introduction of Japanese man-agement practices, as it was felt that this could not have an impact on performance.

The three indices were clearly interlinked: that is, firms which were high on one index tended to be high on the others as well. Therefore, although most of the analysis considers each measure independently, on occasion they are combined to form a single management practice index, when this is more appropriate.

Table 5.1 The elements of the questionnaire

Manufacturing index	*Human resources index*	*Supplier index*
Total Quality Control	Single status facilities	JIT delivery of supplies
Statistical Process Control	Performance appraisal for all	Quality assured supplies
Just-in-time production	Use of temporary workers	Single sourcing of supplies
Kanban materials control	Team briefings	Supplier development activities
Cellular manufacture	Performance-related pay	Supplier involvement in design
Design-for-manufacture	Company council or similar	Reducing number of suppliers
Cross-disciplinary teams	Profit-sharing scheme	Financial stake in suppliers
Quality improvement teams, etc.	Managerial rotation	
Set-up time reduction		
Operator responsibility for quality		

Financial performance measures

Independent financial performance data for each of the sixty-eight companies who had completed a questionnaire were drawn from their accounts over a period of ten years from 1984 to 1993. The performance measures generated by this process were:

- *Total sales*
- *Total stock* – Total value of inventory held at the time when the annual accounts were compiled.
- *Stock days* – This was calculated by dividing 365 by the stock turnover ratio: that is, the ratio of total stocks to total sales.
- *Number of employees*
- *Operating profit as a percentage of sales* – This is the profit level attributed to operations before interest and tax, etc., were subtracted. It is, therefore, a better indicator of the management practice performance than other profitability measures. Exceptional items are included. Therefore considerable restructuring costs appeared in some companies' accounts in the middle of the time period.
- *Return on equity* – This is profit as a percentage of equity capital. Equity was calculated by taking total assets less current liabilities, less long-term loans.

The management practice indices were used to divide the sixty-eight companies into 'high' and 'low' groups according to their use of the methods. Companies for which there were only partial data (for example, those with accounting data missing from some years) were excluded from the analysis. This reduced the number of companies included in the comparisons to forty-four.

RESULTS

Four measures of financial performance are considered in this section: stock (inventory) levels, sales per employee, profit as a percentage of sales, and return on equity.

Stock levels

One of the key aspects of Japanese manufacturing methods concerns the elimination of waste, with JIT and the associated reductions in inventory levels playing a major part in this. The benefits of stock reduction can be substantial, both physically in terms of facilitating visual management (Schonberger 1982, 1986), and in financial terms (Williams *et al.* 1989). Although some commentators have argued that 'Lowering inventory levels releases capital, increases quality, reduces obsolescence and improves flow' (Ingersoll Engineers 1990), many JIT programmes in the UK appeared to have fallen short of expectations (Williams *et al.* 1989; Ingersoll Engineers 1987; Delbridge and Oliver 1991). So have the reforms reported by companies in this study resulted in any real reductions in inventory levels?

Figure 5.1 shows inventory levels, as measured by stock days, for the two groups of companies. During the ten years covered by the study, stock days declined for both groups of companies. Inventories were significantly related to companies' scores on the management practice indices; high users of Japanese methods showed significantly lower stock days than those with lower scores on the management practice indices.

However, careful scrutiny of Figure 5.1 indicates that the picture may be less straightforward than first appears. Although the differences in stock levels between the two groups are statistically significant, the high users showed lower stock levels to begin with. The gap widens during the period 1985–8 (when many implementations were occurring), but then narrows noticeably around 1990–1. This suggests three things. First, it may be the better companies who implement these methods in the first place. Secondly, these companies appear to have begun their programmes of reform earlier; the closing of the gap in 1990–1 may represent a 'catching up' by the more dilatory companies. Thirdly, the 'levelling out' on the part of the high users in 1992–3 suggests that sustaining stock reduction programmes may be difficult.

Sales per employee

Several studies which have compared the productivity of Japanese and Western manufacturers have found that the Japanese firms require about half the direct labour input compared to their Western counterparts (Womack *et al.* 1990; Andersen Consulting 1993; MacDuffie 1989). There is considerable debate about this gap, both in terms of its size and the reasons behind it. Some critics claim that the gap is nowhere near as large as 2:1, and that such a gap, if it exists

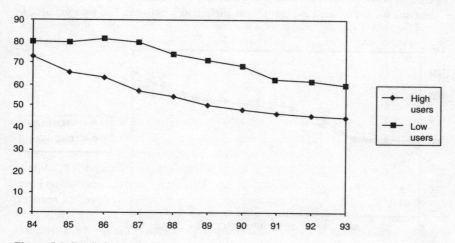

Figure 5.1 Stock days

at all, has more to do with the characteristics of the markets and economies within which firms are located than with management practices, Japanese or otherwise (Williams and Haslam 1992). Sales per employee represent one of the closest equivalent financial measures to such physical measures, although differences in vertical integration can contaminate comparisons. Do high users of Japanese methods show higher sales per employee? These figures are shown in Figure 5.2.

Surprisingly, Figure 5.2 shows there to be no significant differences between the two groups of companies on sales per employee, although both groups show improvements during the ten-year period. The low users actually show slightly (but not significantly) higher sales per employee for five of the ten years. High users are slightly ahead on this measure in 1993.

Profitability and return on equity

One of the criticisms levelled against the research which has focused on physical measures of productivity (such as units produced per labour hour) is that such studies say nothing about how the use of Japanese methods affects the bottom line. Some authors are quite clear in their views on this. For example, Golhar and Stamm assert that the 'productivity advantages of Japanese industry suggest that JIT implementation leads to profitability' (Golhar and Stamm 1991). Other are sceptical, and in an analysis of the cash-generating ability of car assembly firms, Williams and Haslam conclude that the majority of Japanese vehicle assemblers are no better at generating cash than their Western counterparts, and in many cases are worse (Williams and Haslam 1993).

The present study set out to discover if there were any discernible differences in profitability between the high- and low-user groups. Figure 5.3 shows the average annual profit margins of each group. Profit margin refers to the percentage of operating profit on sales to allow comparability between different-sized firms.

Statistically there were no significant differences between the two groups; in

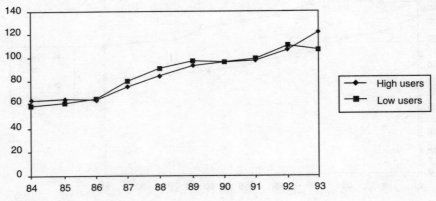

Figure 5.2 Sales per employee (£000s)

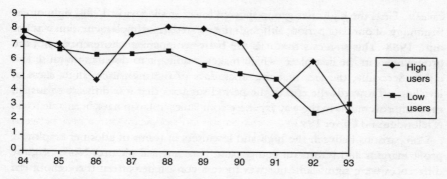

Figure 5.3 Percentage of operating profit

some years the profit margins of the high users were above those of the low users; in some the pattern was reversed, although margins were generally higher for the high users. The profitability of both groups showed a downward trend between 1984 and 1993, with the high users showing much greater volatility, a pattern found in some other measures as well, such as return on equity, which is shown in Figure 5.4.

The figures on return on equity show a similar pattern to those of profit margins, with the high users ahead for five out of the ten years covered, and behind for five. As with profit margins, the return on equity of the high users rises sharply in 1987–9, but plummets between 1989 and 1991, recovering in 1992 and then dropping sharply again in 1993. In contrast, the return on equity of the low-user group is much more stable, albeit on a downward trajectory.

DISCUSSION

The independent financial performance data reveal some surprising patterns. First, the findings on stock turns support the view that the use of Japanese methods can successfully be translated into tangible reductions in inventories, and, by implication, enhanced manufacturing efficiency. However, there are some

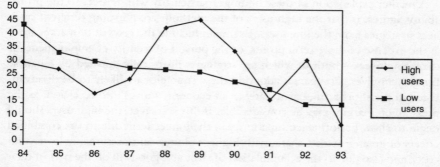

Figure 5.4 Percentage return on equity

caveats. First, the high-user group showed lower stock days in 1984, right at the beginning of our data period, although the mean date of implementation was not until 1988. This suggests that it is the better companies who embark on such programmes in the first place, which makes it difficult to disentangle cause and effect. Secondly, the fact that the stock days of the high users show signs of levelling off towards the end of the period suggests that it is difficult to sustain these improvements in the way Japanese companies in Japan have been able to do (Delbridge and Oliver 1991).

Comparisons between the high and low users in terms of sales per employee, profit margins and return on equity paint an equivocal picture. None of these differences were significant, nor was there a consistent pattern throughout the data period. High users tended to show higher volatility of profits than the low users. Given that many of these methods have been heavily promoted on the grounds that they promote greater competitiveness, some significant differences were expected. Why have these differences failed to materialize?

One possible explanation is that high users were more exposed to international competition than the low users, and that this squeezed their profits, thereby masking any consistent underlying improvement. This effect was examined by separating out those firms with their main markets outside the UK; the same pattern emerged, suggesting that there is not a 'masking' effect of international competition.

In the motor industry, Western and Japanese markets differ markedly, leading some commentators to suggest that the stable, growing market in Japan was a precondition for car manufacturers to use lean production methods successfully. Such commentators maintain that 'lean production techniques are irrelevant and unattainable' in the highly fluctuating Western market (Williams and Haslam 1993). While the findings of the present study do not support this view as far as measures of manufacturing efficiency are concerned, they do raise some serious issues about the robustness of any impact these techniques are making on the bottom line. The greater volatility of the profits of the high users suggests that they prosper more in boom times (such as 1987–9) but suffer more in the bad times (1989–91) relative to their more buffered counterparts.

A further explanation of these findings, particularly with respect to the profitability figures, is that the high users of the methods are pursuing different business strategies from the low users. Examples include the growth of market share at the expense of short-term profits, or the pursuit of security of employment for their employees – both of which are strategies historically pursued by Japanese firms themselves. Companies adopting these strategies are likely to be disadvantaged in the short term, particularly as an economy moves into recession, as the pressure on margins may be considerable. If this is correct, the high users should begin to show performance superiority in the longer term due to the combined effects of greater market share, with higher volumes and presumably lower unit costs, and also due to the accumulation of skills and goodwill on the part of their workforces fostered by long-term employment.

To test this idea, the high and low users were compared in terms of their value of sales and their number of employees over the ten-year period. These figures are shown in Figures 5.5 and 5.6.

The data provide some support for the market share argument, but do not (at first glance) support the employment security thesis. The sales of the high users rose more than those of the others during the same period, suggesting – but not proving – that they may have increased their market share in relative terms. The high users expanded more than the low users, particularly during 1984–5, but showed the same tendency to downsize, albeit a year or two later than the low users. Interestingly, this lag coincided with the period when profits were falling most dramatically for the high users.

CONCLUSIONS

The links between manufacturing practice and financial performance are clearly complex. A number of interpretations of the results of this study are possible, the most plausible of which were detailed in the previous section. Anecdotal evidence

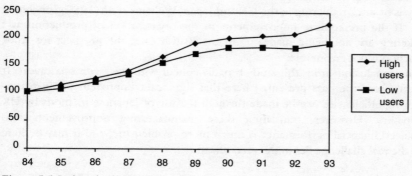

Figure 5.5 Indexed sales (1984 = 100)

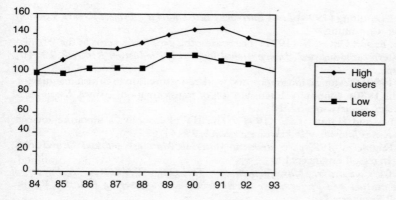

Figure 5.6 Indexed employment (1984 = 100)

collected by the authors lends some support to the idea that it is the 'fragility' created by these methods which may partly explain the patterns of financial performance. A manager from one of the high-user companies in the study recounted how his company's destocking programme had led to problems in their ability to meet customer demands. In the face of unpredictable demand and low inventories, the company had lost orders to competitors because of their inability to supply at the right time. The manager commented: 'Not all stock is evil – only unnecessary stock.' The problem is that the distinction between 'necessary' and 'evil' stock may not be clear until it is too late.

Similarly, the experiences of Nissan UK and its suppliers during 1993 provide a salutary reminder of the fact that competence in the *manufacture* of goods does not automatically translate into financial success. Despite Nissan UK's reputation as a lean manufacturer, and positive reviews of the Primera (one of the two types of vehicle produced by Nissan UK) by the motoring press, marketing failures led to overproduction of the Primera. As inventories of finished vehicles built up, the inevitable adjustment followed, with short-time working and the cancellation of the night shift at the Sunderland plant. This suggests that fragile production, the original term given to lean production, may actually be quite appropriate. In their analysis of stock reduction in the UK and Japan, Williams *et al.* (1989) concluded that 'If the prerequisite improvements in the organisation of production and marketing are not being made . . . in the British case, the prospect for stock reduction is not favourable.'

The conclusions from this study broadly concur with this, with one caveat. It appears from the data presented here that significant improvements in manufacturing efficiencies *can* be made through the use of Japanese methods by UK companies. However, translating these manufacturing improvements into enhanced financial performance is much more problematic, and it may be here that the real challenge lies in the years ahead.

REFERENCES

Andersen Consulting (1993) *Lean Enterprise Benchmarking Project Report*, London: Andersen Consulting.

Delbridge, R. and Oliver, N. (1991) 'Narrowing the gap? Stock turns in the Japanese and western car industries', *International Journal of Production Research*, 29 (10), 2083–95.

Elger, T. (1990) 'Technical innovation and work reorganisation in British manufacturing in the 1980s: continuity, intensification or transformation?', *Work, Employment and Society,* special issue, 67–101.

Golhar, D.Y. and Stamm, C.L. (1991) 'The JIT philosophy: a literature review', *International Journal of Production Research*, 29 (4), 657–76.

Ingersoll Engineers (1987) *Procurement Materials Management and Distribution*, Rugby: Ingersoll Engineers Ltd.

——— (1990) *Competitive Manufacturing – The Quiet Revolution: A Survey of Implementation and Performance Across British Manufacturing Industry*, Rugby: Ingersoll Engineers Ltd.

MacDuffie, J.P. (1989) *Worldwide Trends in Production System Management: Work*

Systems, Factory Practice, and Human Resource Management, IMVP Policy Forum, Cambridge, Mass.: MIT.

Oliver, N. and Wilkinson, B. (1992) *The Japanization of British Industry: New Developments in the 1990s*, Oxford: Blackwell Business.

Parnaby, J. (1987) 'A systems engineering approach to fundamental change in manufacturing', paper presented to the 9th Industrial Engineering Managers' Conference, New Orleans, 9–11 March.

Schonberger, R. (1982) *Japanese Manufacturing Techniques*, New York: Free Press.

—— (1986) *World Class Manufacturing*, New York: Wiley.

Voss, C. and Robinson, S. (1987) 'The application of just-in-time techniques', *International Journal of Operations and Production Management*, 7 (4), 42–5.

Williams, K. and Haslam, C. (1992) 'Against lean production', *Economy and Society*, 21, 321–54.

—— (1993) 'The limits of management: problems of the average car company', paper prepared for the Professions and Management in Britain Conference, Stirling University, Scotland, 26–28 August.

Williams, K., Williams, J. and Haslam, C. (1989) 'Why take the stocks out? Britain vs. Japan', *International Journal of Operations and Production Management*, 9 (8), 91–104.

Williams, K., Haslam, C., Johal, S. and Williams, J. (1994) *Cars*, Providence, RI: Berghahn Books.

Womack, J., Jones, D. and Roos, D. (1990) *The Machine that Changed the World*, New York: Rawson Associates.

6 Leadership in the front line
The changing nature of supervision in UK manufacturing

Ivor Parry and David Tranfield

INTRODUCTION

This case study is a product of an EPSRC-funded research grant into teamworking in manufacturing, and reports early empirical data from a large motor car assembly plant in the North Midlands.[1,2] Its particular focus is a consideration of the implications of changes in organizational structure and manufacturing process for first-line supervision. The company has undergone wide-reaching changes since 1991, and is commencing what many in the company recognize as yet another period of major turbulence, with new technologies, new manufacturing processes and uncertainty over the future permeating through the shop floor and beyond. This research focuses on team leaders as a key group of individuals who have the major task of operating as 'walking archives' (Nonaka and Takeuchi 1995: 152) in the day-to-day running of the business.

CHANGES IN MANUFACTURING: THE WIDER CONTEXT

There is widespread agreement that manufacturing in the UK is undergoing a process of radical change (Storey 1994; Bessant 1991). A range of factors, including increased globalization of markets, newly industrialized nations, advances in technology, and overcapacity in manufacturing, have all contributed to enhanced levels of competition for manufacturers. All this has put a premium on innovative manufacturing strategies which have challenged the existing recipes that have shaped and dominated UK manufacturing since the early part of this century. These were devised at a time when demand for manufacturing goods exceeded supply, there was a shortage of skilled labour, and cost was the main competitive driver (Bessant 1991).

More recently, the advent of new technologies – initially for increased automation (Adler 1986) and latterly for creating flexible manufacturing systems (Bessant and Haywood 1986; Boer *et al.* 1990) – and integration between various parts of the manufacturing process (Clark and Fujimoto 1991; Ettlie 1993) have delivered the potential for different forms of competitive advantage (Draaijer and Boer 1995). These have been based largely on the quest for agility and flexibility of manufacturing response to create a range of products, for the customization of existing products and for time to introduce new products.

At the same time, contemporary manufacturing in the UK has been greatly influenced by those successful Japanese companies who quite simply changed the rules of the game, particularly in the motor industry (Kirosingh 1989; Womack *et al.* 1990; Oliver 1992; Wickens 1995). Such companies focused on waste removal, questioning all aspects of manufacturing processes that added no value, thereby reducing cost, along with emphasizing quality and developing new and different forms of coordination (Oliver *et al.* 1995). Such different approaches to manufacturing developed alternative recipes which can deliver new ways of achieving competitive advantage by challenging the basic premises of traditional manufacturing wisdom – namely, that cost efficiency is best achieved by maximizing utilization of machinery and human assets – and replacing this with the tenet of the pre-eminence of waste elimination. In the old way of thinking, no one denied the existence of work in progress as waste, but it was interpreted as not counting. In such contexts, it was 'buffer stock', a safety margin. In the new paradigm, products made to customer need require factories to make a wider range of goods from the same machinery and plant. Those companies that can achieve maximum flexibility in the deployment of capital equipment are those more likely to achieve and sustain competitive advantage. Although the entities of manufacturing persist, they take on a different meaning and significance once the cognitive frame that contextualizes them alters (Hinings and Greenwood 1988). Thus the concept of waste takes on a new meaning under the new ways of manufacturing, and is construed accordingly.

This search for more efficient forms of manufacturing has apparently begun to coalesce in what Drucker (1990) has termed 'a new theory of manufacturing' which will characterize what he describes as 'the post-modern factory of 1999'. A more practical approach to such organizational change is to be found in the work of Parnaby (1988) at Lucas Industries, where 'a total systems approach' was initiated towards manufacturing systems re-engineering, whose core lies in the formation of a cellular organization structure 'based on natural people and machinery groupings around information and material flows' (Parnaby 1988: 485). Such novel configurations permitted the development of flexible, team-based manufacturing processes which companies have systematically explored and developed during the 1980s (Piore and Sabel 1984). The separate dimensions of this approach are well documented (Schonberger 1982; Oliver and Wilkinson 1992). However, it is important to recognize that such changes are occurring against the backdrop of 'developing idiosyncratic organizational structures in different companies' (Child and Partridge 1982: 196), while detailed accounts of the impact of these changes on the shop floor are still relatively rare.

TEAMWORKING AND PARTICIPATIVE WORKING: MYTH OR REALITY?

It is in the context of the search for new ways of manufacturing that the continued interest and development of teamworking in UK manufacturing must be understood. Given, in particular, the need for flexibility, it is argued that teamworking is a major intervention whereby manufacturing companies can redraw their organizational form and release human potential throughout the organization. Teamworking is thus seen as a major way of offering the key elements of flexibility and responsiveness to ensure competitive advantage.

There has been a long history of interest in teamworking in the UK, and there is much evidence (Peters 1989; Zuboff 1988) of a rekindling of its appeal. We would argue that the emphasis has now changed. Concern for the earlier 'quality of working life' debate (Trist and Bamforth 1951; Blumberg 1968; Davis and Trist 1972) has been largely superseded by an emphasis on improving product quality, reducing lead times, and creating organizational responsiveness to achieve and maintain competitive advantage (although the debate over working-life quality continues within the controversy over the consequences of the lean production system of manufacturing; Schonberger 1982, 1986; Womack *et al.* 1990; Wickens 1995; Garrahan and Stewart 1992; Sewell and Wilkinson 1991). From such a perspective, teamworking can also be seen as having the potential to reshape the organization from shop floor to boardroom, and can be viewed as a core competence in transforming an organization. It can be seen as a possible key to unlocking potential, creating flexibility and integrating across organizational boundaries. Teece *et al.* (1992) argue that dynamic capabilities underpin the competitive performance of an organization in so far as they are the means by which core competencies are developed and transformed. Much of the attraction of teamworking lies in its assumed capacity to produce and develop 'difficult to imitate' competencies that are embedded in the routines by which organizations coordinate their activities. Teamworking then provides a means of restructuring coordination to achieve competitive advantage (Mintzberg 1979). While currently teamworking is often seen as the key intervention through which companies can achieve competitive advantage, there is little theoretical or empirical evidence upon which to draw any firm conclusions of links between it and improved efficiency, particularly where the links and mechanisms interposing between dynamic capabilities and organizational routines transformed through teamworking are concerned.

Managing such wholesale organizational transitions also poses considerable challenges, and Conti and Warner (1994) raise serious questions regarding the skills of most senior managers to implement such complex change programmes successfully:

> The required changes in organization and culture, the scale and scope of supporting activities, the willingness to make long term investments in employee skills, and the daily pressures of 'running lean' without traditional buffers require a combination of technical, behavioural and leadership skills that are seldom found in companies.

(ibid. 181)

Further difficulties for companies in failing to appreciate the strength of particular cultural and historical legacies are acknowledged by Mueller (1994) and Johnson (1992) who highlight the potential political resistance and reaction likely to accompany such wholesale change programmes.

In addition, several sources (Dawson 1994; Elger and Smith 1994; Delbridge *et al.* 1997) have questioned the extent to which notions of flexibility, increased involvement or autonomy are in fact a reality for the shop floor or indeed for first-line supervision. Such caveats gain in importance when we consider the relative paucity of shop-floor accounts of such applications in practice; it might well be argued that some of the contemporary critical response has been more concerned with theoretical issues within the labour process debate rather than exploring the experiences of those involved in such changes in shop-floor practice. Oliver and Wilkinson (1992) present a most even-handed perspective and appraisal of the varying positions taken towards Japanization, while Bonazzi's (1994) work is unusual in exploring the meaning of job changes for the shop-floor workers themselves.

Delbridge and Lowe's work (Lowe 1993; Delbridge and Lowe 1997; Delbridge *et al.* 1997) serves to highlight the structural difficulties faced by manufacturers in attempting to reformulate the role of the first-line supervisor. Lowe's case study of supervisors in an established vehicle producer in the UK concludes that:

> in the face of such weak institutional support [supervisors being responsible for implementing company objectives on the shopfloor, but being divorced from any managerial status or power] for the supervisor's emerging role it is likely that her/his position as the 'marginal man' or 'man in the middle' will remain unchanged or possibly worsen.
>
> (Lowe 1993: 755)

Delbridge and Lowe's (1997) comparative case study of a car assembly plant, Hanwell Motors, and the Japanese-owned Nippon CTV factory demonstrates that the situation of supervisors can vary quite considerably, depending on organizational structures and systems, and on the place of supervisors within these, as well as on individual interpretations, responses and actions to the particular context. Thus Hanwell supervisors experience their marginality daily, while for Nippon CTV there was a clearer alignment between management objectives and supervisory roles (our own current research into first-line supervision in three other manufacturing companies reports similar contrasts).

Finally, their survey of seventy-one automative plants (Delbridge *et al.* 1997) explores the experiences of lean production systems for first-line supervisors. Of particular interest for this discussion is their finding that supervisors' areas of responsibility lie more in production than in management issues, and that the team leader has more responsibility for routine activities rather than skilled maintenance tasks.

A common theme running through Delbridge and Lowe's work is the importance of first-line supervision in any debate on productivity, efficiency or quality concerns, and that its significance and potential for affecting improvements is frequently ignored or downplayed. Again, our ongoing research with supervisors suggests major differences in the degree to which more senior management both recognize this and act accordingly.

THE CHANGING NATURE OF SUPERVISION

Underpinning many UK companies' current efforts to introduce improvement programmes is the attempt to change the organization's social system in order to gain commitment from the workforce. Analysts of the 'lean production' model (Oliver 1995; Andersen Consulting 1993) point out that Japanese companies and their western 'transplants' pay much more attention to honing production systems before attending to social systems, and essentially see social systems as supporting production systems. Whether such a position can be argued in the case of UK manufacturers, who are predominantly ensconced in brownfield sites with historically difficult management–labour relations, is a moot point. Andersen Consulting (1993), in their study of lean production in eighteen automotive component plants, analyse the differences between 'world-class' companies and the rest. They discovered, much to their surprise, that in 'world-class' companies the emphasis, or difference, lay not in empowering workers, but in the significance of the role of the supervisor/team leader:

> These findings suggest that the role of the 'empowered' operator in world class manufacturing may have been overstated and that crucial differences lie at team leader rather than at operator level . . . in most activities, the team leaders played a pivotal role in world class plants.
>
> (Andersen Consulting 1993: 14)

Dawson (1994) points out that in non-Japanese companies, even where changes towards teamworking have been initiated, the tendency has been to ignore supervisory issues that arose during workplace reform: 'Such changes have not been met by a redefinition of supervision, which in many cases remains the neglected function of shop floor operations' (Dawson 1994: 31). Buchanan and Preston (1991: 15), in their case study of first-line supervision, also point out a lack of role change:

> The transition of foreman from policeman to coach had therefore not taken place. Relationships with the shopfloor were characterized by low trust and high intervention. The foreman had made only minimal concessions to participative management.

Dawson (1994) reminds us that managing in the 1990s is likely to be about handling a variety of change initiatives linked with the introduction of new manufacturing techniques and technologies. However, within these initiatives will run a common thread related to developing employee commitment, flexibility and the devolution of quality control to the shop floor. In addition, the nature of coordination and control is likely to change, increasing the development and reliance on the self-managed work team as a major vehicle for improving quality, responsiveness and continuous improvement. There are therefore important implications for first-line managers, as the notion of 'responsible autonomy' reduces management layers and demands new patterns of coordination and control. In such scenarios, teamworking is likely to be seen as a main route towards problem solving through mutual adjustment, which can thereby deliver flexibility and support integrating technologies, while the critical role of first-line supervision in translating company vision into shop-floor reality in such contexts requires acknowledgement.

THE RESEARCH

This case study forms part of an EPSRC-funded three-year research project into 'Teamworking in Manufacturing', which is committed to producing a methodology to inform and improve current practice in our collaborating companies. It focuses upon a specific aspect of the project, namely, the key role of first-line supervision, and it has a particular interest in:

- a comparison of first-line leadership in 'old' and 'new' manufacturing environments;
- the extent of changes in first-line supervision in such contexts;
- the characteristics of the team-leader role in a particular setting; and
- a preliminary assessment of the significance of the team-leader role and some implications for best practice.

Initially, Mintzberg's (1967) managerial roles categorization informed early development of the interview schedule. Later in the interviewing process, Mintzberg's (1994) model of managerial work was used, as this offers a more comprehensive view of the managerial role and greater depth for interviewing. In this more recent work, Mintzberg considers 'the integrated job of managing' by the use of a model which 'builds inside out, beginning at the centre, and working out, layer by layer' (Mintzberg 1994: 12). His model attempts to integrate the job of managing by considering the person, the job 'frame' (its purpose, structure, strategy and conception), the agenda, its context, and the actual behaviours that managers engage in to do their jobs (this can occur at three levels: through direct action, through information and through people). The benefits of using this later model quickly became apparent, enabling increased understanding of how team leaders viewed their experiences of the change process, and so highlighting their sense-making and social interaction within a social setting (Schein 1987; Watson 1995), as well as making explicit their key values and role orientations.

The research considers a small sample of team leaders from this company. As such, it meets Stake's (1995: xi) definition of a case study as: 'The study of the particularity and complexity of a single case, coming to understand its activity within important circumstances'. In all, some nineteen team leaders were interviewed using a semi-structured interview schedule linked to Henry Mintzberg's categories of the managerial role (Mintzberg 1967, 1983, 1994). This was a management-selected group from some 120 team leaders, and we asked for the sample to be differentiated between 'highly effective' and 'merely competent' performers to enable comparisons to be made. In the event, this distinction was rather lost as the sample moved to whomsoever was available. We felt some doubt as to the randomness of this sample, especially given the positive views, but equally, acknowledgement must be made of the drive to gain employee commitment through single-status recognition and clear agreements gained regarding the needs of the company to emerge from the recession in the late 1980s as a strong and competitive manufacturer – what Oliver and Wilkinson (1992) call 'new realist' deals. The outcome of CarCo's negotiations, entitled 'The Future of Manufacturing on the CarCo Site', clearly stated the new arrangements for work organization:

> Shop-floor teams will be led by a Team Leader. Within each team the members will be totally flexible and responsible for all the activities which will take place in that department, including the process (assembly, machining, painting etc.), maintenance, quality/inspection, cleaning up, work records and reporting.

Each interview lasted some 45 to 50 minutes on average, all data were tape recorded with the permission of all interviewees, and brief notes were kept of salient points. Company documentation was also obtained and information gathered from more informal visits and contacts at the plant. Periodic analysis of the interviewing process enabled the continual refinement of the research schedule as well as the questions asked (Meyerson 1991). Throughout, participants 'told their story', so that 'values, goals and aims were all represented'(Schein 1979: 412), even though on occasions that led down unintended paths. Such a process also provided some unexpectedly rich data.

THE DATA

The 'old' and the 'new' – from foreman to team leader at CarCo

In the late 1980s and early 1990s the company was failing, with closure a real threat and possibility. Recessions in the UK and US had a huge impact on sales (vehicle sales plummeting from more than 3,000 in 1990 to 1,750 in 1991), and it is against this economic backdrop that the company undertook a major reorganization of working practices, including teamworking. The speed with which change occurred was extremely rapid, and the new team leaders were quickly presented with a new role to develop and enact. By 1992, the workforce had been reduced from 5,000 to 2,300: 'It was a hard time for us . . . we saw a lot of our friends go down the road' (Team Leader 1).

During this period, three key issues were construed:

1   how to change a culture of 'no change';
2   how to ensure continuous change; and
3   how to build a framework that supports rather than inhibits change (Quality Director).

The company culture moved from 'a hierarchical to a team-based culture, supported by systems, driven by people, with a multidisciplined team of manufacturing engineers, planners and maintenance in each manufacturing zone' (Quality Director). Thus the shift was made extremely rapidly and the new team leaders found themselves starting a new week in a new role: 'We felt it was better to start wholesale change rather than attempt pilots . . . we acknowledged that within that change process there would be lots of opportunities to learn, and to profit from that learning' (Quality Director).

Unlike in Buchanan and Preston's (1991) study, all the team leaders in this sample were fully aware of the role changes they had experienced: 'The foreman's job was basically to sit in the office and if a shop-floor worker had a problem you went to see him. They would discuss with us the type of problem, but they weren't hands on. Where there was anything wrong with machines they'd report it to maintenance' (Team Leader 1).

The past, in terms of its restrictions on workers' knowledge, was also well remembered: 'There was never a next time. We'd get the setter to fix the machine, and when it came round to the crucial bit to set things right he'd always tell you to go and fetch something from the stores. By the time you came back the job was done and you had missed the vital part. They'd only let you know certain things' (Team Leader 2). The implications of the new role were also experienced and understood: 'It was a totally different role. One of the main problems we had, at least initially, was that people tended to see us as foremen, but we weren't. It was a gradual process of change and people slowly became less suspicious. The big improvements were around flexibility, different roles and involvement' (Team Leader 1).

All were aware of the extent and nature of role change that had occurred, and many examples were offered to illustrate the degree of difference. In the next section these differences are presented in the form of two archetypes reflecting the changes in role. In order to best juxtapose these differences, the notion of archetype has been taken from Hinings and Greenwood (1988). In their study of organizational change, they offer an analytical framework that attempts to trace organizational transformation 'brought about by the displacement of central ideas, values and beliefs' (Hinings and Greenwood 1988: 7). While it is not feasible presently to do justice to the complexity and depth of their analysis, the next section has utilized their core idea of 'displacement' to analyse the transformation of the supervisory role from 'Foreman' to 'Team Leader'. Although Hinings and Greenwood's analysis operates at an organizational level, it is our intention to use their analytical framework at the level of individual interpretations of change.

The extent of change

Interviewees were asked to sum up the most significant changes in a few words after they had offered detailed examples to illustrate exactly how the role had altered. This data was then transcribed and a list of key words drawn up encapsulating the significant differences between life pre- and post-1991 as these team leaders saw it. From every example given, a schedule was created of key descriptors produced from actual words and phrases used in the interviews. These were later tabulated in Table 6.1.

Table 6.1 Differences between 'old' and 'new' working practices

Archetype A (*foreman*)	Archetype B (*team leader*)
Hierarchical	Open
Suspicion	Trust
Certainty	Uncertainty
Simplicity	Complexity
Staying the same	Doing it better
Few tasks	Many tasks
Boredom	Interest
Hands off	Hands on
Robotic	Grasping
Management	Leadership

These words provide powerful insights into two differing approaches to the job, and indicate the level of awareness and appreciation of the differences between the 'old' and the 'new'. The 'old' meant getting on with the same old work day after day. The 'new' meant the possibility of sharing knowledge:

> One of the first things I did [on becoming team leader] was to tell the lads that I would teach them how to use every machine in the bay. I had to start by showing them that I was prepared to lose my own knowledge to them. (Team Leader 2)

> You never really talked to a supervisor unless you had a problem, and even then you never felt that they treated you like a human being. Most of us just got on with the work and avoided any trouble. (Team Leader 5)

> It was as though there were two rays at the factory gate. One took out your brain, and the other your heart. We all felt the same over this. (Team Leader 8)

> In all the years I worked here, nobody bothered to ask my opinion about anything. It was as if we were machines ourselves. (Team Leader 12)

Managing the role

One of the most significant points to come from the interviews was the importance the team leaders attached to the ideal and practice of empowerment. The values which people hold dear can and do influence the way they go about their daily work, and for all of our sample the notion of empowerment was of real significance. It was mentioned in every interview and all gave examples of what this meant in practice:

> All my team members have high responsibility. All members can do it, no matter what. Facilitation is important, especially with older members. We had one who wouldn't even answer the phone. We're changing all that. (Team Leader 3)

I've a good team, supportive. We understand each other. We are learning new parts of the new process, and we feel we have the knowledge. (Team Leader 14)

We meet as a team and score each other to identify development needs. The number of D's [development needs] you get determines the training you get. The point is that it's all of us who decide. It's not just me. (Team Leader 5)

It's not so much how I would do it, more how would they do it. (Team Leader 8)

All the sample talked of the benefits of the new way of working for them, although it was always made plain that it was hard work operating in a different way: 'No, I don't think working in this way is easy, but it's more satisfying. There's more to do. We've got more pressure that's for sure, but at least the work is more interesting. I don't mind grafting if it's like that' (Team Leader 9).

The 1994 Mintzberg model distinguishes three ways of getting things done, namely, through information, directly, and through people. All three were raised by the sample as crucial ways of working. The first way – of managing indirectly through information – was seen somewhat ambivalently, as informational control recalled life in the company prior to 1992, when it was felt that managers used information to maintain discipline and to disempower the workforce. Team leaders therefore felt somewhat ambivalent towards this area of their role.

The second way, managing through direct action, was indeed a reality, but in a different sense to that envisaged by Mintzberg. A major way for team leadership was to manage through direct action, but this in fact meant actually doing work alongside everyone else. In other words they were still workers, and felt they needed to demonstrate this continually: 'I'm still a working person on the shop-floor. I work like everyone else. I can act a bit like a dog's body to the team. . . . I'm sometimes told to go and bloody do it myself if there's no one else available. That happens less now, but I still have to graft' (Team Leader 8). Indeed, the role split for team leaders is officially 80 per cent hands-on and 20 per cent coordination. The reality is rather different as all leaders felt it important that they 'maintained the respect' of the team through working as hard as anyone else. Absence from the shop floor could also be difficult: 'I need to go to meetings, and now mostly people will do the work without me there, but it's taken a while to get that trust. It can still be a problem though' (Team Leader 4). Another added: 'I attend a lot of meetings, but I still do my whack' (Team Leader 11).

Clearly, all this creates substantial pressure for team leaders, as they attempt to meet the dual demands of the actual work along with their planning and coordinating roles. Greater experience of the role has also led to more sophisticated ways of dealing with the pressure: 'When I first started the job, I did everything. I simply couldn't learn to delegate. I was rushed off my feet. I've learnt how to do it now, so life is a lot easier' (Team Leader 8).

All the interviewees commented on the need to work alongside team members, particularly when the workload was heavy. This reinforced their view of themselves as shop-floor workers, and guaranteed the maintenance of respect on the

shop floor. It was generally felt that the company would soon be actively considering changing the team-leader role to develop its coordinating and monitoring
role, and to ensure that team leaders viewed and acted less as shop-floor workers,
and more as managers. However, as Delbridge and Lowe (1997) point out, this
can create difficulties if the necessary support is not provided, or insufficient
credence is given to the necessary change in team-leader status to enact that role.
In addition, we found little evidence that this move was wanted by team leaders
themselves, as much as their credibility rested on doing the work as well as, if not
better than, their team members.

It was the third way, managing through people, that was the most frequently
presented and preferred model of working. This was a core value to which all our
sample subscribed. All indicated a strong commitment to working in this style.
The company has stressed empowerment throughout its literature and training,
and it appeared a crucial aspect of the values and goals of this sample. Ways of
encouraging people to become involved were frequently sought, and the origins
of such practice were frequently articulated:

> A while ago we had a foreman from Canada. He was like a breath of fresh
> air. He was very fair. He had a different style, and he was a good model for
> me. I wanted to work in that same way if I ever had that opportunity.
> (Team Leader 7)

> I play a lot of cricket, and I've seen how our captain works, how he gets the
> best out of people. He works in a particular way . . . trusting them . . .
> encouraging and praising them. I'm also a school governor. That's given
> me confidence in dealing with people and running meetings. Before that
> experience I was shy, and I didn't know what to do in meetings. I've learnt
> now. (Team Leader 12)

Nor were the practical benefits of a collaborative style of working ignored:

> In my job, you never know what to expect . . . it's hard to organize what we'll
> be doing. Two heads are always better than one in this situation I believe.
> (Team Leader 4)

> Big jobs become easier if we all work together. If someone's struggling
> with a problem then there's always someone to help. It's easier that way.
> (Team Leader 5)

Mintzberg describes managing by information as essentially empowering, and
there is a sense in which the team leaders, particularly through team meetings, can
have that role to play. Yet managing through information was still seen as a
disempowering reminder of the 'old times' when the power of management lay in
its control of information. Leaders were also especially conscious of the difficulties
of not having all the available information, particularly where the future direction
of the company was involved, as this could pose a threat to shop-floor perceptions
of team-leader commitment to workers, particularly in times of unrest or
uncertainty: 'The whole plant is changing again. We've got the challenge of new

work, but we don't know quite what we'll be doing. We're sceptical about it'. (Team Leader 7).

The more articulate team leaders in this sample recognized that further changes were likely in the future, and understood the benefits of taking every opportunity that presented itself to gain experience of new ways of working: 'I am always looking for new ways of doing things. I think it is in the company's interests as well as my own. I don't think I'll ever be doing the same thing for very long in this company now. Things are changing too much'. (Team Leader 3).

What impressed and to some extent surprised us was the degree to which these team leaders felt so positive about their job. Clearly, they did have concerns regarding increased demands and future uncertainties, but in general, rather like the supervisors in Child and Partridge's (1982) study, they relished the challenge of the new role.

The team-leader role in the CVD – an example of managing change and uncertainty

In the following section, the nature and degree of uncertainty in the role is briefly explored in the light of the experiences and comments of two team leaders in the CVD area (Customer Validation Department). Both these highly experienced team leaders demonstrated high levels of understanding, both about their role and the general strategic direction the company was taking. It is argued that exploration of such working contexts can provide insight into effective practice where flexibility, innovation and creativity can be seen as those distinctive capabilities that firms must seek in order to maintain competitive advantage (McGrath *et al.* 1995).

The CVD is the area where cars, at the rate of eight per day, are road tested and all faults rectified before being passed on to the Coachbuilding Sections. In these sections, teams of around twelve people have the responsibility for diagnosing and solving any mechanical problems a car may present. All are multiskilled, highly experienced, trained in new technologies, and are used to working together to solve any mechanical problem. Increasingly, new technologies are reducing the length of time actually road-testing vehicles, and this entails the learning of new techniques and processes. Alongside this daily work, they can also participate in RATs (Rapid Action Teams) to solve a particularly unusual or reoccurring problem. These teams can also be formed with people from other areas who have a particular expertise or for whom the problem is also of concern.

Being team leader in this area of the shop floor is characterized by high levels of uncertainty and ambiguity:

It's hard to organize this job. We don't know what we'll be doing until the car comes back off the Road Test. Team members have a high responsibility for things here. If I'm away and something needs doing then it gets done. My role is to say that if something needs doing we can all do it. For example, the lads said that they didn't want me filling in the skills matrix, they picked two lads out of the team to co-ordinate it. . . . I just don't say, 'I'm team leader now, you'll do as I'm telling you'. I know that will never work with my team. . . . They'd build a wall right in front of me. (Team Leader 7)

Work in this area is almost impossible to plan for in advance, as no one knows the nature of the problem(s) in the cars arriving for diagnosis and remedy on any particular day. The teams therefore demonstrate high levels of coordination through mutual adjustment (Mintzberg 1983): 'We're all highly skilled. We're trained to handle anything. . . . It could be gear box, engines, cylinder heads . . . we're not doing the same job every day. We're crossed over and interlinked' (Team Leader 7).

Using Nonaka and Takeuchi's (1995) definition, such individuals can be characterized as 'knowledge practitioners' who 'accumulate, generate, and update tacit and explicit knowledge' (ibid. 152). Their personal experience and knowledge add value by ensuring that the customer receives a product that is fault-free. On the other hand, it is recognized within the company that such rare skills need to be removed from what is essentially waste reduction, and that eventual work reorganization needs to tap directly into such skills and expertise.

For Nonaka and Takeuchi (1995), such workers should exhibit the following characteristics:

- high intellectual standards;
- a strong sense of commitment to re-create the world according to their own perspective;
- a wide variety of experience, both inside and outside the company;
- skilled in dialogue with internal and external customers; and
- open to carrying out candid debates and discussions with others.

In their interviews, individuals demonstrated all five of Nonaka's key characteristics of 'knowledge practitioners' to extraordinary levels. Team Leader 5 arrived with a set of characteristics that more than matched Nonaka's. He stressed his roles as 'gofer, problem-solver, networker, passer on and receiver of knowledge, communicator, decision-maker, planner, conceiver and challenger'. He had developed a management style that was solidly founded on an empowerment approach which imbued all that he did. He had a clear view of where the expertise lay:

We're changing our process. All that to tackle . . . people half believe it, but there's a lot of convincing to do. We've challenges of new equipment. We've responsibility for our own process. . . . We're asking to be able to sort it out ourselves. The best person to ask [about changes] is the person on the job. . . . They're the expert. (Team Leader 5)

Hence, he was fulfilling precisely the role of changing implicit to explicit knowledge within a cooperative framework – a major feature of Japanese manufacturing success explored by Nonaka and Takeuchi (1995).

The work of a team leader is demanding at the best of times. In times of uncertainty great pressure can be created for the team leader as team members feel insecure about the future. Such feelings of insecurity 'demand continual readjustment and present unending challenge for all concerned' (Isabella 1990: 7). Nonetheless, Team Leader 6 was equally clear about how the future looked, and how it should be handled:

> We're changing the whole process. There's a lot to tackle . . . half believe it and half don't. There's a lot of convincing to do. There's challenges of new equipment, we've responsibility for the process, and in all this the best person to ask is the bloke who's doing the job. On our team board we have our team motto – 'The team will continuously improve our process as a team' – the team works with that.

Clearly, these team leaders are aware of the real and potential marginality of their position (Child and Partridge 1982; Delbridge and Lowe 1997), and are conscious of the need to manage these tensions creatively.

The actual process in terms of how team leaders do their job is a task for future research, as is the differentiation between highly effective leaders and the merely competent. What is clear is that in this particular area team leaders expect and exhibit high levels of autonomy and individual and collective responsibility. It is a point that Wickens (1993) makes when talking of successful *kaizen*, namely, that it is difficult to prescribe for continuous improvement, and that the process 'relies heavily on the individual, hopefully making the job more meaningful and genuinely devolving both responsibility and authority' (ibid. 47).

However, the insights gained from such interview data need to be supplemented with observational data to establish what such leaders actually *do* in practice. A number of questions come to mind, all of which centre on applying Mintzberg's model to team leaders' actual work processes. Thus the idea of 'best practice' needs observational evidence to assess what exactly its 'ingredients' are. From this interview data there is clear evidence of the more articulate team leaders explaining that they can operate with all three of Mintzberg's ways of managing, with a clear preference for managing 'through people', as well as being able to switch styles as and when appropriate, but we need to know more about how this is actually achieved on the shop floor.

In addition, this particular sample of team leaders was chosen by management. It is therefore impossible to assess the degree to which the relatively positive view of these team leaders is typical or otherwise of the other 100, or indeed the extent to which the rest are able to operate within and between Mintzberg's three levels of managerial behaviour. Some indication of the existence of differing viewpoints and practice can be ascertained from the following two quotes. The first was from our major source of contact, a fairly senior manager within the STRIVE Team who pointed out that: 'The company's real problem is the 20 per cent of team leaders who haven't really got a clue about what they are doing. Those are the ones who really give us concern' (Senior Manager). He went on to explain that the concern lay within this sizeable minority's incapacity to work in the ways now needed by the new work organization.

The second example was from a team leader whom we met briefly on the shop floor. His comment was: 'Don't be fooled by what management are telling you . . . nor by the pretty pictures around the place. [He was referring to the company slogans and logos placed around the shopfloor.] It's not as good as they make out, believe me. You're only getting half the story here!' This individual went on to stress clearly that he was by no means alone in having these views, and that many on the shop floor were unwilling to say what they really felt. Indeed, there were occasions when one sensed in interviews that people were being careful about sounding critical, or being careful over their precise use of particular words, as, for example, when the word 'problem' was 'translated' into 'challenge' (although it must also be stated that the particular company language style, deriving as it did from the sayings of one of the co-founders of the company, was much in evidence in talking to company 'associates' – indeed, we found that such words and phrases were slipping into our own usage after spending time at the plant!).

In this plant – as with Delbridge and Lowe's (1997) Nippon CTV example – the nature of workplace relations, the non-existence of difficult union relations, along with what was felt by the sample to be a generally supportive plant management, have enabled first-line supervision to align its own concerns with those of senior plant management, and hence to negotiate successfully a path through the dilemmas of managing on the front line. However, this cannot be assumed to be always so, particularly as pressure in the future is likely to shift the team-leader role into a more explicitly managerial mode. Indeed, Child and Partridge (1982) make the very same point in their case study, but we would argue that the position is different in this situation for two reasons. First, most of these team leaders have come from the shop floor, identify with these roots, and rely on this to manage the role successfully. Secondly, they feel that they do have the support of more senior managers – a different situation to Child and Partridge's sample. Their concern rests with the future, not with marginality. To that extent, they are the 'new realists' identified by Oliver and Wilkinson (1992).

THE FUTURE

Team leaders acknowledge the extent of current changes within the company: outsourcing has meant closures for several manufacturing areas; bodies will be produced in a plant assembly shop; a modern single-powered line with feeder areas located alongside is being trialed; and more continuous improvement processes are being brought into operation. For some team leaders this has meant closure of their section, and the chance to retrain:

> The machine shop is closing. I was a skilled machinist, and I am now retraining. In fact, I'm undergoing a massive change. I've been on fast-track training, and am working to be eventually on the new model production line. There are major changes ahead. At the moment cars are physically pushed, man-handled from one station to another, but soon there will be a continuous moving track for the new model. This new track will be mobile, height adjustable, so a more

amenable height for us to work on the car. As the picture becomes clearer so anxiety reduces. For me this special project offers me alleyways to get somewhere. It provides a major skills expansion. (Team Leader 9)

The increasing demands to reduce lead times, improve quality and reduce waste in the future will augment the pressure on this key group of workers, but how this may be interpreted and hence managed is likely to be dependent on how the ambiguity of such changes in terms of both increasing pressure of work and reduction of physical effort will be mediated through team leaders' and workers' interpretations of the work in relation to prior expectations, rewards and experiences (Bonazzi 1994). Team leaders at CarCo are all too aware of the possible impact of such factors on their relationships with the shop floor.

CONCLUDING REMARKS

This case study has examined the changing nature of first-line supervision in this car assembly plant, with a particular focus on changes post-1991, the year in which the company undertook a major restructuring programme. The aim has been to highlight some of the most significant changes that have occurred in the supervisory role, commencing with the appointment of team leaders some five years ago, along with an examination of how team leaders have understood, experienced and managed the change process. Above all, it has tried to present a view of the changes in this company which are the team leaders' own. The analysis of the data from a series of semi-structured interviews was centred around Mintzberg's (1994) model of the managerial role, from which the importance of both value and practice of an empowerment model of managerial practice was acknowledged. In this vital sense, there appear to be high levels of congruence between company objectives and the team leaders in this sample. Also, the significance of interpretation and 'sense making' was explored, particularly in the consideration of future developments, both within the company as well as for the team-leader role. These team leaders demonstrated high levels of understanding and skill regarding the management of their role. They were first and foremost shop-floor workers, and always stressed this, but are much more. They are able to move confidently within and between different ways of managing, underpinned by a commitment to and practice of empowerment. This came from a strong sense of both the practical benefits of this approach for the task of leading the team, alongside an awareness and appreciation of its benefits for workers' jobs and their futures in the company. The empowerment model also reduced tension by encouraging commitment. In their view, it was a more effective way of working, particularly because it recognized where expertise and insight lay, but also because it meant that they could manage their teams without going back to the 'old' ways so detested by all on the shop floor. To do that would guarantee failure. How future tensions between this empowerment model of managing and ever-increasing emphasis on 'leanness' in the company will be managed by team leaders is a matter for future research, but clearly there are crucial implications for this group of key workers, who will be charged with the responsibility of managing technological innovations, increasing workloads and new work practices, while also ensuring shop-floor commitment in such a scenario.

NOTES

1 The research project into Teamworking in Manufacturing is a three-year programme supported by the CPD of the EPSRC. Fund holders for the project are Professors Stuart Smith and David Tranfield, and Morris Foster, Senior Research Fellow. The first stage involves fieldwork to develop case studies with the collaborating companies. In the later stages, a prototype methodology for the introduction of teamworking will be developed.
2 The CarCo company's STRIVE Team is a continuous improvement team, created from a cross-section of company associates usually seconded to this team for 18 to 24 months. It includes shop-floor workers. We wish to thank the collaborating company for its commitment to the project and to this research area, the STRIVE Team for organizing interviews, and the team leaders for sharing their time, energy, and knowledge with us.

REFERENCES

Adler, P. (1986) 'New technologies, new skill', *California Management Review*, **291**, 9–28.

Andersen Consulting (1993) 'Entering the business of business integration', INSEAD.

Argyris, C. and Schon, D.A. (1996) *Organizational Learning*, vol. 11, New York: Addison-Wesley.

Atkinson, P. (1990) *The Ethnographic Imagination*, London: Routledge.

Bessant, J. (1991) *Managing Advanced Manufacturing Technology: The Challenge of the Fifth Wave*, Oxford: Blackwell.

Bessant, J. and Haywood, B. (1986) 'Flexibility in manufacturing systems', *Omega*, **14** (6), 465–73.

Blumberg, P. (1968) *Industrial Democracy: The Sociology of Participation*, London: Constable.

Boer, H., Hill, M.R. and Krabbendam, J.J. (1990) 'FMS implementation management: promise and performance', *International Journal of Operations and Production Management*, **10** (1), 5–20.

Bonazzi, G. (1994) 'A gentler way to total quality? The case of the "integrated factory" at Fiat Auto', in T. Elger and C. Smith (eds), *Global Japanisation: The Transformation of the Labour Process*, London: Routledge.

Buchanan, D.A. and Preston, D. (1991) 'The floggings will stop when morale improves: benefits and pitfalls of manufacturing systems engineering', Research Paper no. 20, Loughborough University.

Byham, W.C. (1988) *Zapp! The Lightning of Empowerment*, Century Business, London: Century Business Books.

Child, J. and Partridge, B. (1982) *Lost Managers: Supervisors in Industry and Society*, Cambridge: Cambridge University Press.

Clark, K.B. and Fujimoto, T. (1991) 'Product development performance: strategy, organization and management in the world auto industry', Working Paper, Harvard Business School.

Coghlan, D. (1994) 'Research as a process of change: action science in organizations', *International Bulletin of Action Research*, **15**, 119–30.

Conti, R.F. and Warner, M. (1994) 'Taylorism, teams and technology', *New Technology, Work and Employment*, 9, 2.

Davis, L.E. and Trist, E.L. (1972) 'Improving the quality of working life: experiences in the socio-technical approach', US Department of Health, Education and Water, Washington, DC.

Dawson, P. (1994) *Organizational Change: A Processual Approach*, London: Paul Chapman.

Delbridge, R. and Lowe, J. (1997) 'Manufacturing control: supervisory systems on the "new" shopfloor', *Sociology*, 31 (3).

Delbridge, R., Lowe, J. and Oliver, N. (1997) 'Who does what under team working? Managerial perceptions of employee roles and responsibilities in contemporary manufacturing', paper submitted to Teamworking Workshop, Nottingham University.

Delbridge, R., Turnbull, P. and Wilkinson, B. (1995) 'Pushing back the frontiers: management control and work intensification under JIT/TQM regimes', *New Technology Work and Employment*.

Draaijer, D.J. and Boer, H. (1995) 'Designing market-orientated production systems: theory and practice', *Integrated Manufacturing Systems*, 6 (5), 305–34.

Drucker, P.F. (1990) 'The emerging theory of manufacturing', *Harvard Business Review*, 68 (3).

Elger, T. and Smith, C. (1994) *Global Japanisation: The Transformation of the Labour Process*, London: Routledge.

Garrahan, P. and Stewart, P. (1992) *The Nissan Enigma*, London: Mansell.

Hinings, C.R. and Greenwood, R. (1988) *The Dynamics of Strategic Change*, Oxford: Blackwell.

Hunt, J.G. (1991) *Leadership: A New Synthesis*, London: Sage.

Isabella, L.A. (1990) 'Evolving interpretations as a change unfolds: how managers construe key organizational events', *Academy of Management Journal*, 33 (1), 7–41.

Johnson, G. (1992) 'Managing strategic change: strategy, culture, action', *Long Range Planning*, 25 (1), 28–36.

Kirosingh, M. (1989) 'Changed working practices', *Employment Gazette*, August, 422–9.

Lazonick, W. (1990) *Competitive Advantage on the Shop Floor*, Cambridge, Mass.: Harvard University Press.

Lowe, J. (1993) 'Manufacturing reform and the changing role of the production supervisor: the case of the automobile industry', *Journal of Management Studies*, 30 (5).

McGrath, R.G., MacMillan, P. and Venkaturaman, S. (1995) 'Defining and developing competence: a strategy process paradigm', *Strategic Management Journal*, 16, 251–75.

Meyerson, D.E. (1991) 'Normal ambiguity? A glimpse of an occupational culture', in P.J. Frost *et al.* (eds), *Reframing Organizational Culture*, London: Sage.

Mintzberg, H. (1967) *The Nature of Managerial Work*, New York: Harper & Row.

—— (1979) *The Structuring of Organizations*, Englewood Cliffs, NJ: Prentice-Hall.

—— (1983) *Structure in Fives: Designing Effective Organizations*, Englewood Cliffs, NJ: Prentice-Hall.

—— (1994) 'Rounding out the manager's job', *Sloan Management Review*, fall, 11–26.

Mueller, F. (1994) 'Teams between hierarchy and commitment: change strategies and the internal environment', *Journal of Management Studies*, 31 (3), 383–403.

Nonaka, I. and Takeuchi, H. (1995) *The Knowledge Creating Society*, Oxford: Oxford University Press.

Oliver, N. (1993) *Making it in Britain: Japanese Manufacturers in the UK in the Nineties*, Cambridge: Cambridge University Press.

Oliver, N. and Wilkinson, B. (1992) *The Japanization of British Industry*, 2nd edn, Oxford: Blackwell Business.

Oliver, N., Delbridge, R. and Lowe, J. (1995) 'Lean production and manufacturing performance: international comparisons in the auto components industry', refereed paper at the British Association of Management Conference.

Parnaby, J. (1988) 'A systems approach to the implementation of JIT methodologies in Lucas industries', *International Journal of Production Research*, 26 (3), 483–92.

Peters, T. (1988) *Thriving on Chaos: Handbook for a Management Revolution*, New York: Harper & Row.

Pfeffer, J. (1977) 'The ambiguity of leadership', *Academy of Management Review*, 2 (1).

Piore, M.J. and Sabel, C.F. (1984) *The Second Industrial Divide: Possibilities for Prosperity*, New York: Basic Books.

Pondy, L.R., Boland, R.J., Jr. and Thomas, H. (1988) *Managing Ambiguity and Change*, New York: Wiley.

Schein, E.H. (1969) *Process Consultation: Its Role in Organization Development*, New York: Addison-Wesley.

—— (1987) *Process Consultation*, vol. 2, *Lessons for Managers and Consultants*, New York: Addison-Wesley.

—— (1992) *Organizational Culture and Leadership*, New York: Jossey-Bass Inc.

Scholes, K. (1995) 'Core competencies and strategic capabilities', mimeo, Sheffield Business School.

Schonberger, R.J. (1982) *Japanese Manufacturing Techniques*, New York: Free Press.

—— (1986) *World Class Manufacturing*, New York: Free Press.

Senge, P.M. (1990) *The Fifth Discipline*, London: Century Business.

Sewell, G. and Wilkinson, B. (1991) 'Someone to watch over me: surveillance, discipline and the just-in-time labour process', mimeo, UMIST, Manchester.

Shimada, H. (1993) 'Japanese management of auto production in the United States: an overview of "human technology"', in *Lean Production and Beyond*, Geneva: International Labour Organization.

Smith, P.B. and Peterson, M.F. (1988) *Leadership, Organizations and Culture*, London: Sage.

Stake, R.E. (1995) *The Art of Case Study Research*, London: Sage.

Storey, J. (1994) *New Wave Manufacturing Strategies*, London: Paul Chapman.

Teece, D. and Pisano, G. (1994) 'The dynamic capabilities of firms: an introduction', *Industrial and Corporate Change*, 3 (3).

Teece, D.J., Pisano, G. and Shuen, A. (1992) 'Dynamic capabilities and strategic management', Working Paper, Harvard Business School.

Thompson, J.K. and Rehder, R.H. (1996) 'The gap between vision and reality: the case of Nissan UK', *Journal of General Management*, 21 (3).

Tranfield, D.R. and Smith, S. (1990) *Managing Change: Creating Competitive Edge*, Kempston: IFS Publications.

Tranfield, D., Smith, S., Whittle, S. and Martin, V. (1994) 'Strategy, regeneration and routines in manufacturing', Working Paper, Sheffield Business School.

Trist, E. and Bamforth, R. (1951) 'Some social and psychological consequences of the long wall method of coal getting', *Human Relations*, 4, 3–38.

Unterweger, P. (1993) 'Lean production: myth and reality', in *Lean Production and Beyond*, Geneva: International Labour Organization.

Watson, T.J. (1995) 'Management of technology: issues of skill and effectiveness', paper presented to 13th International Labour Process Conference, Blackpool.

Wickens, P.D. (1993) 'Lean, people centred, mass production', in *Lean Production and Beyond*, Geneva: International Labour Organization.

—— (1995) *The Ascendant Organization*, London: Macmillan.
Womack, J.P. and Jones, D.T. (1994) 'From lean production to the lean enterprise', *Harvard Business Review*, March–April.
Womack, J.P., Jones, D.T. and Roos, D. (1990) *The Machine that Changed the World*, New York: Rawson Associates.
Yukl, G.A. (1981) *Leadership in Organizations*, London: Prentice-Hall.
Zuboff, S. (1988) *In the Age of the Smart Machine: The Future of Work and Power*, London: Heinemann.

7 Mature firms in the UK mid-corporate sector

Innovation strategies and employment prospects

Oswald Jones and Nelson Tang

INTRODUCTION

Schumpeter (1943) argued that smaller firms were an essential element in the cycle of creative destruction which fuels economic growth. This view was developed by Freeman (1982) and Rothwell and Zegveld (1985) who linked the role of small firms to fluctuations in the Kondratiev cycle: large firms carry out basic research; small, entrepreneurial firms continue the pioneering work; and finally, as the sector begins to mature, large firms exploit their superior resources to dominate the market. Hence, public policy has placed considerable emphasis on 'start-up' firms, or what are more generally described as new technology-based firms (NTBFs), which are found in sectors such as biotechnology and software (Oakey 1994; Oakey *et al.* 1988). In recent years the DTI (Department of Trade and Industry) has introduced a number of initiatives such as the Teaching Company Scheme, Business Links and the Carrier Technology Programme which are intended to help SMEs (small and medium-sized enterprises) improve their innovative capacity (Jones and Tang 1997). The creation of university science parks has also been a key element in policies designed to increase the numbers of dynamic, innovative, high-technology small firms (Massey *et al.* 1992). Westhead and Storey (1994) found that 'high-technology' small firms on science parks had higher growth rates and lower failure rates than those in mature sectors. Shearman and Burrell (1988) differentiate NTBFs from what they describe as 'complex, high-technology SMEs'. NTBFs are generally technology-led, have simple organization structures and single products, are found in emerging industries (e.g. microelectronics, biotechnology, new materials, medical lasers), and are therefore few in number. In contrast, high-technology-based SMEs generally have sophisticated organizational structures, are committed to R&D and manufacturing processes, are market-oriented, and may have a wide variety of products. NTBFs are associated with the notion of reindustrialization, whereas high-technology-based SMEs are strongly associated with the idea of industrial regeneration (Shearman and Burrell 1988).

In this chapter we are concerned with the potential for industrial regeneration rather than reindustrialization: that is, we examine the potential for medium-sized firms operating in traditional manufacturing industries to create new employment opportunities. It has been common to categorize successful smaller firms according to their ability to increase levels of employment (Storey *et al.* 1987) or economic performance in terms of increased sales/turnover (Feeser and Willard 1990). While we acknowledge the importance of both profitability and employment generation throughout the mid-corporate sector, we are concerned to examine mature firms which are well established and appear to have prospects of surviving in the medium term. However, we note the work of Phillips and Kirchhoff (1989) who found that the survival of small firms was strongly associated with growth in employment – although, the rate of growth measured as low (four workers or less), medium (five to nine workers), or high (ten or more) was not significant to the prospects of survival. As Storey (1994: 98) comments: 'the key to survival is for new firms to achieve growth; the rate of that growth is of secondary importance.'

Traditionally, high levels of SMEs in an economy have indicated low levels of economic performance but this perception has changed in recent years. Small firms in Japan account for a higher share of employment, sales and added value than in other developed economies, and this is particularly apparent in the manufacturing sector (United Nations 1993). The report produced by the United Nations (1993: 13) also claims that manufacturing SMEs are increasingly important sources of innovation and employment in most developed economies. Hutton (1995: 267) argues that medium-sized, family-owned firms, known as the *Mittelstand*, have been central to the strength of German manufacturing (see Pike and Tomaney in Chapter 10 in this volume). Dodgson and Rothwell (1993) also claim that SMEs make important contributions to industrial regeneration and the creation of employment opportunities. Allen *et al.* (1983: 199) acknowledge that the introduction of new technology in the form of product changes or new manufacturing techniques to those small, unsophisticated companies that make up the majority of firms in any country is 'the most difficult problem in technology transfer'. Generally, such firms have little commitment to R&D and lack employees with scientific and technological training. In fact, '[j]ust becoming aware of the possibility of improvement and the means to bring it about is often the most difficult and important step in the transfer of technology' (Allen *et al.* 1983: 200).

MANUFACTURING AND GOVERNMENT POLICY

There are many theories which attempt to explain why the UK is 'bad' at manufacturing (Williams *et al.* 1983; see also Chapter 1 in this volume). Much New Right rhetoric concentrates on the Luddite role of trade unions in resisting new technology while bidding-up the price of labour. Other weaknesses include: damaging underinvestment in capital stock; a lack of skills as a result of poor education and training; excessive military spending; broader macroeconomic policies which have resulted in high interest rates; and an overvalued exchange rate (see Kitson and Michie in Chapter 2 in this volume). In 1979 the first Thatcher Government came to power promising that a combination of monetarist economic policies and anti-trade union legislation would transform the British economy. The effect on manufacturing industry was devastating as output fell by over 10 per cent between 1979 and 1983 and this reduction was inevitably accompanied by a massive shake-out of jobs. At the end of 1979 manufacturing industry employed almost seven million, but by 1984, numbers had declined to less than five million. The most rapid reduction occurred in the period from mid-1980 to mid-1982 when more than one million manufacturing jobs were lost (*Employment Gazette*). Although there was an increase in the numbers of 'micro' firms (1–9 employees) during this period, those firms with between 20 and 499 employees decreased in number from approximately 37,000 to 31,000 (see Tables 7A.1 and 7A.2 in chapter appendix).

The weakening of trade union bargaining power and fewer jobs meant that manufacturing productivity did increase dramatically. Crafts (1996) and Eltis (1996) claim productivity improvements provide evidence that government policies were successful, while Kitson and Michie (1996: 24) believe that they seriously debilitated an already weak sector: 'Britain's manufacturing base is too small and uncompetitive.' Some critics argue that the dominance of finance capital in the UK has created a climate of chronic short-termism which is the most important cause of the UK's persistent industrial and economic decline (Ingham 1984; Hutton 1995). Low levels of demand for British products and weak manufacturing competitiveness will continue, 'as long as the Government sticks to its free-market approach to policy and its belief that competitiveness can only be achieved by cost-cutting measures pursued *via* product and labour market deregulation' (Kitson and Michie 1996: 24).

In the early 1990s the CBI (Confederation of British Industry) and the Engineering Employers Federation began to demand that the Conservative Government adopt a more active approach towards manufacturing. When Howard Davies became CBI Chairman in 1992 he argued that Michael Heseltine must develop an industrial policy to regenerate the UK's manufacturing sector (Cassell 1992). On becoming Prime Minister, John Major apparently rejected his predecessor's free market approach to manufacturing. Major claimed to have been in a 'minority' which had defended industry and argued that there was now a 'majority' in government committed to regenerating the UK's manufacturing base (*The Independent*, 4 March 1993). The Business Links scheme, launched in 1993, was designed to assist smaller firms improve their manufacturing capabilities and access new technologies by bringing together a wide range of regional support services (Jones and Tang 1997). Setting up the Office of Science and Technology (OST) and establishing the technology foresight programme were also tangible indications that the Government was serious about improving industrial competitiveness by encouraging firms to make better use of science and technology. When Ian Lang succeeded Heseltine as trade and industry secretary following the mid-1995 government reshuffle he acknowledged that earlier Tory administrations had placed too much emphasis on services at the expense of manufacturing. Lang claimed that the DTI was now allocating 'enormous amounts of time and resources . . .

to sustain and encourage our manufacturing base' (*Financial Times*, 1 February 1996).

The election of New Labour in May 1997 is unlikely to lead to any substantial changes in industrial policy as Margaret Beckett the new trade and industry secretary paid tribute to the success of Tory competitiveness policies. At the same time Beckett suggested that there was a need to find a 'middle way' between the dogmas of the free market and state direction by bringing together government and the business community (Wagstyl 1997).

The shrinkage of manufacturing began in the mid-1960s, accelerated in the 1980s, and by 1993 employment was less than half that of 1966 (Kitson and Michie 1996: 35). According to Wolf (1996), UK manufacturing employment declined by 2.5 million between the economic cycles of 1964–73 and 1979–89 compared with 0.5 million in France and 1.1 million in Germany. Since 1989, a further 850,000 jobs have been lost in manufacturing industry and the sector now accounts for only 18 per cent of UK employment (Taylor 1996). Recent indications confirm that pessimism about employment prospects in manufacturing is entirely justified. The CBI reported that 16,000 manufacturing jobs were lost in the first quarter of 1996 and forecast that a further 11,000 would be lost in the second quarter (Wolf 1996). Specific examples are provided by two of the UK's leading manufacturing companies, Pilkington Glass and Lucas Varity, which announced respective job losses of 1,900 and 3,000 late in 1996.

The total number of manufacturing firms increased from 119,000 in the late 1970s to over 184,000 in 1994 (see chapter appendix). However, almost all the new firms were located in the smallest sizeband (1–9 employees), with a small increase in the 10–19 sizeband. In every other sizeband the number of firms and the number of employees declined significantly between 1977 and 1994. Also, while the number of small firms did increase, there was no *pro rata* expansion in employment levels. In 1977, firms in sizeband 1–9 had an average of 4.7 employees, but by 1994 this figure had declined to 2.6.

Although the UK's manufacturing output remained stagnant during the 1970s and 1980s productivity did improve, with output per person increasing by 78 per cent between the first quarter of 1979 and the end of 1995. The combination of fast productivity growth with virtually no increases in output was certainly extraordinary. It has also had two inevitable consequences: job losses and a declining share of manufacturing in gross domestic product. Unskilled workers were the main victims of these job losses as manufacturing industry sought to make more with less. The philosophies of lean production and Business Process Re-engineering (BPR) have played important roles in reducing manufacturing employment (Hammer and Champy 1993; Womack *et al.* 1990). Recently, those who consistently advocated marginalizing the workforce by re-engineering and outsourcing during the 1990s have begun to question the effectiveness of such policies. Stephen Roach (1996), a key advocate of the 'virtual organization', now acknowledges that sustained productivity is dependent on improvements in the quality of the workforce: 'Tactics of open-ended down-sizing and real-wage compression are ultimately recipes for industrial extinction.' Moreover, Michael

Hammer now recognizes that the 'theory' of BPR was flawed because it did not consider the human dimension (Keegan 1996).

MID-CORPORATE MANUFACTURING

The National Westminster Bank describes the 90,000 companies which have a turnover between £1 million and £130 million as the 'mid-corporate sector' and they account for 40 per cent of private sector output (value added) and employ an estimated 7.7 million people (Bannock and Partners 1994/5). According to NatWest data approximately 21,000 of these 90,000 firms are manufacturing-based and this broadly encompasses all those firms with between 50 and 999 employees (see chapter appendix). Hutton (1995) claims that Germany's middle-sized business sector is 'nearly twice the size of its counterpart in Britain'. Comparative data suggest that there are strong similarities between the UK and German medium-sized manufacturing sectors. In sizeband 1–99 the UK has 36.2 per cent of its total manufacturing employment compared to 33.7 per cent in Germany. While firms with between 100 and 499 employees account for 35.6 per cent of UK manufacturing employment compared with only 27.3 per cent in Germany, these percentage figures disguise the absolute strength of German manufacturing companies. Taking the small firm sector as a whole (1–499) Germany has 334,000 firms employing 4.5 million workers whereas the UK has 183,000 firms employing 3.3 million. The main discrepancy is in sizeband 1–19 where there are 292,000 German firms compared with 124,000 UK firms. In the category 20–499 the difference is much less apparent: 42,000 German firms employ just over 3 million and 31,000 UK firms employ 2.7 million (*Annual Abstract of Statistics* 1996; *Statistisches Jahrbuch* 1996). Therefore, German mid-sized manufacturing firms, the *Mittelstand*, do not have a significant advantage over the UK in terms of size nor in terms of employment. Nevertheless, German manufacturing strength is confirmed by the number of firms and employees in the 500-plus sizeband. There are 1,850 large German manufacturing firms with a total employment of over four million, whereas the 1,360 large UK firms employ 1.48 million: that is, average employment in large manufacturing firms is almost 2,200 in Germany compared to 1,060 in the UK.

We believe that the innovation strategies pursued by companies in mature sectors will have direct implications for their ability to create or sustain employment. To examine this proposition, research was carried out in two mid-corporate manufacturing companies, Stern Automotive and Peak Automotive Controls (PAC), who supply components to the major motor manufacturers. Stern was founded as an aircraft company in 1938, but by the late 1940s had started to seek customers in the growing UK automotive industry. In 1982 the company was the subject of a management buyout and now has sales of £25 million and over 500 employees involved in designing and manufacturing two main product ranges. The first product range based on driver control components includes: parking brake systems, pedal box assemblies, gear-change mechanisms, steering columns and clutch systems. The second product range is based on structural chassis and suspension members including: highly stressed suspension members, hinges, radius rods, watts links and tie-rods. PAC, founded in 1946, is a privately owned company which had 750 employees and an annual turnover of approximately £31 million in 1996/7. The business is based on the manufacture of control devices for the automotive and small domestic appliance industries. PAC supplies DC (direct current) cut-outs to over forty countries, including the leading Japanese and German auto manufacturers, and this accounts for approximately 65 per cent of business. Cut-outs for small domestic appliances such as kettles, battery chargers, cable reels, hair dryers, transformers and washing machine motors account for the remaining 35 per cent of PAC's turnover.

Both companies are the subject of a longitudinal study which is investigating the role of innovation management and technology strategy in medium-sized manufacturing firms. Initially, data on the activities of Stern were obtained *via* six MBA dissertation projects which examined a number of organizational issues, including: payroll process redesign; inventory planning and control process; outbound logistic process; new product introduction process; and a just-in-time system development. Since the MBA projects were completed in 1995 the authors have carried out regular interviews with senior managers and engineers about the role of innovation in maintaining the company's long-term viability. Data collection on PAC began in 1993 with an MBA group research project which analysed the firm's technology strategy. This was followed in mid-1994 by an extended study to establish the way in which PAC managers had set up a small number of technological alliances (Jones and Beckinsale 1994). In the intervening period, contact has been maintained with PAC and interviews with managers and engineers have been conducted at regular intervals by the authors.

INNOVATION STRATEGY IN STERN AUTOMOTIVE

Stern Automotive was founded in 1938 to produce light aircraft, diversified into the manufacture of automotive products in 1949, and by the early 1960s had become a successful supplier of high-quality components to leading car and truck manufacturers. Stern was acquired by British Leyland in the mid-1960s but regained its independence in 1982 as the result of a management buyout. The Stern product range is based on mechanical components for the vehicle's steering, braking and suspension. Managers have focused on process innovations such as *kanban* to minimize transportation, inspection, storage and handling. The *kanban* principle encourages direct liaison with customers which confers responsibility for quality control and product improvement on cell operatives. Welding is one of the primary manufacturing processes and a wide range of techniques are utilized by the various production cells: gas-shielded arc, electric arc, computer-controlled robot welding, projection resistance welding and friction welding. The company also has an extensive press shop and a modern machine shop which utilizes CNC (computer numerically controlled) vertical and horizontal machines as well as CNC robot-loaded and bar-fed turning centres which complement special purpose machines. A direct numerical computer (DNC) links Stern's CAD (computer-aided design) system to a modern, fully equipped toolroom CNC facility, allowing the rapid transfer of data to speed tool development. The tool-room workshop is staffed by skilled specialists who are responsible for producing new components on 'soft tooling' that ensures a strong correlation between prototype and production parts. Increasingly, the company is introducing very early hard tooling trials to ensure the maximum possible comparability between prototype and production. The DNC link permits both product design and tool design to be carried out on the company's CAD systems.

The stated strategic focus of the company is to provide a top-quality design and manufacturing service to their customers by investing in people and modern technology. Senior managers recognize that to be productive employees must be trained and motivated to generate positive attitudes towards quality and cost. Present policy on quality is centred on the ISO 9000 quality standard, and accreditation was gained in early 1994. The company has undertaken active improvements by integrating quality control into manufacturing and assembly production cells. Quality standards are maintained by means of two three-dimensional coordinate measuring machines based on a statistical process control (SPC) data-logging network. At present, managers are introducing a number of initiatives designed to improve the core business activities, including a revised new product introduction process and a just-in-time system to improve overall effectiveness and competitiveness. Stern managers want the company to remain at the forefront of process technology by investing in a more sophisticated CAD system as well as new developments in information technology and robotics.

INNOVATION STRATEGY IN PEAK AUTOMOTIVE CONTROLS

Despite bimetallic technology being in the mature phase of its life cycle, constant product and process innovation has enabled PAC to remain competitive since the company was founded more than fifty years ago. A wide range of technologies are used in product design and manufacture including: insert moulding; DC and high-frequency welding; ultrasound welding; infrared sensing; encode/decode software; thick-film circuitry for sensors; electronic-based pressure and tempera-ture sensing. PAC has been particularly successful in integrating product and process development with its production capabilities. This is certainly apparent in the manufacture of bimetallic switches in which applications knowledge is com-bined with a deep understanding of snap action and contact technologies. Con-sequently, the company is extremely flexible in response to changes in customer requirements, and this is a key source of competitive advantage over larger, bureaucratic rivals. The constant commitment to market-led improvements in products and processes has enabled PAC to develop an impressive range of cus-tomers amongst the world's leading auto-manufacturers. However, in the early 1990s managers estimated that the market for electronic cut-outs would be increas-ingly competitive by the year 2000. It was thought that PAC would find it difficult to compete with specialist electronics companies, and managers began to consider alternative products and markets. The technical director was given responsibility for identifying new technologies, and eventually he set up collaborative projects with two universities in the north-west of England. The first project followed a proposal from an independent inventor who had patented a bimetallic device for sensing the pressure of pneumatic tyres. The commercial potential was obvious but PAC engineers felt that the technology was too primitive to be acceptable to leading automobile manufacturers, and University A was commissioned to develop a more sophisticated tyre pressure sensor (TPS) based on transmitter/receiver technologies (Jones and Smith 1995). The second alliance involved a depth of anaesthesia monitor (DAM) developed by University B to ensure that patients were not conscious during surgery. Initially, PAC entered into a manufacturing agreement with the university but found that the underdeveloped prototype could not be manufactured consistently. Consequently, PAC took a more direct involvement and agreed to invest in the development of a new software algorithm to replace the unreliable DOS-based package developed by University B. Gradually, the DAM venture shifted from a straightforward manufacturing exercise into a highly sophisticated design and development project.

Initially, both products were relatively simple and PAC managers felt that they were well within the organization's capabilities. Gradually, the TPS and the DAM became increasingly sophisticated and began to extend beyond existing areas of technical and market competence. The technical director remained confident that both products would be successful; however, in January 1996 the TPS and the DAM were discontinued. Senior managers decided to focus on the company's core competencies in bimetallic technologies, rather than risk further expenditure on radically new products. Abandoning an innovation strategy that had been pursued for the previous four years was related to doubts about PAC's ability to compete in highly specialized markets. The finance director believed that a relatively small company such as PAC was running a massive commercial risk by moving into areas that were potentially vulnerable to litigation. In addition, PAC's main competitor was pursuing a 'more active' strategy that threatened existing markets for bimetallic cut-outs.

Managers are now attempting to 'add value' to existing products by developing a 'brushcard' which is complementary to the bimetallic cut-out. This will enable PAC to move the product upstream from motor manufacturers who presently make the brushcard themselves or buy it in from other suppliers. Offering an integrated cut-out and brushcard means that the value to PAC increases from approximately 20 pence per cut-out to £1 for the complete assembly. Managers believe that buying the complete assembly is also attractive to the motor manufacturers because it is difficult for them to economically automate the production of such a low-value item. Future diversification will be much more 'focused' than efforts with the TPS and the DAM, and growth is more likely to be based on acquisition rather than organic expansion. There has recently been a complete restructuring of the company's activities. The functional structure based on engineering, accounts, marketing and production have been reorganized into three divisions: Automotive Products, Domestic Appliances and Operations. The main objective of the change is to improve communications between marketing, engineering and production as well as ensuring that employees are more 'customer-focused'. Despite difficulties which led to the discontinuation of the two products, sales increased by almost 16 per cent in the 1996/7 financial year and turnover is expected to double to £60m by the year 2000. More significantly for employment prospects, it is planned to boost 'sale value per head' from its present level of £700 per week to £2,000 per week. Hence, expansion will be based on improvements in productivity through investment in new process technologies, rather than through the creation of new jobs. For example, the company's current investment in Surface Mount Technology (SMT) will make a substantial improvement to output without increasing the level of employment.

STRATEGIC INNOVATION AND INDUSTRIAL REGENERATION

The phenomenon of 'post-industrial society', in which employment and wealth creation shifts from manufacturing to services, was identified in the early 1970s (Bell 1974). Although the trend, first identified in the US, is apparent in all industrialized economies, the decline in manufacturing's contribution to gross domestic product has been most pronounced in the UK. Kitson and Michie (1996; see also Chapter 2 in this volume) believe that underinvestment in capital stock has been a major contributory factor to this reduction in manufacturing capacity. Between 1979 and 1989 the UK was the only industrialized country not to increase its manufacturing capital stock (increases in other countries included 2.0 per cent in the US, 1.2 per cent in Germany, 2.1 per cent in France and 5.2 per cent in Japan). As Kitson and Michie (1996: 41) point out, this indifferent record not only restricted growth in manufacturing output, but it also constrained growth in demand and technological progress. The importance of incorporating decisions about technological innovation into corporate strategy was certainly apparent by the mid-1980s (Ford and Jongerius 1986). However, Clark et al. (1995) suggest that only a small minority of UK companies actually include a technological element in their strategic decision making (see Ackroyd and Procter in Chapter 3 in this volume). It is argued that US and UK managers are primarily concerned with improving financial ratios by downsizing and restructuring, rather than by innovating new products to increase sales and develop new markets (Hamel and Prahalad 1994). Technology must be managed strategically if firms are to innovate the new products and processes which are central to long-term competitive advantage (Dussauge et al. 1992). Zahra et al. (1994) identify six major dimensions of technology strategy: technological innovation posture (first-to-market, fast-follower, imitator and late-entrant); dominant technological thrust and goals; globalization of technology strategy; technology sourcing; technological investments; and organizational mechanisms. Zahra et al. (1994) also emphasize the importance of companies maintaining consistency in their technology strategies. For example, a 'first-to-market' posture focuses on cutting-edge research that leads to the introduction of new technologies ahead of competitors. A 'fast-follower' posture requires an agile response to innovation by industry pioneers and may include modifications to those technologies. A 'me-too' posture is aimed at imitation of widely available technologies by the introduction of close substitutes. Finally, a 'late-entrant' posture is concerned with making incremental changes to existing technologies for limited applications (Zahra *et al.* 1994: 176). As well as displaying 'internal' consistency, technology strategy must be aligned with competitive strategy. In conceptualizing competitive strategy Zahra *et al.* utilize the work of Segev (1989), who integrated the frameworks developed by Miles and Snow (1978) and Porter (1980) to give five generic strategic types as shown in Table 7.1.

Stern managers have consistently pursued a 'cost leadership' strategy for twelve years as they sought to charge the lowest possible prices to the large auto-assemblers. The technology posture is that of 'late-entrant' or 'me-too' as they attempt to copy changes introduced by larger rivals or suggested by their customers. The narrow range of technologies are not state-of-the-art and are acquired internally and externally to minimize costs of development and implementation (Zahra *et al.* 1994). In line with the cost-leader approach, organizational structure is functional and places considerable emphasis on integrating marketing, production planning and control to provide strong elements of a 'lean' operation (Womack *et al.* 1990). There is some divergence from the framework described by Zahra *et al.* (1994) which may be a result of the relatively small size of Stern Automotive. The company certainly does not spend the industry average on R&D, as most process improvements are instigated by production engineering, and there is no 'global' element to the firm's technology posture. Japanese car manufacturers are only willing to build long-term relationships if first-tier suppliers demonstrate commitment and performance by reducing costs and improving quality. However, Stern's major customer has provided direct help by sending teams of engineers to implement new processes, designed costs cut and improve quality (cf. Bresnen and Fowler in Chapter 8 in this volume).

Following an assessment of the long-term prospects for bimetallic technologies, PAC switched from a 'cost-leader' to an 'analyser' strategy. Hence PAC tried to ensure that it remained competitive within its traditional markets at the same time as it was developing two radically new products. The posture was first-to-market based on orthogonal technologies: the TPS employed radio frequency technology, while the DAM utilized software technologies. Other activities also adhered to the analyser typology: technology was sourced internally and

Table 7.1 Strategic types, technological posture and emphasis

Strategic types	*Technological posture*	*Emphasis*
Defender	Fast-follower	Process innovation
Cost leader	Me-too	Process innovation
Analyser	First-to-market	Process/product innovation
Cost differentiator	Fast-follower	Product innovation
Prospector	Fast-follower/me-too	Product innovation

externally; investment in technology was high; and a project team structure was adopted. PAC does not exactly fit the analyser model because there was no global focus to its technology posture, nor was there a sustained commitment to basic research. Ultimately, this ambitious strategy was unsuccessful and both products were abandoned early in 1996 because managers were concerned about the company's ability to compete in new markets. As Green *et al.* (1995) point out, there are four dimensions to radical innovation: technological uncertainty, newness to the firm, business uncertainty and financial risk. It certainly appears that PAC was pursuing a strategy which meant that the company was taking radical risks on at least three of the dimensions. R&D employees were attempting to utilize existing technologies to develop radically new applications. However, the technologies were certainly new to the firm and, given limited resources, uncertainty was high. The potential threat of 'product liability' in markets where PAC was unknown meant that there were also considerable business risks. Finally, financial risks associated with the development of the TPS in particular were very high because much of the development work was subcontracted to a university. Consequently, PAC managers have shifted from an analyser to a defender strategy, and technology strategy has changed from first-to-market to fast-follower. Hence there is now an emphasis on the core competence in bimetallic technologies, with focus on process rather than product innovation. Organizational mechanisms have been changed to give greater managerial control over the transfer of new technologies by emphasizing the need for 'market focus'. In addition, twenty software and electronics engineers lost their jobs, as managers made a substantial reduction in their expenditure on R&D.

MID-CORPORATE FIRMS AND EMPLOYMENT CREATION

Influential research by Birch (1979) indicated that US firms with less than twenty employees provided a disproportionate share of new jobs. Burrows (1991) argues that these finding encouraged Thatcher's first administration to create an 'enterprise culture' in the UK. Much of the policy thrust was designed to reduce regulations that were perceived to be an inhibiting factor on the dynamism of smaller firms (Aston Business School 1991; Curran and Blackburn 1991). As Atkinson and Storey (1994: 2) point out, 'for much of the 1980s government saw its role as being to liberate the small firm sector from trade union membership, legislation involving workers' safety, workers' rights etc.'. Throughout the 1980s and 1990s there has been considerable discussion about the extent to which SMEs contribute to job creation. The main evidence supporting the view that smaller firms are a key source of new jobs has been a series of studies based on the Dun & Bradstreet database (Doyle and Gallagher 1987; Gallagher *et al.* 1990; Daly *et al.* 1991). Atkinson and Storey (1994) are 'unpersuaded' by this data because Dun & Bradstreet are a credit rating agency and are more likely to include expanding firms (also see Storey and Johnson 1986). The main criticism of the small-firm job creation thesis is that a small number of fast-growing firms have an asymmetrical impact on the data (Storey *et al.* 1987; Gallagher and Miller 1991).

Johnson (1989) suggests that throughout the 1980s there was an increase in the number of establishments with less than 200 employees. Unfortunately, this increase was the result of a decline in the size of large firms rather than a genuine increase in the number of small firms (see chapter appendix). North *et al.* (1994) examined the potential of mature manufacturing SMEs to create employment. Firms in the study had been in existence for more than ten years, were independent, and had less than 100 employees. The firms were located in three geographical regions: London, Hertfordshire and Essex, and rural areas of northern England. The longitudinal study examined survival and employment patterns between 1979 and 1990. Of the London firms, 42 per cent failed to survive and they accounted for 36.6 per cent of lost jobs, while the remaining 58 per cent of firms increased their levels of employment slightly. Across the three regions, the survivors increased employment by 18.4 per cent although there were significant sectoral differences. North *et al.* (1994) confirm that a small number of 'sectoral leaders' contributed heavily to job creation and that there was a strong correlation between increases in sales turnover and job creation. But because of increases in productivity, 'firms needed to at least double their output in real terms in order to make much employment impact' (North *et al.* 1994: 221).

Recent government figures (*Annual Abstract of Statistics*) indicate that between 1989 and 1994, 375,000 (7.8 per cent) jobs were lost in UK manufacturing industry despite the creation of 25,000 new firms. The growth in the number of new firms was entirely in the two smallest categories (1–9 and 10–19), and the numbers employed in such firms increased from 560,000 to 620,000. Firms employing between 20 and 199 remained broadly stable in terms of numbers (30,000) and the amount of employees (approximately 1.74 million). The number of firms in sizeband 200–499 fell from 3,200 to 3,000 and jobs were reduced by 100,000. In both the 500–999 and the > 1,000 sizebands the number of firms and employment decreased by similar amounts: 17 per cent and 25 per cent respectively. Mid-corporate manufacturing firms such as PAC and Stern which fall into the 500 – 999 category lost 108,000 jobs and the number of firms declined from 930 to 770 between 1989 and 1994. Large firms (> 1,000) fell in number from 433 to 324 and employment decreased from 851,000 to 642,000 (see years 1989 and 1994 in chapter appendix).

Following the UK's economic recovery in the early 1990s, manufacturing output improved in 1993 and 1994, but then began to decline again (Wolf 1996). Unfortunately, better economic prospects in the UK led to a steady rise in the pound sterling to the extent that by August 1997 the National Institute of Economic and Social Research estimated that it was overvalued by at least 15 per cent. The consequence of this overvaluation was that UK manufacturing industry became less competitive in export markets, and imported goods became more attractive to consumers (see Chapter 1). According to Kitson and Michie in Chapter 2, the total increase in manufactured output between 1973 and 1992 was a derisory 1.3 per cent. Over the same period, manufactured output rose 68.9 per cent in Japan, 68.6 per cent in Italy, 55.2 per cent in the US, 32.1 per cent in West Germany and 16.5 per cent in France. Throughout the 1980s there were significant improvements in manufacturing productivity. Crafts (1996) points out that in 1979 West German output per person was 40 per cent above UK levels but by 1989 this advantage was down to only 17 per cent. According to IMD (1997) data this improvement has continued, with the UK moving from nineteenth to eleventh in the world competitiveness league. However, the report also confirms traditional managerial weaknesses, with UK recording low scores for in-company training and for employee flexibility and adaptability (IMD 1997).

The two manufacturing firms that are the subject of our study certainly recognize the value of investing in employee training at all organizational levels. However, our argument is that even well-managed mid-corporate manufacturing firms such as Stern and PAC are unlikely to generate new jobs in the future. Rather, the likeliest scenario is that employment in manufacturing firms will continue a steady decline. Well-established firms seem certain to concentrate on cost reduction rather than job creation. Within PAC there is optimism about the company's future prospects, but, at the same time, there is a determined desire to increase turnover without employing more staff. PAC managers plan to double output from £30m to £60m by the year 2000 primarily through investment in new process technologies such as SMT to improve productivity. Companies such as PAC and Stern that directly or indirectly supply components to the auto-industry are under considerable pressure from their main customers. The leading auto-assemblers have instigated a regime of annual price reductions which forces all companies in the value-added chain to ensure that costs are kept as low as possible. Managers in both companies are constantly seeking to improve productivity and reduce labour costs. Consequently, it is extremely unlikely that either company will increase overall levels of employment.

CONCLUSIONS

Lamming (1993) argues that manufacturing organizations have been forced to look more closely at developing closer integration between suppliers and customers externally and between functions internally as a means of improving their competitive advantages. Whether this integration can contribute to the success of the organization depends on the effective use of current product and process technology, as well as an awareness of new and emerging technologies. The two companies that are the subject of this study have adopted very different innovation strategies. For the last twelve years Stern has consistently pursued a 'cost leadership' strategy as managers have sought to charge the lowest possible prices to the large auto-assemblers. Over the last five years PAC has made two major changes in its strategic direction: switching from cost-leader to analyser to defender. Having abandoned the attempt to develop new products, managers are now concentrating on a less ambitious strategic position based on the consolidation of PAC's position in its core competency of bimetallic technologies. Although the phrase 'lean production' has not been used by managers in either organization it is clear that future growth in turnover will not generate new job opportunities. Despite pursuing different generic strategies both PAC and Stern are following the same employment strategy: increase turnover without a concomitant increase in employment.

The view expressed in this chapter is that employment opportunities are declining in mid-corporate manufacturing firms. This is confirmed by data from two case study organizations and by government figures indicating a steady reduction in the number of medium-sized firms. It appears that managers in medium-sized manufacturing companies have decided that long-term survival depends on implementing strategies designed to reduce costs and levels of employment. Even when there is an explicit expansionist strategy, as in the case of PAC, there is no expectation that doubling turnover will create new jobs. Nevertheless, we believe that mature manufacturing firms do still have an important role to play in the UK economy. Developing effective innovation and technology strategies will enable such firms to sustain existing employment levels while attempting to reverse the decline in manufacturing's contribution to GDP, which fell from 28 per cent in 1979 to 21 per cent in 1993. Finally, although neither company is likely to increase their level of employment, safeguarding existing jobs is as important as creating new ones. Halting the decline in smaller manufacturing firms would make a valuable contribution to retaining a meaningful level of industrial capacity in the UK.

APPENDIX: UK MANUFACTURING INDUSTRY, 1977–94

Table 7A.1 Number of firms ('000)

Year	Total	Size of firm by number of employees							
		1–9	*10–19*	*20–49*	*50–99*	*100–199*	*200–499*	*500–999*	*> 1,000*
1977	119.0	61.5	17.4	17.4	9.1	6.1	4.6	1.50	0.964
1979	118.7	62.4	18.5	16.8	8.5	5.8	4.3	1.40	0.908
1985	150.0	98.9	19.1	15.4	7.1	4.7	3.2	1.01	0.511
1989	159.2	107.2	17.3	17.5	7.7	4.9	3.2	0.93	0.433
1994	184.2	129.8	20.2	17.6	7.6	4.7	3.0	0.77	0.324

Table 7A.2 Number of employees ('000)

Year	Total	Size of firm by number of employees							
		1–9	*10–19*	*20–49*	*50–99*	*100–199*	*200–499*	*500–999*	*> 1,000*
1977	7,090	288	248	551	636	845	1,399	1,036	2,089
1979	6,747	288	266	516	594	815	1,330	969	1,969
1985	4,937	328	262	475	497	654	967	693	1,061
1989	4,806	319	241	540	532	684	1,012	626	851
1994	4,431	342	278	544	532	663	912	517	642

REFERENCES

Allen, T.J., Hyman, D.B. and Pinckney, D.L. (1983) 'Transferring technology to the small manufacturing firm: a study of technology transfer in three countries', *Research Policy*, **12**, 199–211.

Annual Abstract of Statistics (1990 to 1996) London: HMSO.

Aston Business School (1991) *Constraints on the Growth of Small Firms*, London: HMSO.

Atkinson, J. and Storey, D. (1994) 'Small firm and employment', in J. Atkinson and D. Storey (eds), *Employment, the Small Firm and the Labour Market*, London: Routledge.

Bannock, Graham and Partners (1994/5) 'A quarterly review of enterprises in the £1 million to £130 million turnover sizeband', *Mid-Corporate Directions*, **1** (2).

Bell, D. (1974) *The Coming of Post-Industrial Society*, London: Heinemann.

Birch, D.L. (1979) *The Job Generation Process*, Project on Neighborhood and Regional Change, Cambridge, Mass.: MIT.

Burrows, R. (ed.) (1991) *Deciphering the Enterprise Culture: Entrepreneurship, Petty Capitalism, and the Restructuring of Britain*, London: Routledge.

Cassell, M. (1992) 'No going back to the bad old days', *Financial Times*, 1 July.

Clark, K., Ford, D., Saren, M. and Thomas, R. (1995) 'Technology strategy in UK firms', *Technology Analysis and Strategic Management*, **7** (2), 169–90.

Crafts, N. (1996) 'Deindustrialisation and economic growth', *Economic Journal*, **106** (434), 172–83.

Curran, J. and Blackburn, R.A. (eds) (1991) *Paths of Enterprise: The Future of Small Business*, London: Routledge.

Daly, M., Campbell, M., Robson, M. and Gallagher, C. (1991) 'Job creation 1987–89: the contribution of small and large firms', *Employment Gazette*, November, 589–96.

Dodgson, M. and Rothwell, R. (1993) 'Technology-based SMEs: their role in industrial and economic change', *International Journal of Technology Management*, special edition, *Small Firms and Innovation*, 8–22.

Doyle, J.R. and Gallagher, C. (1987) 'The size distribution, growth potential and job-generation contribution of UK firms', *International Small Business Journal*, **6** (1), autumn.

Dussauge, P., Hart, S. and Ramanansota, B. (1992) *Strategic Technology Management*, Chichester: Wiley.

Eltis, W. (1996) 'How low profitability and weak innovativeness undermined UK industrial growth', *Economic Journal*, **106** (434), 184–95.

Employment Gazette (various years) London: HMSO.

Feeser, H.R. and Willard, G.E. (1990) 'Founding strategy and performance: a comparison of high and low growth high-tech firms', *Strategic Management Journal*, **11**, 87–98.

Ford, D. and Jongerius, C. (1986) *Technology Strategy in British Industry*, Milton Keynes: Base International.

Freeman, C. (1982) *The Economics of Industrial Innovation*, London: Pinter.

Gallagher, C. and Miller, P. (1991) 'New fast growing companies create jobs', *Long Range Planning*, **24** (2), 96–101.

Gallagher, C., Daly, M. and Thomason, J. (1990) 'The growth of companies 1985–87 and their contribution to job generation', *Employment Gazette*, February, 92–8.

Green, S.G., Gavin, M.B. and Aiman-Smith, L. (1995) 'Assessing a multidimensional measure of radical technological innovation', *IEEE Transactions on Engineering Management*, **42** (3), 203–14.

Hamel, G. and Prahalad, C.K. (1994) *Competing for the Future*, Boston: Harvard Business School.

Hammer, M. and Champy, J. (1993) *Re-engineering the Corporation: A Manifesto for a Business Revolution*, London: Brealy.

Hutton, W. (1995) *The State We're In*, London: Jonathan Cape.

Ingham, G. (1984) *Capitalism Divided? The City and Industry in Britain*, London: Macmillan.

IMD (1997) *World Competitiveness Yearbook*, World Economic Forum, Geneva: Institute for Management Development.

Johnson, P.S. (1989) 'Employment change in the small establishment sector of UK manufacturing', *Applied Economics*, **21**, 251–60.

Jones, O. and Beckinsale, M. (1994) 'Alliances between SMEs and HEIs: technology management in PAC', *DTI (Innovation Unit) Report*.

Jones, O. and Smith, D. (1995) 'Strategic technology management in a mid-corporate firm: the case of PAC', Research Paper no. RP9511, Birmingham: Aston Business School.

Jones, O. and Tang, N. (1997) 'Networks for technology transfer: linking HEIs and SMEs', *International Journal of Technology Management*, **12** (7), 820–30.

Keegan, V. (1996) 'Cut downsizers down to size', *Guardian*, 9 December.

Kitson, M. and Michie, J. (1996) 'Manufacturing capacity, investment and employment', in J. Michie and J. Grieve Smith (eds), *Creating Industrial Capacity: Towards Full Employment*, Oxford: Oxford University Press, 24–51.

Lamming, R. (1993) *Beyond Partnership: Strategies for Innovation and Lean Supply*, London: Prentice-Hall.

Massey, D., Quintas, P. and Wield, D. (1992) *High-Tech Fantasists: Science Parks in Society and Space*, London: Routledge.

Miles, R.E. and Snow, C.C. (1978) *Organizational Strategy, Structure and Process*, New York: McGraw-Hill.

North, D., Smallbone, D. and Leigh, R. (1994) 'Employment and labour process changes in manufacturing SMEs during the 1990s', in J. Atkinson and D. Storey (eds), *Employment, the Small Firm and the Labour Market*, London: Routledge.

Oakey, R. (1994) *High Technology Small Firms*, London: Pinter.

Oakey, R., Rothwell, R. and Cooper, S. (1988) *Management of Innovation in High Technology Small Firms*, London: Pinter.

Phillips, B.D. and Kirchhoff, B.A. (1988) *The Survival and Quality of Jobs Generated by Entrepreneurial Firms*, Boston: US Small Business Administration.

Porter, M.E. (1980) *Competitive Strategy: Techniques for Analysing Industries and Firms*, New York: Free Press.

Roach, S. (1996) 'America's recipe for industrial extinction', *Financial Times*, 14 May.

Rothwell, R. and Zegveld, W. (1985) *Reindustrialization and Technology*, New York: Longman.

Schumpeter, J.A. (1943) *Capitalism, Socialism and Democracy*, New York: Harper & Row.

Segev, E. (1989) 'A systematic comparative analysis and synthesis of two business-level strategic typologies', *Strategic Management Journal*, **10** (5), 487–505.

Shearman, C. and Burrell, G. (1988) 'New technology based firms and the emergence of new industries: some employment implications', *New Technology, Work and Employment*, **3** (2), 87–99.

Statistisches Jahrbuch 1996: Für die Bundesrepublik Deutschland, Metzler Poeschel.

Storey, D. (1994) *Understanding the Small Business Sector*, London: Routledge.

Storey, D. and Johnson, S. (1986) *Job Generation and Labour Market Change*, London: Macmillan.

Storey, D.J., Keasey, K., Watson, R. and Wynarczyk, P. (1987) *The Performance of Small Firms: Profits, Jobs and Failures*, London: Croom Helm.

Taylor, R. (1996) 'Flurry of P45s will continue: job losses can be expected across many sectors', *Financial Times*, 27 June.

United Nations (1993) *Small and Medium-Sized Transnational Corporations: Role, Impact and Policy Implications*, New York: United Nations.

Wagstyl, S. (1997) 'Beckett invites industry input on White Paper', *Financial Times*, 24 July.

Westhead, P. and Storey, D. (1994) *An Assessment of Firms Located On and Off Science Parks in the UK*, London: HMSO.

Williams, K., Williams, J. and Thomas, D. (1983) *Why Are the British Bad at Manufacturing?*, London: Routledge.

Wolf, M. (1996) 'The ills of manufacturing', *Financial Times*, 14 May.

Womack, J., Jones, D. and Roos, D. (1990) *The Machine that Changed the World*, New York: Rawson Associates.

Zahra, S.A., Sisodia, R.S. and Das, S.R. (1994) 'Technological choices within competitive strategy types: a conceptual integration', *International Journal of Technology Management*, 9 (2), 172–95.

8 Continuity and change in buyer–supplier relations
Case evidence from manufacturing supply chains

Mike Bresnen and Carolyn Fowler

INTRODUCTION

In recent years, a considerable amount of attention has been directed towards changes that have been occurring within manufacturing supply chains (e.g. Imrie and Morris 1992; Lascelles and Dale 1989; Rubery *et al*. 1987; Sako 1992; Thomas and Oliver 1991; Turnbull *et al*. 1992, 1993; Williams *et al*. 1987, 1989). As part of a general trend towards greater collaboration between industrial companies (e.g. Best 1990; Grabher 1993; Thompson *et al*. 1991), it has been suggested by some that new forms of 'obligational contracting' in sectors such as the car industry represent a new, more cooperative approach by manufacturers towards supply-chain management that is also increasingly necessary to ensure continued commercial success (e.g. Bessant *et al*. 1984; Dore 1983; Lamming 1989; Womack *et al*. 1990). On the other hand, however, there are others who query the actual nature and extent of change and who insist instead upon the importance of continuing to view buyer–supplier relations as still involving the exercise of power and control by dominant manufacturers over their dependent suppliers (e.g. Morris and Imrie 1992; Rainnie 1985, 1991; Turnbull 1989, 1990).

In this chapter we set out to contribute to this debate by examining the nature of contemporary changes in buyer–supplier relations, focusing in particular upon the position of suppliers located within manufacturing supply chains. We do so by drawing upon the literature that explores this territory from a power-dependence perspective (see Pfeffer and Salancik 1978) and then applying the issues raised to the examination of two case studies of medium-sized firms situated in manufacturing supply chains (in the food and metal-processing sectors). Elsewhere, it has been argued that critical accounts which emphasize the exploitation and control of suppliers, although they provide extremely valuable insights, nevertheless are often based upon data drawn from only one or two segments of manufacturing industry. Moreover, there is seldom much attempt made to view conditions from the perspective of suppliers, or to complement an analysis of market relations with a consideration of the *organizational* aspects of interfirm dealings (Bresnen 1996). This chapter is an attempt to redress these imbalances, by using these themes to guide the analysis of the case studies. The case data is drawn from two companies which, on the face of it, are subject to the sorts of pressures and constraints on suppliers that are often identified in the empirical literature. Indeed, they are seemingly caught in a cleft stick between powerful customers and powerful suppliers. The analysis therefore charts the consequences of, and reactions to, this predicament with the intention, more generally, of contributing towards knowledge about the factors that affect or determine the nature and quality of interorganizational relations and thus the prospects for change.

CHANGE OR CONTINUITY IN BUYER–SUPPLIER RELATIONSHIPS?

The questions of whether or not and to what extent buyer–supplier relations are undergoing a transformation towards more collaborative ways of working are part of a much broader debate about the nature and direction of organizational change in late twentieth-century capitalism (e.g. Best 1990; Hirst and Zeitlin 1989; Piore and Sabel 1984). Essentially, it is argued by some that greater economic pressure due to more intense competition in world markets is forcing firms to drop the adversarial stance they have traditionally adopted in dealings with their suppliers and to develop instead a new approach based upon partnership and cooperation (e.g. Best 1990). Many commentators have looked to Japan to provide models of best practice in this respect (e.g. Dore 1983; Womack *et al.* 1990). Indeed, the Japanese approach of forming close operational links between firms to complement the use of just-in-time (JIT) systems of production has provided an exemplar that is increasingly being adopted or emulated by western manufacturers (Oliver and Wilkinson 1988; Sako 1992). Together with accumulating evidence of closer interfirm cooperation in other sectors of activity, such developments are taken to suggest that we may be witnessing the emergence of a new mode of organizing, based upon norms of reciprocity and trust and manifested in networks of autonomous organizations linked contractually with one another (e.g. Grabher 1993; Thompson *et al.* 1991).

Such a prognosis can also be seen in the literature on 'flexibility', where considerable emphasis is placed upon collaborative interorganizational relations between manufacturers and their suppliers and subcontractors. Such networks provide the local infrastructure of economic relations that are said to help make flexible specialization possible (Best 1990; Piore and Sabel 1984). They also provide the numerical flexibility necessary for the operation of the so-called flexible firm (Atkinson 1985; Atkinson and Meager 1986). Although there is, of course, considerable debate surrounding the theoretical validity and empirical justification for these theories and their prophecies (e.g. Pollert 1988, 1991; Williams *et al.* 1987; Wood 1989), nevertheless empirical evidence continues to demonstrate the increasing significance of various forms of interorganizational relationship consistent with the network phenomenon (e.g. subcontracting).

Institutional economists too have increasingly recognized the importance of 'hybrid' forms of organization that involve close, long-term relationships between autonomous firms (Powell 1990; Williamson 1985, 1991, 1993).

Powell (1990), for instance, has proposed that the interorganizational network, based as much upon cooperation and trust as on formal contracts, should be regarded as a discrete structural alternative to either pure market or pure hierarchical forms of governance. Similarly, Stinchcombe (1990) has argued that contracts between firms in sectors such as construction and oil extraction often contain elements which are synonymous with hierarchical mechanisms of control (see also Eccles's (1981) discussion of the quasi-firm in the construction industry). Such hybrid forms combine market transactions with hierarchical or quasi-hierarchical mechanisms of coordination and control (Powell 1990).

In the sphere of manufacturing, empirical research over the last decade has also fuelled the debate about network forms of organization by charting the emergence of new forms of 'obligational contracting' based upon partnership and close, long-term relationships between buyers and their suppliers (e.g. Bessant *et al.* 1984; Dore 1983; Lamming 1989; Womack *et al.* 1990). Quite often these new approaches to contracting are related to the adoption of Japanese-style manufacturing systems and methods such as JIT. However, whatever their origins, they are said to embody a 'new philosophy' which, in practical terms, means a wider range of criteria than simply price being used in the award of contracts; close collaboration occurring at an operational level between contractual partners; and the development of long-term strategic alliances, in the form of preferred supplier status or single sourcing agreements (e.g. Imrie and Morris 1992; Rubery *et al.* 1987; Williams *et al.* 1987, 1989). To many commentators, such new practices are, increasingly, a prerequisite for long-term business success (e.g. Best 1990; Dore 1983; Womack *et al.* 1990). However, despite the growing evidence of such developments, which leads many to claim that we are witnessing a volte-face in manufacturers' attitudes and approaches to supply-chain management, other commentators remain rather more sceptical about the nature and extent of change.

First, critics point to the very uneven distribution and piecemeal evidence of change to suggest that the new 'best practice' is the exception rather than the rule (Morris and Imrie 1992; Rainnie 1991; Turnbull 1989, 1990). Examples of such practice also tend to be concentrated in specific sectors, notably the car industry (Imrie and Morris 1992: 644). Furthermore, change is often introduced in an ad hoc manner (Imrie and Morris 1992). Research on Japanese-style production systems, for instance, has found that British companies often only partially adopt them (Bessant *et al.* 1984; Lamming 1989; Oliver and Wilkinson 1988). The reasons for this include manufacturers' tendencies to implement only selected elements of complete packages and their preferences for blending in new systems with their existing policies and practices. More generally, many commentators question the transferability of such practices to the West, given the very different forms of industrial structure found in Japan, as well as major differences in the culture of relations within industry (Boyer 1987; Cusumano and Takeishi 1991; Oliver and Wilkinson 1988; Turnbull 1990; Turnbull *et al.* 1992). As a consequence, questions are raised about the practical applicability and efficacy of such forms of interfirm collaboration, when compared with how they operate in Japan.

Second, it is evident that changes such as rationalizing supply bases are often driven by narrower, more pragmatic concerns simply to reduce costs and increase production efficiency (Turnbull 1990; Turnbull *et al.* 1992; Wilson and Gorb 1983), rather than being part of a coherent and consistent shift in strategy and philosophy (Imrie and Morris 1992; Wood 1989). Indeed, much of the empirical evidence suggests that the label of 'partnership' is misleading, since any changes to terms and conditions of supply are often simply those imposed by powerful producers on dependent suppliers (e.g. Rainnie 1991). Consequently, producers' gains in efficiency are made at the expense of suppliers who incur greater costs in holding inventory (Rainnie 1991; Turnbull 1989, 1990; Turnbull *et al.* 1992). Moreover, price and cost calculations appear to remain central to the process of awarding contracts, and manufacturers seem reluctant to increase their dependence upon single suppliers, preferring instead to keep their options open in order to take advantage of price competition and more favourable deals (Bessant *et al.* 1984; Imrie and Morris 1992: 644; Lascelles and Dale 1989; Rainnie 1991). Thus the greater security for suppliers that supposedly comes from single sourcing often results instead in heightened dependency and forced price reductions. Similarly, integrated production systems can be seen simply as more explicit and obtrusive (and costly) control mechanisms imposed by powerful manufacturers upon small, dependent suppliers, rather than an expression of true interfirm collaboration (Rainnie 1991; Turnbull 1990). Not surprisingly, then, suppliers continue to be sceptical about manufacturers' motives and remain unwilling to increase their dependence by tailoring their production systems to the demands of individual customers (Imrie and Morris 1992: 649–50; Lascelles and Dale 1989; Rainnie 1991; Turnbull 1990).

The main critical argument therefore presented is that the image of closer, more collaborative and more mutually beneficial relations between buyers and suppliers masks attempts by powerful producers to exert greater control over dependent firms and achieve efficiency gains at their expense. Hence true interfirm collaboration is largely a myth and, in reality, so-called partnerships between (usually large) manufacturers and (usually small) suppliers essentially reflect the imbalance in market power between them (Morris and Imrie 1992; Rainnie 1991). Suppliers can, of course, be powerful producers in their own right, in which case this alters the balance of power in their favour (Oliver and Wilkinson 1988; Rainnie 1985; Turnbull *et al.* 1992). However, this is the exception to the rule, and the more common scenario is one characterized by the exploitation and control of small dependent firms.

INTRODUCING AN ORGANIZATIONAL PERSPECTIVE

In spite of all this empirical research, however, there remain many aspects of buyer–supplier relations that are still relatively unexplored. It has been argued elsewhere that, despite the usefulness of a power-dependence framework for critically examining new developments (e.g. Pfeffer and Salancik 1978), existing research falls short of examining the complexity of buyer–supplier relations on a number of key counts (Bresnen 1996). In particular, the research is often narrowly focused on certain sectors (notably, the car industry) and, as a result, suffers from being grounded within very specific organizational and institutional contexts. Perhaps more importantly, comparatively little tends to be said about the orientations, attitudes and actions of organizations occupying positions further down supply chains. Most commonly, research either takes a 'top-down' perspective, examining conditions from the viewpoint of focal manufacturers (e.g. the major car firms); or suppliers are presumed to be dependent by virtue of their position – without any real attempt being made to examine directly their perceptions and attitudes. In other words, there tends to be a strong emphasis upon examining the structural relations linking firms together, but rather less attention is paid to exploring the interpretation and enactment of these relations (cf. Silverman 1974).

One particular omission is the tendency to discount or ignore suppliers' motivations, perceptions, interpretations and attitudes towards what appear to be conditions of dependency (Bresnen 1996: 133–5). For example, it may be the case that actors lower down the supply chain are able to make strategic choices or manoeuvre tactically to react to, and hence cope with, manifest dependency. Another particular omission relates to the treatment of suppliers as, to all intents and purposes, homogenous, unitary organizations. Again, it has been argued elsewhere that the inherent complexity of suppliers as organizations must be taken into account to obtain a fuller picture of the nature and dynamics of interorganizational dealings (Bresnen 1996: 135–9). More specifically, one might expect the nature and conduct of interorganizational dealings to depend on (and, in turn, affect) internal organizational factors, such as the locus of influence in decision making, the degrees of horizontal and vertical differentiation and integration, key cultural characteristics and the like. For example, more centralized control may enhance the ability to negotiate successfully with external parties (e.g. Kochan 1975; Schmidt and Kochan 1977). The potential number of contributory factors is, of course, considerable. However, the main point here is that the influence of such internal factors on external dealings has not really begun to be assessed.

In this chapter an attempt is made to develop a more interpretative analysis of interorganizational relationships within manufacturing supply chains and to study these relations from an organizational, rather than economic, perspective. The research is exploratory and based upon evidence collected from case studies of medium-sized firms that occupy positions as first- and second-tier suppliers to major customers in two industrial settings. It departs from more standard investigations of buyer–supplier relations in three important respects. First, it focuses upon manufacturing settings that seldom receive the same amount of attention from researchers as do companies in other, so-called leading-edge sectors such as automotives or electronics. As such, it examines developments in quite different organizational and institutional contexts from those which are commonly investigated. Second, it considers buyer–supplier relations from the perspective of the supplier, in contrast to much of the research on this topic, which tends to examine conditions from the viewpoint of (usually large-scale) manufacturers. Third, the research seeks to open up the 'black box' of decision making and other internal organizational processes that often receive little attention in more economistic analyses. As such, emphasis is placed upon exploring the nature of interrelationships between contractual dealings and internal organizational structures, cultures and processes. The case evidence is then used to explore the ways in which such firms – often dependent on both major customers *and* major suppliers – react and respond to the conditions that they face. In particular, it explores their own perceptions and interpretations of patterns of power and dependency, and their strategic and tactical responses to these conditions.

THE CASE STUDIES

The case studies are of two medium-sized firms operating in two distinct industrial sectors (food and metal-processing). These two sectors were chosen to enable comparisons and contrasts to be drawn across firms facing quite different market conditions and employing quite distinct technologies (cf. Bresnen 1996: 127–31). The case studies form part of a larger data set of six case study firms in these two industrial sectors (see Bresnen and Fowler 1993, 1996 for further details). Data on buyer–supplier relations were also collected from these other firms, but are not reported here due to space restrictions. The two firms described were also positively selected because, of the six, they faced more extreme pressures in their input and output dealings.

The research was conducted between 1992 and 1993 and involved several visits to each firm, during which interviews were conducted with staff from all main departments and across all managerial levels. The interviews each lasted about an hour and approximately a dozen interviews were conducted in each firm. As well as general information about the firm and its environment, information and views were obtained concerning the business strategies and structural and cultural attributes of each firm. The specific data reported here were drawn mainly from interviews with senior managers and production, marketing and materials management staff. The names of the firms have been changed to protect confidentiality, and outline details of the firms studied are presented in Table 8.1.

Beta Bread

Beta Bread is one of three bakeries that are wholly owned by a group (with a turnover of around £30 million in 1992) that specializes in making sliced bread for the lower end of the market and which it sells to retailers as own-label produce. It is a profitable company and has changed little since it was established in 1983, although the group as a whole was restructured in the 1980s in order to decentralize operations as much as possible to each factory site, with the result that the head office establishment was cut from fifty to ten staff.

The company mass manufactures a limited range of loaf sizes based on its own recipe and standard size specifications. There are two automated lines that mix the

Table 8.1 The case studies

	Beta Bread	Sigma Steel
Date established (taken over)	1983	1959 (1989)
Status of establishment	Profit centre (1 of 3 group factories)	Profit centre (1 of several group factories)
Turnover (% group)	£10 million (36%)	£20 million (1%)
Full-time employees		
male:	148	68
female:	6	3
Net assets	£1.3 million	£2 million
Pre-tax profits	£153,000	£358,000
Products (% output)	Sliced bread (100%)	Alum-coated steel coils (100%)
Customers (% sales)	4 retailers (40%, 30%, 8%, 5% +17% others)	Parent (51%) 3 auto tube companies (15%, 10%, 7%) 20 other (14%)
UK market share	4.5%	50%
Exports (% sales)	–	20%
World market share	–	10%
Main competitors	2 large nationals 4 small locals	10 international
Unit prime costs:		
raw materials	47%	82%
labour	10%	10%
distribution	17%	–
other	26%	8%
Main raw materials (% input)	Flour (75%)	Steel coils (95%)
Main suppliers (% from each)	2 millers (90%, 10%)	Parent (100%)

Note: All figures relate to financial year ending in 1992.

ingredients, cut, shape and bake the dough, and automatically wrap the bread; one of these is dedicated to baking the most popular product, which accounts for 60 per cent of output. The factory operates around the clock and has fourteen operators on each shift: seven on the line and seven packers. Turnaround is quick and, because of the perishable nature of the product (twelve to fourteen hours' storage maximum), production and deliveries are scheduled on the basis of daily (and even more frequent) orders from customers. Weekly throughput is about 500,000 loaves and, at the time of research, the plant was operating at approximately 15 hours undercapacity with a breakeven target of 650,000 loaves per week. Waste levels were reported as very low and stock levels were estimated at £100,000.

The company holds only a small market share (about 4.5 per cent of national sliced bread sales) and faces competition from Mother's Pride and Sunblest as well as from four small local independents. Of its total output, 70 per cent is sold to its two largest customers, both of which are retail chains. One of these accounts for 40 per cent of sales (Beta being sole supplier); the other accounts for 30 per cent of sales (with Beta supplying 80 per cent of bread purchases). Two other retail chains account for 13 per cent of sales (Beta is sole supplier to one and main supplier to the other). The remainder of Beta's sales (17 per cent) goes to a number of smaller, local independent bakers (in many cases Beta is again sole supplier). This concentration of sales has increased substantially from five years previously, when only 20 per cent of sales went to their five largest customers. This has been mainly due to the growth of larger retailer chains and the collapse of many small businesses. Beta have also consciously tried (as yet, unsuccessfully) to reduce their level of dependence on any one firm to 20 per cent or less of sales. At the same time, the managing director described the company as being 'flexible' and 'responsive' to customers' needs.

Forty-seven per cent of unit prime costs are accounted for by raw materials, over three-quarters of which is accounted for by flour (the other main ingredients being yeast, improver and salt). Due to a recent takeover of one of their flour suppliers by another, they now depend on one company for 90 per cent of their flour (it also supplies 40 per cent of all group flour) and on one other company for the remaining 10 per cent. Beta is a relatively small customer for both of these millers (accounting for about 17 per cent and 0.5 per cent of sales respectively). Beta also single sources its yeast and salt and dual sources its improver (most of which it buys from its main flour supplier). In all cases again, Beta is a minor customer, and managers there expressed their concern at being highly dependent on particular suppliers. The chairman of the group negotiates flour contracts for the group as a whole and, since millers produce to the same specification, the key criterion is price. With the exception of yeast (where the quality of different strains can differ), there are no formal contracts for any of the raw materials. The company receives about four tanker-load deliveries of flour per day and employs an independent organization to conduct monthly lab tests to check quality.

Sigma Steel

Sigma Steel is a wholly owned subsidiary of a British steel company which has a turnover in excess of £1 billion. Sigma specializes in the aluminium coating of steel coils supplied by the parent which it then supplies on to stockholders (54 per cent of sales) or direct to manufacturers (46 per cent). The company is profitable and is one of only ten firms worldwide that do this type of work. Consequently, it has no British competitors, holds about half the UK market and a tenth of the world market (it exports a fifth of its output). The company had been part of a steel stockholding group until it was taken over by the parent in 1989. In the early 1980s, it began cutting coils and building up its direct business with manufacturers, rather than simply supplying to stockholders.

The plant is highly automated and consists of one continuous production line which has three main machines that coat, level and then cut the coil into the lengths and widths required. The coating process is to a standard specification, the changeover time to different width coils is about one hour, and waste levels from the cutting process are minimal. Weekly throughput is about 1,000 tons (breakeven level is about 580 tons) and production is scheduled on a weekly basis. A computer system is used to log sales orders and record daily output and deliveries. The line operates around the clock, five days a week, and is manned by thirteen operators, plus supervisors and fitters, per shift.

Sigma Steel is sole supplier to all of its customers. Its main customer is its own parent stockholder (who purchases 51 per cent of output; other stockholders account for 3 per cent). The remainder of its business is through direct sales of cut coils to manufacturers. In recent years, the company has substantially increased its direct business to car component suppliers that are tied into the main car companies' JIT systems of production. It has about twenty-five 'live' customers at any one time, of which three automotive component producers account for 32 per cent of total sales (15, 10 and 7 per cent respectively) and twenty other car component suppliers and household appliance manufacturers account for the rest (i.e. 14 per cent). Contracts with these companies are 'open-ended', although the company is subject to regular and in-depth audits of all aspects of its production process by many of their more prominent customers and factory visits and other forms of communication are frequent. Deliveries to customers are generally required weekly, although they do often have to respond to changing daily demands. At the same time, however, they regarded their business as a 'soft sell game' (works director), and it was emphasized that rarely had they been tested on their JIT deliveries and that, although these customers could go to stockholders, they chose not to.

Nevertheless, the company does face severe problems in handling the logistics of production scheduling and materials management. Eighty-two per cent of its unit prime costs are raw materials, of which 95 per cent is 'tied' steel coil purchases from the parent. Sigma account for only a very small amount of parent sales and, more significantly, parent production is scheduled on a six-week cycle basis (in order to maximize production economies), the time lag for steel delivery to Sigma being approximately ten weeks. Integrating materials delivery with the short-term demands of many of their direct customers therefore requires accurate anticipation of short-term demand based upon prior experience (although the works director did point out that larger customers tended to order on a monthly basis and that meeting their requirements was easier).

Nevertheless, these constraints did have a number of important effects. First, and most significantly, stock levels are high, with about 500 tons in process, 1,000 tons of raw material and 3,500 tons finished stock. At an estimated value added of £100 per ton, this represents about £0.5 million. Secondly, the structure of the organization is highly specialized: the crucial functions of matching sales orders to production and distribution is handled by a production manager who works closely with a sales assistant manager, steel stock control clerk, transport manager and two quality control staff. Purchasing and sales are also highly centralized activities: one joint managing director negotiates steel prices quarterly (including rebates for bulk purchase), while the works director buys aluminium direct from dealers on the London metal exchange. The other joint managing director is responsible for sales and is supported by four staff in two sales offices that handle home and export sales. Contracts for gases are negotiated annually via the parent; other consumables are purchased from small local companies.

CASE STUDY COMPARISONS AND CONTRASTS

On the face of it, these two firms occupy difficult positions within their respective supply chains. Although part of a group of three factories, Beta Bread has a small market share, faces competition from major nationals and is heavily dependent upon a relatively small number of powerful retailers for the majority of sales. Although the company acts mainly as sole supplier, this translates into a perceived or felt dependency, leading to attempts being made to broaden their customer base. As buyers of raw materials, they rely quite heavily too upon major corporations for the supply of key ingredients and so operate as small players in essentially oligopolistic commodities markets. Although the company exercises some countervailing power through group purchasing, it is still a relatively minor customer for the millers who supply it.

Sigma Steel is somewhat different. It has a sizeable market share, faces much less direct competition and has a more distinctive product. However, it too faces pressures to adapt to customers and suppliers which lead to problems in scheduling production and managing materials effectively. In particular, the company is faced with demands placed on it by its automotive component customers which do not at all match the delivery schedules of its main supplier. Moreover, it too has consciously attempted to reduce its dependence on key customers, despite being sole supplier to many of these firms. On the supply side, the company is obviously heavily dependent upon its parent for the supply of its main raw material, although through its parent it is also able to secure more favourable deals with suppliers of minor items (e.g. gases).

Under such circumstances, one would expect the quite strong pressures on both companies to result in a heavy reliance upon stocks to cope with variable customer demands and constraints in materials supply. And, indeed, the case evidence points very clearly to absorbing slack as an almost inevitable outcome of these pressures (particularly at Sigma Steel, where the nature of the production process itself also leads to considerable inventories of work-in-progress). However, at the same time, these companies are fairly profitable and, when one explores their situation in depth, there are subtleties and complexities in their responses to these constraints that belie a simple explanation based upon exploitation and control by dominant customers and intransigent suppliers.

First, it is important to consider each company's business strategies. Both have specialized in producing one main standardized product for bulk manufacture and sale, reflecting their distinctive competence in particular manufacturing processes and resulting in the development of a specific market niche. Sigma Steel are one of the few manufacturers worldwide of their product and, during recent years, have intentionally integrated forward into processing (having previously acted only as stockholders). Beta Bread's niche is as producers of a low-price product targeted at the lower end of the market (the managing director reported that Beta were probably seen by their competitors as the 'cheap and expanding cowboys' of the industry). In both cases, moreover, their products are manufactured to their own specifications and involve standard specification raw materials – hence reducing some of the potential uncertainty associated with variability in input and output transactions. Furthermore, apart from some minor diversification (Sigma Steel had tried marketing alum-coated wires, and Beta Bread merchandized some cakes), they have both concentrated upon their core activities. The point to be made here is simply that the outcomes, in so far as inventory levels are concerned, are in part the second-order consequences of first-order strategic decisions, made historically about which markets to target and which production technologies to employ (cf. Child 1972).

Second, there are some observations to be made regarding these companies' perceptions of their input and output transactions. Managers at both companies were obviously very aware of their plight and concerned to avoid further dependence upon dominant buyers and suppliers. On the supply side, they were both constrained in choice – Sigma by being tied to their parent, and Beta by now being highly dependent on one miller (the managing director was 'unhappy' about this and reported that the company had originally made a conscious decision not to single source and that they were now looking at alternative sources of supply, including imports). On the demand side, both firms too were keen to widen their customer base. Sigma Steel was trying to extend its direct business to auto tube suppliers, despite (and because of) the fact that sales had increased to the parent stockholder since the takeover, whereas the number of 'live' domestic customers had fallen. At Beta Bread, the concentration of sales over the last five years was the cause of some concern, as already noted.

Interesting too, however, were the orientations of the companies to 'managing' these situations. The impression gained from interviews with both sets of managers was, on the one hand, a desire to be accommodating and responsive to customers' needs, but, on the other hand, a felt need to maintain an arm's-length relationship with both customers and suppliers. For both companies, the ability to do this was strengthened by the fairly standardized nature of the product and thus the relatively routine nature of their input/output transactions. However, what was perhaps of more interest was the companies' motivations for maintaining some distance. Sigma Steel is here the better example. Despite having to respond to JIT customers' delivery requirements and auditing regimes, senior managers reported that these demands were less pressing than one might suppose and that they had rarely been tested yet on their deliveries. There was therefore much more 'slack' in the relationship than at first appeared. Similarly, auditing requirements, though viewed as important, were treated with a certain amount of savoir-faire. This may, of course, have reflected the company's relatively strong position as sole UK producer – a fact that certainly explains what can only be described as a degree of complacency in marketing (the works director described the sales function as 'sitting back and waiting for the phone to ring'). However, it does also suggest that, depending upon circumstances, a company might have the motivation and the ability to avoid the depth of penetration of customer demands that one would associate with supplying to a JIT regime.

The constraints that both firms faced also had a number of effects upon their organizational and management practices. Neither firm was sufficiently internally differentiated (in terms of tasks performed) to allow it to create self-contained units to cope with specific external demands (cf. Galbraith 1977). However, not surprisingly there was some limited evidence of 'stratification' (cf. Lascelles and Dale 1989), in the form of priority scheduling to respond to urgent orders. There was also, of course, some (limited) use of computerized information systems to help integrate customer orders, production scheduling and deliveries. More interesting perhaps were other structural features. In particular, marketing, scheduling and purchasing/materials management activities were not only critically important, but also (and probably as a result) highly centralized and integrated activities (cf. Hickson *et al.* 1971). At Beta Bread, the chairman and managing director purchased supplies on behalf of the group and production scheduling was effectively determined by sales contracts negotiated by head office staff. At Sigma Steel, purchasing and production planning were among the main responsibilities of the works director, and one of the two joint managing directors was responsible for sales. Added to this, was the relatively high number of specialist support staff in these areas for firms of this size: at Sigma Steel in particular, a production manager (who was responsible for scheduling) was supported by an engineering stores buyer, a transport manager and a steel stock control clerk.

Further details about the structural and cultural characteristics of these firms can be found elsewhere (Bresnen and Fowler 1993, 1996). The important point to stress here is that the responses to external constraints in both cases included the centralization of key activities and decisions and the concentration of staffing support around the logistics of procurement, scheduling and supply (although this was much less evident at Beta Bread, where there were fewer support staff anyway following the reduction in numbers at head office and the attempt to make the bakeries fully responsible for profitability and controlling costs). These structural responses, in turn, did have consequences for management within these firms, affecting the balance of influence within management and between departments. These consequences have been explored in some depth elsewhere, as have the consequences for lower-level supervisory staff (Bresnen and Fowler 1996). However, in so far as employment relations generally at these firms are concerned, there was little evidence of any direct effects due to external constraints and pressures. Both firms were consciously pursuing strategies related to labour utilization. Sigma Steel had a long-term policy of gradually reducing labour costs through natural wastage; they also claimed that 'flexibility' in labour use had always been the norm (although this had not as yet extended to incorporating engineers within production teams). At Beta Bread, the restructuring of the company had put greater pressure upon bakery managers to control costs, the result being work intensification at the plant, with supervisors and managers also sometimes having to work directly on the line.

However, the point to be made here is that, although such strategies could be interpreted as complementary to broader business objectives and therefore associated with the immediate external constraints the companies faced, there was no direct and obvious causal connection. The intent behind these strategies was essentially to cut costs and achieve flexibility in manning. Neither of the firms had gone further than this in regarding any form of human resource management as important to the development of their activities within their respective supply chains; and their labour-use strategies were clearly introduced independently of any change in the external locus of influence and control within their immediate environments. In other words, both firms exercised considerable discretion in their employment policies and practices – implementing strategies and policies that may have complemented their broader business goals, but which were not directly the result of their positions within their respective supply chains.

CONCLUDING DISCUSSION

The foregoing analysis has drawn out a number of points that are consistent with other, critical accounts of the effects of dependency upon supplier organizations. It was quite clear that the constraints that these firms operated under resulted in absorbing slack as an almost inevitable outcome of the need to integrate variable customer demand with fixed patterns of supply (Rainnie 1991; Turnbull 1989, 1990). Not only was this evidenced in high levels of stock, but also in the relatively large overheads attached to the activities of procurement, scheduling and delivery. The analysis has also highlighted the orientations of these firms, including their continued scepticism about relationships with customers and suppliers (cf. Lascelles and Dale 1989; Rainnie 1991); the tendency to rely upon their own frames of reference and systems of operation when responding to customers' needs (cf. Lamming 1989); and an unwillingness to orient their systems to the demands of specific customers. At one level, such findings suggest that, if there are continuing difficulties in changing suppliers' orientations in as prominent a sector as the car industry (e.g. Imrie and Morris 1992; Lascelles and Dale 1989; Thomas and Oliver 1991), then the difficulties in doing so elsewhere may be much more pronounced. At another level, these findings offer support for the notion that the reality of buyer–supplier transactions often continues to be characterized by one-sidedness and a degree of 'semi-detachment' in relationships. It remains questionable, therefore, whether what we are witnessing in manufacturing supply chains amounts to a transformation in the culture of relations between buyers and suppliers.

On the other hand, the analysis has also drawn out a number of features reflecting the other, more positive side of the same coin: namely, the choices and actions that such firms take to avoid (or at least cope with) conditions of dependency. In particular, emphasis has been placed upon exploring their situations in the light of the strategic and tactical choices and decisions they have historically made (and continue to make) about which products to produce and which markets to target. Although such firms have in common with car component suppliers a tendency towards limited product diversification and therefore perhaps fewer strategic options (cf. Delbridge *et al.* 1990), the point here is precisely that their positioning is the result of conscious first-order strategic choices. In both cases, moreover, they have managed to secure specific and, to judge from the figures, profitable niches as first-/second-tier suppliers (cf. Delbridge *et al.* 1990: 22). Furthermore, they continue to monitor and reflect upon their circumstances with a view to attempting to limit their actual dependency. This is not meant to suggest that one should overemphasize their proactivity or underemphasize the constraints they face; merely that they are not entirely the victims of circumstance they may be made out to be in some critical accounts of the changing nature of buyer–supplier relations. More specifically, they are able to make choices about whether to be 'locked into' manufacturers' sourcing programmes (cf. Thomas and Oliver 1991: 615) and clearly have something to gain from the positioning choices they make (cf. Delbridge *et al.* 1990: 25; Thomas and Oliver 1991; Turnbull *et al.* 1993).

Reinforcing this theme are the points made about organizational coping strategies. In particular, the analysis has highlighted the tendencies towards centralization of critical activities and decisions, as well as the integration of specialized activities associated with these activities, as structural/cultural mechanisms to cope with conditions of dependency (cf. Hickson *et al.* 1971). The point here is that, although such tactics can perhaps be interpreted simply as reactions to external constraints and pressures, at the same time they suggest a variety of internal adaptive responses that, in other types of firm in other types of circumstances, may extend to include a wide range of different organizational responses to cope with environmental constraints and contingencies (Bresnen 1996; cf. Galbraith 1977). The analysis has, at the same time, also noted how *other* policies and practices – including those developed for the management of labour – may effectively be disengaged from the pressures generated in the surrounding milieu. In other words, contingent upon circumstances, there may be a fairly loosely coupled connection between external relationships and internal management practices – a prospect that strategic contingency theories have long acknowledged and allowed for (e.g. Pugh *et al.* 1969), if not some current critical accounts of buyer–supplier relations which tend to presume a much more deterministic relationship between external conditions and internal management practices (e.g. Rainnie 1985, 1991).

Taken together, these findings suggest important elements of continuity, as well as change, in the position of suppliers in manufacturing supply chains that revolve around their preferred level of autonomy and the degrees of freedom they continue to exercise in their strategic and operational decision making. In many ways, such firms are increasingly expected to adjust to the requirements of major buyers (and perhaps even powerful suppliers) in ways which reflect a new, more flexible orientation to changing customer (and supplier) demands. Although the companies in this study have not been drawn fully into the types of regime encountered nowadays by many first-tier suppliers in the car industry, they are still engaged, for the most part, as sole suppliers and are, as a result, highly dependent on major customers and suppliers. They are also commonly subject to some specific and very obtrusive forms of monitoring and control. Perhaps most importantly, they *perceive* themselves as being involved in (and expect to be involved in) non-adversarial contractual relationships. At the same time, however, there is still plenty of evidence of a more traditional approach towards the management of transactional relationships: price is still very much the major criterion in awarding contracts; relationships are relatively informal but still arm's-length; and there is precious little evidence of close operational and strategic connections with either buyers or suppliers (cf. Imrie and Morris 1992). The lack of such integration with their contractual partners may be explained in part by the standardized nature of the products they offer and the comparatively routine nature of their production systems (cf. Delbridge *et al.* 1990: 18–19; Williams *et al.* 1987: 427), as well as by the companies' relatively strong market position or distinctive niche (cf. Delbridge *et al.* 1990: 22; Rainnie 1985). Whatever the combination of reasons, however, they are obviously not only able, but also very willing, to create or maintain some distance between themselves and their immediate contractual partners.

The fact that they are able and willing to do so, in turn, raises a number of questions about prospects for their performance in both the short and long term (as well as about the prognosis for the development of manufacturing supply chains as a whole). In many contemporary accounts of changing buyer–supplier relations, it is almost taken as given that, if firms are to remain competitive, they need to respond more positively than they have in the past to attempts to forge closer, more collaborative relationships with other industrial and commercial organizations. The benefits of doing so include the commercial or financial gains that can be made (through, for example, repeat orders and reduced tendering costs); they also include less immediate benefits that can accrue from practices such as the transfer and sharing of technical or managerial knowledge and expertise. It could therefore be argued that the very survival of such companies in the long term is dependent in part upon the competitive edge that they gain through being committed, willing and flexible contractual partners. The research reported here, however, has shown that, in the short term at least, companies which are in ostensibly dependent positions *may* nevertheless perform quite effectively and profitably without having to commit themselves to closer operational or strategic links with their contractual partners. Indeed, there are clearly other less tangible, but nevertheless important, perceived benefits of maintaining some distance and keeping the company's strategic options open. Ironically, such an approach by suppliers almost perfectly mirrors the tendency among many of their customers to keep their procurement options open by retaining various elements of competition in tendering arrangements (e.g. Imrie and Morris 1992: 644). It also reinforces the point that, as well as potential benefits, there are many direct and indirect costs associated with closer interorganizational collaboration (e.g. Lascelles and Dale 1989; Rainnie 1991; Turnbull 1990). Taking these points together and relating them to the performance of supply chains as a whole, it is also evident that, if the circumstances are right, supply chains can operate quite effectively without the need for closer integration or 'coupling' between firms. In other words, new and more collaborative forms of contracting relationship also have a number of costs associated with them that may make a more traditional approach to supply-chain relationships appear equally, if not more, beneficial in the short term.

On the other hand, the companies investigated here do face a particular set of conditions, and there are, of course, many other, more competitive types of environment where closer collaboration may be both more desirable and more necessary. Furthermore, for the firms looked at here there are clearly many costs associated with adopting an arm's-length approach and a number of benefits that are forgone as the price paid for greater autonomy and freedom of action. Not only are such firms likely to be operating at less than optimum levels of performance (particularly due to sizeable overheads), but they may also lose out in other ways – such as in not gaining the knowledge, skills and experience that can enhance their future capabilities. Consequently, one might question whether such an approach is sustainable in the long term.

Clearly, the answer to such a question requires a great deal more research that traces through the long-term effects of different forms of contractual relationship on different types of supplier. However, there are some useful and direct pointers that can be drawn from the research reported here. In particular, much clearly depends upon the scope that firms have to select from a range of goals and objectives, of which profit maximization may be only one (and upon the relative values and importance that are attached to each of those goals and objectives). Similarly, it also depends a great deal upon the scope that companies then have to develop business strategies and internal structural mechanisms to cope with external pressures (and their relative preferences and desires in adopting these different courses of action). Other companies in other environments may not have the luxury afforded these firms by their relatively strong commercial position. Nor may they express any preferences other than to maximize profitability. However, to the extent that they do have some flexibility in their pursuit of goals, objectives and strategies, they can continue to manoeuvre in such a way as to avoid some of the potential problems and costs associated with dependence upon other organizations and perhaps even succeed in exerting more direct control over critical elements of their environment.

As far as supply chains as a whole are concerned, the prospects are similarly likely to depend upon the particular conditions of demand and supply affecting the range of transactions among firms. However, one might nevertheless conclude that, where supply chains as a whole exhibit some degree of 'slack' (for whatever reason), then the prospect emerges that a more traditional approach to buyer–supplier relations becomes a feasible and sustainable prospect in the long run. The implication is that, although the emergence of newer, more collaborative approaches to managing buyer–supplier relations may be an important contemporary development, it is not the only possible future trajectory for interfirm relationships within the manufacturing sector: it is instead more than likely that fairly traditional approaches to managing buyer–supplier relations will continue quite successfully to co-exist with newly emerging, more collaborative approaches, as firms continue to calculate the specific benefits and costs to them of alternative ways of dealing with their supply-chain relationships.

REFERENCES

Atkinson, J. (1985) 'The changing corporation', in D. Clutterbuck (ed.), *New Patterns of Work*, Aldershot: Gower.

Atkinson, J. and Meager, N. (1986) 'Is flexibility just a flash in the pan?', *Personnel Management*, September, 26–9.

Bessant, J., Jones, D., Lamming, R. and Pollard, A. (1984) 'The West Midlands automotive component industry: recent changes and future prospects', Sector Report no. 4, West Midlands County Council, Economic Development Unit.

Best, M.H. (1990) *The New Competition: Institutions of Industrial Restructuring*, Cambridge: Polity Press.

Boyer, R. (1987) 'Labour flexibility: many forms, uncertain effects', *Labour and Society*, **12**, 107–29.

Bresnen, M.J. (1996) 'An organizational perspective on changing buyer–supplier relations: a critical review of the evidence', *Organization*, **3** (1), 121–46.

Bresnen, M.J. and Fowler, C.M. (1993) 'Flexibility and management change: case evidence from medium-sized firms in two industrial sectors', in *Proceedings of the Conference, Professions and Management in Britain*, School of Management, University of Stirling, 26–28 August.

—— (1996) 'Professionalisation and British management practice: case evidence from medium-sized firms in two industrial sectors', *Journal of Management Studies*, **33** (2), 159–82.

Child, J. (1972) 'Organizational structure, environment and performance: the role of strategic choice', *Sociology*, **6** (1), 1–22.

Cusumano, M.A. and Takeishi, A. (1991) 'Supplier relations and management: a survey of Japanese, Japanese-transplant, and US auto plants', *Strategic Management Journal*, **12**, 563–88.

Delbridge, R., Oliver, N., Turnbull, P. and Wilkinson, B. (1990) 'Supplier relations in the UK automotive components industry in the 1990s: developments in the Welsh sector', special report, Japanese Management Research Unit, Cardiff Business School, UWCC.

Dore, R. (1983) 'Goodwill and the spirit of market capitalism', *British Journal of Sociology*, **34** (3), 459–82.

Eccles, R.G. (1981) 'The quasi-firm in the construction industry', *Journal of Economic Behaviour and Organization*, **2**, 335–57.

Galbraith, J.R. (1977) *Organization Design*, Reading, Mass.: Addison-Wesley.

Grabher, G. (ed.) (1993) *The Embedded Firm: On the Socioeconomics of Industrial Networks*, London: Routledge.

Hickson, D.J., Hinings, C.R., Lee, C.A., Schneck, R.E. and Pennings, J.M. (1971) 'A strategic contingencies theory of intraorganizational power', *Administrative Science Quarterly*, **16** (2), 216–29.

Hirst, P.Q. and Zeitlin, J. (eds) (1989) *Reversing Industrial Decline? Industrial Structure in Britain and Her Competitors*, Oxford: Berg.

Imrie, R. and Morris, J. (1992) 'A review of recent changes in buyer–supplier relations', *OMEGA International Journal of Management Science*, **20** (5/6), 641–52.

Kochan, T.A. (1975) 'The determinants of power of boundary units in an interorganizational bargaining relation', *Administrative Science Quarterly*, **20** (3), 434–52.

Lamming, R. (1989) 'The causes and effects of structural change in the European automotive components industry', International Motor Vehicle Programme, Massachusetts Institute of Technology, Cambridge, Mass.

Lascelles, D.M. and Dale, B.G. (1989) 'The buyer–supplier relationship in total quality management', *Journal of Purchasing and Materials Management*, summer, 10–19.

Morris, J. and Imrie, R. (1992) *Transforming Buyer–Supplier Relations: Japanese-Style Industrial Practices in a Western Context*, London: Macmillan.

Oliver, N. and Wilkinson, B. (1988) *The Japanization of British Industry*, Oxford: Blackwell.

Pfeffer, J. and Salancik, G.R. (1978) *The External Control of Organizations*, New York: Harper & Row.

Piore, M. and Sabel, C. (1984) *The Second Industrial Divide: Possibilities of Prosperity*, New York: Basic Books.

Pollert, A. (1988) 'The flexible firm: fixation or fact?', *Work, Employment and Society*, **2** (3), 281–316.

—— (ed.) (1991) *Farewell to Flexibility?*, Oxford: Blackwell.

Powell, W.W. (1990) 'Neither market nor hierarchy: network forms of organization', in B.M. Staw and L.L. Cummings (eds), *Research in Organizational Behaviour*, vol. 12, Greenwich, Conn.: JAI Press.

Pugh, D.S., Hickson, D.J., Hinings, C.R. and Turner, C. (1969) 'The context of organizational structures', *Administrative Science Quarterly*, **14** (1), 91–114.

Rainnie, A. (1985) 'Small firms, big problems: the political economy of small businesses', *Capital & Class*, **25**, 140–68.

—— (1991) 'Just-in-time, subcontracting and the small firm', *Work, Employment and Society*, **5** (3), 353–75.

Rubery, J., Tarling, R. and Wilkinson, F. (1987) 'Flexibility, marketing and the organization of production', *Labour and Society*, **12**, 131–51.

Sako, M. (1992) *Prices, Quality and Trust: Interfirm Relations in Britain and Japan*, Cambridge: Cambridge University Press.

Schmidt, S.M. and Kochan, T.A. (1977) 'Inter-organizational relationships: patterns and motivations', *Administrative Science Quarterly*, **22** (2), 220–34.

Silverman, D. (1974) *The Theory of Organizations*, 2nd edn, London: Heinemann.

Stinchcombe, A.L. (1990) *Information and Organizations*, Berkeley: University of California Press.

Thomas, R. and Oliver, N. (1991) 'Components supplier patterns in the UK motor industry', *OMEGA International Journal of Management Science*, **19** (6), 609–16.

Thompson, G.F., Frances, J., Levacic, R. and Mitchell, J. (eds) (1991) *Markets, Hierarchies and Networks: The Co-ordination of Social Life*, London: Sage.

Turnbull, P. (1989) 'Now we're motoring? The West Midlands automotive component industry', Working Paper, Japanese Management Research Unit, Cardiff Business School, UWCC.

—— (1990) 'Buyer–supplier relations in the UK automotive industry', in P. Blyton and J. Morris (eds), *Flexible Futures? Prospects for Employment and Organization*, New York: De Gruyter.

Turnbull, P., Oliver, N. and Wilkinson, B. (1992) 'Buyer–supplier relations in the UK automotive industry: strategic implications of the Japanese manufacturing model', *Strategic Management Journal*, **13**, 159–68.

Turnbull, P., Delbridge, R., Oliver, N. and Wilkinson, B. (1993) 'Winners and losers: the "tiering" of component suppliers in the UK automotive industry', *Journal of General Management*, **19** (1), 48–63.

Williams, K., Cutler, T., Williams, J. and Haslam, C. (1987) 'The end of mass production', *Economy and Society*, **16**, 405–39.

Williams, K., Williams, J., Haslam, C. and Wardlow, A. (1989) 'Facing up to manufacturing failure', in P. Hirst and J. Zeitlin (eds), *Reversing Industrial Decline? Industrial Structure in Britain and her Competitors*, Oxford: Berg.

Williamson, O.E. (1985) *The Economic Institutions of Capitalism*, New York: Free Press.

—— (1991) 'Comparative economic organization: the analysis of discrete structural alternatives', *Administrative Science Quarterly*, **36**, 269–96.

—— (1993) 'Transaction cost economics and organization theory', *Industrial and Corporate Change*, **2** (2), 107–56.

Wilson, P. and Gorb, P. (1983) 'How large and small firms can grow together', *Long Range Planning*, **16** (2), 19–27.

Womack, J., Jones, D. and Roos, D. (1990) *The Machine that Changed the World*, New York: Rawson Associates.

Wood, S. (ed.) (1989) *The Transformation of Work*, London: Unwin Hyman.

Part III

Policy implications for future development

9 Opening Pandora's box

De facto industrial policy and the British defence industry

John Lovering

INTRODUCTION: THE 'MANUFACTURING MATTERS' DEBATE AND THE DEFENCE SECTOR

It has long been argued that manufacturing has been treated unfairly in Britain. The institutional dominance of finance capital within the economic policy-making arms of the state has allegedly resulted in interest rate and exchange rate policies which have favoured financial activities – 'the City' – rather than productive ones – 'industry'. The bias towards short-term financial management has also been reflected in the distinct lack of attention at the level of the state to other preconditions for manufacturing growth and competitiveness, such as investment in human capital and in technological innovation.

The idea that the state–finance–industry nexus in Britain has presented a structural bias against manufacturing goes back at least a century to Marx's comments that Britain is ruled by 'the gang who know nothing about production' (cited in Brown 1988: 49). For some this represents an enduring fact of British cultural life: British elites have looked to the civil service or to the City rather than to industry, and industrialists and engineers have been given lower status than in other countries. This line of thought entered popular consciousness a century ago when advocates of government support for industry, and those who wished Britain to enter a competitive arms race with Germany, found common purpose in the claim that Britain was threatened economically and militarily by the better organized military–industrial apparatus then being constructed under Bismarck (Morris 1984). The idea that manufacturing has been unfairly discriminated against in Britain, and that this is a bad thing for the nation as a whole, has persisted. Since the 1930s it has been an influential current within both the 'British-state-developmentalist' strand within the Labour Party and the 'corporatist-one-nation' strand in the Conservative Party.

In the 1960s, it was revived in a new context. For the neo-Gramscian New Left, the absence of a (German-style) economic development apparatus in the British state was a manifestation of a more fundamental specificity of British capitalism, namely, the absence of a 'proper' bourgeois revolution (Anderson 1992). This absence explained the enduring opposition to 'modernization' in Britain, in sharp contrast to other late-developing capitalist states. Similar ideas, shorn of their

Leftist connotations and focusing on 'culture' in a broadly neo-liberal light, became common currency in the 1980s, taking their bearings from the influential account of Weiner (1981). In the early 1990s, the collapse of the formal confrontation between capitalism and Communism prompted a new interest in the relationship between uneven national economic performance and the 'varieties of capitalism' (Storper 1993). Within this framework Britain is seen as an exemplar, or perhaps a casualty, of the 'Anglo-Saxon' model, which is supposedly inferior to other versions of capitalism, especially the Rhineland model, or even some of the more statist versions of Southeast Asian countries (Singapore?). Although they are characterized by enormously crude generalizations and an almost complete disregard for contemporary historical change, such stories have been invoked to provide some intellectual legitimacy for the view that Britain could and should learn from more 'successful' countries, especially by adopting a deliberate strategy to promote manufacturing.

In the mid-1990s, pieces of several of these arguments were appropriated and served up to *Guardian* readers by Will Hutton, whose book-length résumé became a best seller in the run-up to the 1997 General Election. For Hutton, the promotion of manufacturing is part and parcel of a wider bundle of reforms, including constitutional change, which are vitally necessary to 'modernize' Britain. Some of these ideas were briefly echoed by the Labour leadership during their pre-election flirtation with 'stakeholder capitalism' (see Kelly *et al.* 1997). But New Labour avoided any serious commitment to any particular industrial strategy, just as it picked up and then dropped Euro-Keynesianism at the macroeconomic level (Anderson and Mann 1997). In the months after being elected, Labour concentrated on financial management conceived in a firmly neo-liberal mould, as manifested in its formal abdication of control of interest rates and prevarication over entry to the EMU. By the autumn of that year the regime of interest and exchange rates was seen by many manufacturing businesses as once again threatening investment and growth, and thereby their competitive position vis-à-vis foreign competitors.

Despite Labour's initial apparent lack of interest, the debate over manufacturing support is likely to become increasingly influential over the next decade. The extreme 'free market' policies of the 1980s are unpopular and discredited even by their own former advocates (J. Gray 1997) while the idea of targeting so-called strategic industries continues to attract influential support amongst industrialists and politicians in the US and in Europe (Tyson 1992; CEC 1993). The main reason why manufacturing is thought to be particularly deserving of support is that it is regarded as the main source of internationally tradable outputs and the main field of economic activity in which it is possible to significantly increase productivity (Mayes and Soteri 1994; see also Chapter 1 in this volume). The growth of manufacturing output, and especially exports, is therefore uniquely likely to reduce the prime constraints on national economic growth and to contribute to rising standards of living. A closer and more responsive relationship between government and industry, resulting in a more market-sensitive and reflexive system of economic governance, would help to raise levels of investment and lift the national (or regional) economy up to a higher league of flexible growth based on economies of scope and institutionalized learning.

Against the background of claims such as this the experience of the defence industry is of some interest. As noted above, the defence industry was invoked in the original debates over British industrial policy – or the lack of it. From the middle of the twentieth century the defence sector became the focus of the most elaborate and enduring system of governmental support (followed perhaps by agri-business and the health industry). As a result it has had an unusually large presence in the British economy. More relevantly, the defence industry has recently undergone a wide-ranging modernization that can be attributed directly to the new form of de facto industrial policy which has been applied in this sector since the mid-1980s. In this chapter, I suggest that recent experience in the defence industry offers some instructive lessons for the 'Manufacturing Matters' debate. A supportive industrial policy has been reasonably successful in the limited sense that it has enabled British defence companies to survive and recon-struct themselves in the context of the internationalization of the arms market and changing international state relationships. But it is doubtful that this has spun off any benefits for other UK industries, or resulted in any increase in national economic welfare. What it has done is set off a number of indeterminate processes which may have negative effects in the longer run. Intervention to boost the competitive viability of the British arms industry has resulted in the creation of a new decision-making nexus which is inherently uncontrollable and largely beyond public accountability, and the longer-term effects may be counterproduc-tive in terms of both economic and social goals, prosperity and peace.

THE UK DEFENCE INDUSTRY

The UK defence industry consists of a small number of companies specializing in developing and assembling products for military customers, plus a much larger group producing a wide range of products, some of which are consumed by armed services, but the bulk of which are sold to civilian markets. It is customary to regard the former as the core of the defence industrial base (Taylor and Hayward 1989). In this group British Aerospace and GEC-Marconi dominate the defence-aerospace sector, GEC-VSEL and Vosper Thorneycroft the warship and submarine sector, GKN-Westland the helicopter sector, GKN and Vickers the armoured vehicles sector, and Royal Ordnance (a BAe subsidiary) the munitions sector. A number of medium-sized companies, notably Dowty, Smiths Industries, the Hunting Group, and the FR Group, have important stakes in particular weapons and related equipment niches and receive over £25m annually in MoD contracts. In addition to this defence-specialized core, a large number of other suppliers are primarily civilian producers. Prominent examples include Rolls-Royce, Amec, Esso and ICI.

The UK defence industry supplies around 90 per cent of the MoD expenditure on equipment procurement (£9,430m in 1997), and earns over half as much again from exports. In 1996 exports orders worth £5.1 billion were received

(Parliamentary Answers, *Hansard*, 30 June 1997). According to the most recently available MoD estimates, UK industrial employment dependent on defence spending amounted to 415,000 people in 1995/6,[1] some 237,000 fewer than in 1990. Employment related to exports is estimated at around 145,000 jobs, one-third of the total.

In the early years of the Cold War the defence industry was generally regarded as one of Britain's industrial jewels, reflecting its nurturing of the jet engine, radar, and other modern technologies which became iconic in the 'Golden Age' of capitalist growth. But from the late 1950s a less celebratory view became influential, following the failure of a number of defence programmes, the revelation of a series of procurement scandals, and the wider emergence of a liberal 'anti-Establishment' culture of economic commentary (thanks in particular to a number of economic journalists from a liberal economics background such as Andrew Shonfield and Mary Goldring). By the 1970s a new critical orthodoxy had emerged. The defence sector was seen as diverting investment and scarce-skilled labour from the rest of industry and misusing the resources at its disposal (Kaldor *et al.* 1986; Sandler and Hartley 1995). Its sheltered position within the British state encouraged inefficiencies, which not only resulted in unworkable weapons, but also tended to seep out and infect British industry (and workers) generally.[2] The 'Cold War' defence industry was seen as paradigmatic of many of the characteristic failings of British manufacturing. Not for nothing was the Peter Sellers' film about the idiocies of the British class system and their reflection in poor industrial relations and corporate corruption – *I'm All Right Jack* – set in an arms factory.

The generally negative assessment of the impact of defence spending on the UK economy has been reproduced by most observers in recent years (e.g. Lee 1996). But few have devoted much attention to the radical nature of the restructuring within the defence industry over the past decade, and it would be easy to get the quite false impression that nothing much has changed since the 1950s. In fact, after a series of modest but unsuccessful attempts to reform defence procurement under both Labour and Conservative governments, state–industry relations began to change significantly in the second term of the Thatcher Government. In the mid-1980s a new emphasis on competitive procurement was introduced in the form of the 'Levene Reforms' (Dunne and Schofield 1995). These aimed not merely to reduce costs, but also to encourage firms to take a more imaginative, active and long-termist approach to future markets, rather than continuing to rely on their friends within the British military-industrial establishment and on privileged access to UK public spending. The impact of the reforms was greatly strengthened in the later 1980s as UK defence procurement spending fell at a rate unprecedented since the end of the Second World War (Dunne and Smith 1993; Lovering 1993).

This new policy towards the defence industry was not derived from any new analysis of defence strategy or defence-industrial needs, but was essentially derivative of the wider neo-liberal strategy towards manufacturing and the public sector. Central to this was the attempt to reduce the power of state-dependent elites and bring about a new market order closer to the Liberal vision associated with Hayek and his disciples (see Cockett 1995). For economic liberals in the Thatcher Government the defence industry – characterized by corporatism, high level of unionization, lax industrial relations, and managements which were more concerned with engineering elegance than commercial criteria – was a prime example of the malign effects of the growth of a class dependent on public spending (see, for example, Alan Clark's *Diaries*, 1993). The particular character of the recent restructuring of the British defence industry would be profoundly influenced by the fact that it was near the forefront of the Thatcher Government's neo-Hayekian assault on 'collectivism'.

At first glance, the strategy was remarkably successful. The industry has been transformed in terms of its corporate structure, management behaviour and corporate culture, employment levels, marketing strategies, the organization of production and use of manufacturing technologies, and location. In the space of one decade, the defence sector has had to make adjustments which took other industries two or three. Not all companies have changed at the same pace, of course, but the leading survivors, especially the small number of major key contractors, have been through a revolutionary transformation and are now global players in the arms market.

But the reforms failed to realize the Hayekian goal of a withdrawal of the state. Instead, the state still plays a fundamental role, but one that differs in *form* from that of the Cold War era. The clue to the enduring scale of the state commitment to the defence sector lies in the contradictions of Thatcherism. In internal policy it attempted to impose a cultural revolution in economic affairs based on the liberal distaste for statism and high public spending. But in its external relations it was anxious to maintain the image of a powerful state and military actor within the 'Atlanticist' mould which had been endorsed by all postwar governments (with a brief exception under Edward Heath). To this end, it was felt to be essential that Britain retain a large and powerful arms industry. Consequently, while the government made great play in public of breaking with the traditional forms of support for the defence industry the reality was somewhat different. The Thatcher administration and its successors gave clear priority to the leading – now privatized – 'national champion' companies which were the beneficiaries of a number of large-scale national development or procurement programmes, in particular the Eurofighter. In addition, they were the main beneficiaries of a new export drive. A major increase in export sales was sought to help to square the circle: that is, to maintain a large and increasingly expensive defence industry without adding to public spending. The result was a series of huge government-to-government arms launched at the highest political levels (see WDM 1995; CAAT 1996). The Al Yamamah ('Dove') contracts with Saudi Arabia were followed by package deals with Malaysia and Indonesia, and then by numerous smaller contracts, especially in Pacific and subcontinental Asia. The Defence Export Services Organization (DESO) established by Labour in the 1960s was beefed up under the Conservatives in the 1980s and 1990s with the aim of promoting the British Defence Industry as a package, emulating similar policies in the US and in France. A number of large banks, notably the Midland, were successfully encouraged to be more supportive of defence exports. The Export Credit Guarantee Department became a major player in smoothing export deals, so much so that it was eventually implicated in both the 'Arms to Iraq' and the 'Pergau Dam' scandals (Norton-Taylor *et al.* 1996). Britain overtook France to become the world's second-largest arms exporter, behind only the US (although the US share also rose – from a quarter to a third – and the total volume of trade is below the late 1980s peak).

The New Labour Government in 1997 announced that it was committed to 'ending instability' in defence procurement and to reinforcing the Atlanticist defence strategy. But it marked a consolidation of, rather than a change in, the de facto industrial policy for the defence sector (Lovering 1998a). Without waiting a few months for the results of its own Defence review, the Blair Government promised to complete the Eurofighter project, approved the investment of £200m to underpin British participation in the forthcoming US Joint Strike Fighter programme (JSF), and announced that it would maintain existing substantial arms export programmes and support future ones (except to exceptionally nasty regimes, which fortunately are not major buyers).

THE RESTRUCTURING

It would be difficult to find any other industrial sector in Britain which has been through such a radical, rapid and wide-ranging transformation. Although there remain a number of problems and the future of individual companies is susceptible to a number of imponderables, there can be no doubt that the leading companies have become much more 'modern', robust and competitive in the 1990s. At the risk of oversimplification, these developments can be summarized as follows (see also Lovering 1996; OST 1995).

First, and most visibly, the companies have shed labour on a massive scale. If the British defence industry was one of the most overmanned in Europe in the early 1980s, the reverse is now the case (Wulf 1993). Whole layers of management have been removed, partly under the influence of the generic tendency to flatten hierarchies, and partly due to the reform of procurement practices that has allowed companies to remove bureaux which previously mirrored Ministry of Defence procurement departments. Table 9.1 illustrates the changing employment levels in some large producers (the increase in Hunting in 1993 was due to taking on responsibility for management of the British atomic weapons establishments under contract).

Second, a significant change has taken place in the way in which corporate strategies are developed in the industry. Defence companies are now much less like extramural government agencies and much more like market-responsive corporations in the civil sector. Corporate strategies clearly pay much more attention to marketing considerations than in the past, and the emphasis is firmly on *international* markets. Increasingly, domestic contracts are important less because they are sufficient in their own right than because they are a stepping stone

Table 9.1 Employment change in UK defence companies (000)

	1989	1990	1991	1992	1993	1994	1995	1996	1997	
BAe (defence)		49.8	46.7	33.5	33.5	31.5	30.8	30.0		end year
BAe (all)		127.4	123.2	87.4	87.4	46.5	44.0	47.0		annual averages
GEC (all)	102.7	74.7	84.9	75.4	64.9	59.1	56.4	57.1	52.3	
Hunting (defence)	2.07	2.66	2.33	2.05	6.84	7.96	7.45	7.14		
Hunting (all)	6.92	7.33	7.3	7.65	12.93	13.588	12.68	12.744		
Smiths (aero)	8.79	8.77	7.71	7.07	6.17	5.44	4.95	4.75		
Smiths (all)	13.61	13.61	2.11	11.58	11.54	10.98	11.72	12.2		
RR (aero)			33.8	30.7	27.9	24.5	25.5	25.1		
RR (all)			61.4	55.0	49.2	43.5	43.2	42.6		
Racal (UK only)		19.47	19.53	8.36	7.589	6.9	6.7	8.48	10.9	
Sum of above companies										
Defence or related			82.21	65.24	65.98	62.63	60.12	59.02		
Sum of total employees			308.44	245.39	233.559	180.568	174.7	180.14		

Defence divisions only	1991	1992	1993	1994	1995	1996	1997	
BAe (defence)	46.7	33.5	33.5	31.5	30.8	30.0		end year
RR (aero)	33.8	30.7	27.9	24.5	25.5	25.1		
Smiths (aero)	7.71	7.07	6.17	5.44	4.95	4.75		
SUM	88.21	71.27	67.57	61.44	61.25	59.85		

towards export sales. The product validation indicated by home sales is virtually essential when seeking arms export orders. Much of the debate over involvement in long-term collaborative programmes illustrates a clear desire to escape 'short-termism'.

Third, there has been a striking cultural change throughout the sector (although, naturally, considerable differences remain between individual companies). This is even evident in the physical work environment: offices once cluttered with photographs and models of science-fiction-like creations have been transformed into workplaces much like those which could be found in any company seeking to project a high-technology or modern image. The fashionable discourses of contemporary management are heard everywhere, including talk of the 'learning company', the imperative of 'globalization', and the need for 'networking' and 'partnerships' both within firms and across them. The executive suites which were populated a decade ago almost exclusively by men, many of them ex-generals or admirals from the armed services to which the companies traditionally sold their products, are now likely to be peopled by much younger people, including women, with accountancy, finance or marketing backgrounds. The key spokesperson on British Aerospace's defence investment strategy in recent years has been a young woman.

Fourth, at the level of production technologies and the technical division of labour, the industry has been intensely busy rationalizing capacity, installing new technologies, and reorganizing employment. In the larger companies this has often involved relocation and consolidation of the capacities of the constituent smaller companies, which has enabled the creation of units with larger production runs, in turn enabling the introduction of FMS and related 'neo-Fordist' patterns (a good example is the BAe plant at Lostock, Lancashire, a former propeller factory which is now a key site in the Anglo-French BAe-Matra missiles venture). It used to be said that the defence sector stood out as a field of craft skills and low-volume batch production. This may still be the case relative to consumer electronics, but it is much less the case than in the past. As the companies gradually replace work left over from Cold War contracts with new work developed in the context of large-scale international collaborative projects, the trend towards mass production (albeit in 'lean' forms) is likely to accelerate. If British firms secure their expected place in the forthcoming US Joint Strike Fighter programme, for example, the defence sector will find itself adopting production techniques linked to scales of production undreamed of before: the JSF programme, which is promised to be to the defence industry what the 'world car' was to the motor industry,[3] aims to achieve huge economies of scale by producing just one basic model, with production runs up to several hundred times greater than those the British military aircraft industry experienced in the Cold War period.

Fifth, these changes have been closely connected to the reform of industrial relations and employment practices, symbolized in the ubiquitous replacement of personnel departments by Human Resource Management, and the narrowing of the collective bargaining agenda. The massive job-shedding of the late 1980s and early 1990s enabled not only the reform of pay and incentive systems, but also purged the defence industry workforce of its more militant members, and had a salutary effect on the trades union leaderships. As the phase of de-manning came to an end the priority in employment policy shifted to attracting and retaining skills and building teamworking. Accordingly, some of the companies have abandoned the severe styles of labour management which characterized the early 1990s in favour of a new caring-sharing approach. In 1996–7 many of the major companies participated in a series of seminars hosted by the trades unions, at which they set out information concerning markets and competitors in the hope of encouraging union members to contribute their energies and ideas to the collective effort of building competitiveness. Several such sessions were hosted independently by MSF, the IPMS, and the TGWU, the latter under the heading of 'Partnership in Progress'.

In sum, if some defence firms are still characterized by relatively out-of-date production methods, lax employment systems and industrial relations, duplication of capacity, and pervasive inefficiency, then they are increasingly unrepresentative of the industry. Although many inefficiencies remain in the defence procurement system – especially on the part of the Ministry of Defence procurement executive and in some lingering Cold War weapons programmes (NAO 1997) – the core British defence companies have been through an extraordinary convulsion over the past decade, more revolutionary than at any time since the defence industry emerged in its modern form in the years immediately after the Second World War (Lovering 1996). One result is that they now find themselves to be leaders in their fields in Europe, and they are seeking to exploit this lead in shaping the restructuring of the European defence industry as a whole.

Europe versus America

The restructuring strategies adopted by UK companies have been heavily influenced by events in the US where the post-Cold War reconstruction of the arms industry began early and rapidly took an extremely radical form. In the space of three years following the 'Last Supper' conferences hosted by the Pentagon, a series of mega-mergers absorbed a dozen major contractors in the space into an enormously concentrated group of three very large companies: Lockheed-Martin-Loral, Boeing-McDonnell Douglas, and a third and looser group around Raytheon (the Lockheed group alone has annual sales of $30 billion, $47 billion of orders, and an annual R&D budget of $1 billion). Within Europe, only the UK has come close to emulating the dynamics of the US model, although at a much more modest level and pace. Here the industry has coalesced around two poles: GEC-Marconi, and British Aerospace, each of which is set within a complex network of collaborative production and development deals with other European and US companies, plus companies in Pacific Asia, South Africa, Australia, South America, and elsewhere.

The restructuring of the rest of the European defence industry has been extremely slow and somewhat directionless. Given that US defence procurement is almost twice as large that of Europe, while there are fewer than half as many prime contractors, a major rationalization of capacity is inevitable (CEC 1996). But attempts by companies to seize the moment and crystallize new cross-national corporate alliances have been hindered by uncertainties at national government levels and national variations in the nature of the industry, especially in employment terms (Grant 1997). In particular, the rationalization of the French defence industry has been delayed by lingering Gaullist protectionism. BAe and GEC, for example, have made several attempts to form new alliances with Thomson-CSF, Matra, GIAT, Aerospatiale, and Dassault, but the more radical plans have collapsed in the absence of clarification of the French government's procurement intentions, and the need to shed labour (many French defence workers have civil service status and UK companies are unwilling to become ensnared in the process of rationalization, having just completed it at home). Nevertheless, it would seem inevitable that the European combat aircraft industry will eventually be reformed early in the next decade around BAe, while GEC will have a central role in the reconstruction of European defence electronics (in 1997, GEC set up three joint ventures with Alenia Difensa, thereby gaining influence over 70 per cent of the Italian defence industry).

Yet at the same time, and even more probably, British companies are set to be significant actors within the American defence industry. Much of the so-called globalization of the arms industry is in fact the extension of linkages to US firms (Gold 1994; Lovering 1998a). British defence companies are well ahead of most of their European competitors in this race, with some 250 British companies already contracting directly to the US defence industry. While BAe has been tentatively exploring new alliances with European companies, it has also been working to transform its existing collaborative ventures with Lockheed into a full-scale transatlantic aerospace-defence company (B. Gray 1997).

The new relationship with the City

The British arms industries have ceased to be little more than a reactive industrial expression of decisions made within the armed service and the state. They have rapidly evolved into independent corporate actors, with much in common with civilian firms engaged in high technology oriented to international markets. One important signifier of this is that they have begun to establish a new relationship with finance capital.

As the creatures of national government protectionism, the defence industries of the Cold War were largely insulated from 'normal' capital markets. During the 1980s, as they began their painful transition, the defence firms had a hard time convincing the City that they really were viable profit-generating entities, and their share performance was markedly inferior to that of civilian firms (Dunne and Smith 1993). But more recently this seems to have changed. Finance capital has begun to look more favourably upon the leading edge of the arms industry (although the collapse of a major project could still trigger a relationship breakdown in a particular case). In this respect a lesson seems to have been learned from the US, where Wall Street eagerly embraced the government-triggered concentration of the defence industry into giant corporations. In Britain, the City's coolness towards defence companies took longer to thaw. But it now appears that GEC is beginning to replicate BAe's recent success in finding new allies in the City.

THE EVOLUTIONARY DYNAMICS OF INDUSTRIAL RESTRUCTURING

The modernization of defence manufacturing has involved more than improvements in the technical efficiency of the industry and changes in its corporate structure: it has also transformed its political economy. A key aspect has been the creation of privatized corporations out of formerly nationalized or effectively state-dependent units. This is part of a wider process of 'marketization' in defence, which has also seen private firms playing a role in providing military training, providing security at bases, and participating in government-funded R&D in the reformed Defence Evaluation and Research Agency, DERA (which has been given the new role of advising the MoD on procurement 'from a global defence industry').

In turn, the companies have become active players in the construction of new networks linking producers and customers internationally. In this respect, the modernization of the arms industry provides an illustration of the inherently unpredictable end-point of an evolutionary process. If the first effect of government support for the UK defence industry was to create new corporate entities empowered to act as autonomous decision-making actors, the second was to trigger a new dynamic as these companies – quite rationally – began to use this power according to their own assessment of opportunities and threats. As such, they are motivated by their survival interests as capitalist entities rather than by their role as the industrial embodiments of the social or national interest that was the rationale for government support in the first place. It is through the success or failure of the current flood of proposals for mergers, cross-national alliances, and the formation of real transnational companies that the shape of the defence industry of the next century – a cluster of core defence firms embedded in a new set of networks – will be determined.

It is important in the present context to notice that these experiments are not derived from any overall strategy for production – or for defence – imposed from above by any single public authority. They are driven by a diversity of corporate considerations and a corresponding variety of perceptions as to future possibilities. In short, the defence companies are active participants in the construction of their own future market- and policy-environment. They have become the key actors in the construction of a new globally concentrated arms industry. And one influence on this construction is the attempt to insulate the companies as far as possible from the vagaries of national democratic politics. Long-term cross-national collaboration can help companies to overcome what many of them see as the primary problem facing the defence industry in the 1990s: 'technical problems are not the issue, the fundamental point is the unreliability of politicians' (see Lovering 1998a). Collaboration protects both the arms industry and its customer armed forces against the risk of project cancellations by surrounding defence programmes with legal-technical formalities (subject to withdrawal penalties) and foreign policy agreements.

The irreducibly political nature of the defence market, plus its emphasis on secrecy and esoteric technologies, and the elevated role of professional 'experts' mean that the opportunities for companies to secure 'market closure' are likely to be greater than in most civilian markets. Since the companies are themselves the greatest repositories of technical knowledge on defence products, they have a major impact on the assessments of future equipment requirements that military planners must make (Kaldor 1990). The modernization of the defence industries has involved the construction of a new – internationalized – framework which is inherently susceptible to 'corporate capture'. One unintended feedback effect of the restructuring of the UK arms industry around a group of private corporations has been that the industry has devoted a considerable part of its efforts to seeking to influence government policy, both in its own right and as a step towards influencing other potential customers.

INDUSTRIAL MODERNIZATION IN AN OLD COUNTRY: COMBINING ELEMENTS OF THE OLD AND OF THE NEW

Neoclassical critics of defence industry policy have long maintained that the protectionism it has traditionally involved is likely to create a platform for special interests both within industry and also within the apparatus of the state (the armed services) (Hartley 1991; Sandler and Hartley 1995). It is now evident that similar effects can arise from a new-style industrial policy which focuses not on classic exclusionary protectionism, but on promoting the global competitiveness of a 'strategic industry'.

In the case of the British defence industry, one striking consequence has been that Britain's relative specialization in military production has increased while global defence spending has fallen (by a third since the mid-1980s peak). The changing political economy of arms production exhibits a curious example of 'path dependence', in which a rather ancient orientation towards militarism within the British state and British industry (Edgerton 1991) has been reinvented in a new era of globalization, information technologies and corporate autonomy. Britain has secured a larger share of a shrinking cake, but there is little to suggest that this has generated significant economic benefits. Modernization has turned around the major companies, as indicated in the growth of their export order books, share prices and corporate cash mountains. But it is unlikely to have improved their economic impact in the regions in which they are located. And it is unlikely that it has brought considerable benefits to the rest of British industry. While there is no comprehensive research to draw upon here, it seems inevitable that the increased emphasis on internationalizing inputs, and the political need to locate some production facilities in main export markets, implies that a greater share of the shrinking volume of work remaining in the defence industry is being done outside the UK.

One consequence of this is a 'hollowing-out' of the defence companies. Large prime contractors such as British Aerospace (like competitors such as Daimler Benz Aerospace) are increasingly losing their manufacturing identity, and deliberately so, as they seek to become global specialists in systems integration drawing on component production and assembly skills on the international level. BAe for example is becoming more of a management structure and design facility than a set of manufacturing units. This has implications for both the level, and the type, of employment within the defence industry in Britain. The emphasis is shifting to the recruitment and retention of core groups of engineers, and related marketeers, rather than classic production skills. As cross-national alliances and companies become the core structures in the defence industry, subject to their own corporate governance rather than controlled by national governments, the allocation of labour to tasks falls under new principles. Symptomatically, BAe, for example, has insisted that within Airbus Industry (which is likely to develop a military offshoot) senior executives should be selected on 'objective' commercial criteria, rather than 'a European version of Buggins turn' (Shapinker and Gray 1997). The modernization of manufacturing in the defence sector clearly implies a reduction in the employment impact at the national and regional levels, and the consolidation of an emergent international labour market elite (both in the sense that a number of individuals build careers by moving through a variety of sites involved in international collaborative projects, and in the sense that a cohort of skilled individuals are marketable internationally rather than solely in their home country). It also raises the question of how long it will remain meaningful to describe these as 'manufacturing' companies.

The recent history of the defence industry challenges a number of simplistic assumptions about British industry. It shows, for example, that supposedly sluggardly British manufacturers can modernize themselves very rapidly in terms of internal organization, and of external behaviour, once it is recognized that the old ways of doing things are no longer viable. It also reveals the 'balancing act' which British firms – probably uniquely – have to perform as between European and non-European markets. For most defence firms, the consolidation of the Europe defence market is a tantalizing possibility, but, as noted earlier, the costs of getting involved with European companies are off-putting and the gains are imponderable. Access to the much larger US market is difficult, but the potential rewards are clearly much greater.

The defence industry case also throws some instructive light on changing government–industry relations. Although the arms companies are rapidly ceasing to be deviants from industrial norm as they adopt styles of management, marketing, and employment which are generic in modern industry, they continue to rely on the active support of the home state. But this is not unique to defence. There is much about evolving state–industry relations in this sector which echoes relations in other sectors where the customer is a major public body and the high-technology nature of the product requires long-term large-scale investment (see, for example, Cawson *et al.* 1990). The leading defence companies cite international *civil* companies such as GEC-Alsthom or Airbus Industries, which combine uncompromisingly commercial internal practices with close cooperation with a plurality of national governments, as models which the defence industry is likely to emulate.

DEFENCE INDUSTRY MODERNIZATION AND THE UK ECONOMY

The modernization of the defence industry has kept Britain as a major military actor, and has, moreover, created new pressures to influence government policies and to further encourage the leading defence companies to deepen their specializations in military production. One does not have to be a signed-up member of the Peace Movement to conclude that this is not entirely a Good Thing.

For example, if one wanted to maintain the present level of defence-industrial capacity, it would probably have been better to achieve it differently. Rather than creating a defence-specialized group of companies, defence production could have been diluted into a wider pool of generic high-technology capacity, as is the case in Japan, for example (Samuels 1994). This would reduce the exposure of individual companies to changes in particular defence markets or contract cancellations. More importantly in view of the discussion above, it would reduce the companies' interest in seeking out purely military markets and also reduce their ability to exert pressure on governments by presenting themselves as vital national security assets.

Alternatively, if the goal is to secure the best weapons at least cost, the 'internationalization' could have taken a much more radical form – buying the much cheaper Russian aircraft, or American missiles, for example. The promiscuous internationalization pursued by British defence companies and underwritten by defence-industrial policy has given 'internationalization' a very different slant. As a result, it may not be long before the question, 'What contribution does the defence sector make to British manufacturing and the wider national economy?', is of less practical interest to the decision makers who determine the development of the industry than the question, 'What contribution does the British economy make to the international defence industry?', the latter being largely a euphemism for a US-centred corporate network.

In some important respects the defence industry has exemplified the kinds of 'modernization' which the 'Manufacturing Matters' school would like to see adopted more widely. But the effects, I suggest, have hardly been what they would hope for. Some of the leading companies have been transformed and are no doubt good models in various fields, but the industry as a whole probably generates fewer real benefits to British firms and employees in return for the lavish funding it still receives, than it did in the past. The benefits of improved competitiveness, other than to a small constituency of senior staffs and shareholders in the leading companies and their major UK subcontractors, are not obvious. The most commonly cited national economic benefit is to the balance of payments through export earnings. But even here the true net effect is a matter of considerable doubt, since it is necessary to take into account complex flows of aid, credit guarantees, and so forth, on which the evidence is lacking (see WDM 1995; Cooper 1997). One of the few things that is clear about the defence industry is that the practical governance of the sector, and hence its future direction of investment, product development, employment, and relationships to other UK industry and service sectors, has become more opaque and less accountable.

CONCLUDING THOUGHTS

One conclusion to be drawn from recent experience in the defence industry is that the idea that British economic problems can be attributed to conflicts between industry and the City is grossly simplistic. It confirms Barratt Brown's (1988) point, against Perry Anderson, that it is quite wrong to suggest that the state and the City have been consistent enemies of British industry. Not all of British industry is floundering in a policy vacuum, or lagging behind its German or Pacific Asian competitors. It is not helpful to talk of industry or manufacturing as if it is a homogenous entity, or as if it is entirely autonomous of finance capital. The defence industry case also shows that it is increasingly questionable to generalize about 'manufacturing', as some of the leading British examples are in effect becoming business-service industries rather than direct producers.

At a policy level, the defence industry case provides plenty of fuel for the suspicion of liberal critics such as Krugman (1996) that a 'strategic trade' bias in favour of manufacturing can easily end up conferring arbitrary favours on particular firms, to the detriment of everyone else. The risk of 'corporate capture' is not exclusive to defence. This suggests that it is not enough to insist that 'Manufacturing Matters' without first clarifying the criteria that determine *which* industries should be addressed, *which* of the many possible routes to competitiveness they should be encouraged to adopt, and what costs are acceptable to these ends.

Perhaps the most interesting feature of the defence industry case is the 'Pandora's box' effect, whereby a new and inherently indeterminate corporate evolutionary dynamic has been set in motion as a result of a supportive industrial policy. This too is not likely to be exclusive to the defence sector; given the current context of an international search for markets and the ubiquity of corporate networking, it is increasingly difficult to predict the long-term effects of any policy intended to boost industrial competitiveness. The defence industry case illustrates the dangers of a 'minimalist' version of such a policy which promotes the modernization of manufacturing without framing this within a broader regulatory context. It shows the dangers of developing supportive structures to enable firms to adapt better to market forces without considering how such interventions may impact on those market forces.

To borrow an analogy from the defence field, to urge greater support for manufacturing from government, the City, and industry, and service providers ranging from private business services to the educational system, in the cause of something called 'Competitiveness', is rather like encouraging troops to fight harder without devoting adequate attention to the question of what battles they are going to fight. They may respond by moving on to fight very different battles from those their supporters had in mind. If there is a case for special measures to promote manufacturing, it needs to be articulated within much more searching debate over the purpose and likely effects of industrial intervention than that which is encouraged by the current discourse centred on the extremely woolly concept of 'Competitiveness,'[4] and the increasingly questionable category of 'manufacturing'.

NOTES

1 If the industry is defined more narrowly as the production of equipment items only (i.e. excluding non-equipment items such as fuels, clothing) it employs some 305,000 people. These figures are generated by MoD calculations based on estimates of the employment intensity of defence contracts, estimates which are derived from a sample of prime contractors and are therefore approximate.

2 Against this, a Marxist counter-orthodoxy held that defence spending and the defence sector played a useful role in resolving capitalism's contradictions by exerting a counter-cyclical macroeconomic effect, and by legitimizing state involvement in the creation of new technologies which the free market would otherwise fail to bring about (Kidron 1970)

3 JSF will be the largest arms project in the world in the new century. US sales of $100 billion are anticipated on a production run of 2,900 aircraft, and some suggest that as much again could be earned from exports.

4 The notion of the competitiveness of a territory elides the profitability of individual firms located on it with the economic interests of the resident population (a crudity repeated every year by the UK government in the annual White Papers on Competitiveness). To advocate national or regional development policies to raise competitiveness by promoting businesses is to fudge the question; which businesses? At the regional and urban level, with the establishment of new development agencies in order to promote local competitiveness, this question is now becoming acute.

REFERENCES

Anderson, P. (1992) *English Questions*, London: Verso.

Anderson, P. and Mann, N. (1997) *Safety First: The Making of New Labour*, London: Granta Books.

Brown, M. B. (1988) 'Away with all the great arches: Anderson's History of British Capitalism', *New Left Review*, 167, 22–51

CAAT (1996) *Killing Jobs*, Campaign Against Arms Trade, 11 Goodwin Street, London N4 3HQ.

Cawson, A., Morgan, K., Webber, K., Holmes, P. and Stevens, A. (1990) *Hostile Brothers: Competition and Closure in the European Electronics Industry*, Oxford: Clarendon Press.

CEC (1993) *Competition, Growth, Employment*, Brussels: Commission of the European Communities.

—— (1996) *The Challenges Facing the European Defence-Related Industry: A Contribution for Action at European Level*, Brussels: Commission of the European Communities, COM(96) 10 final.

Chalmers, M. (1985) *Paying for Defence: Military Spending and British Decline*, London: Pluto.

Clark, A. (1993) *Diaries*, London: Phoenix House.

Cockett, R. (1995) *Thinking the Unthinkable: Think-Tanks and the Economic Counter Revolution 1931–1983*, London: HarperCollins.

Cooper, N. (1997) 'The cost of UK defence exports', paper to conference on The Globalisation of European Military Industry and the Arms Trade, Middlesex University, 19–20 September. (Consult author for draft, c/o Dept of Politics, University of Plymouth.)

Dunne, J.P. and Schofield, S. (1995) 'Contracts, competition and performance in the UK defence industry', Discussion Paper series no. 16, School of Economics, Middlesex University.

Dunne, J.P. and Smith, R.P. (1993) 'Thatcherism and the UK defence industry', in J. Michie (ed.), *1979–1992: The Economic Legacy*, London: Academic Press, 91–111.

Edgerton, D. (1991) 'Liberal militarism and the British state', *New Left Review*, **185**, 138–69.

Fine, B. and Harris, L. (1985) *The Peculiarities of the British Economy*, London: Lawrence & Wishart.

Gold, D. (1994) 'The internationalisation of military production', *Peace Economics, Peace Science, and Public Policy*, **1** (3), 1–12.

Grant, C. (1997) 'Linking arms: survey of the global defence industry', *Economist*, 14 June.

Gray, B. (1997) 'BAe takes a billion-dollar gamble', *Financial Times*, 19 June.

Gray, J. (1997) *Endgames: Questions in Late Modern Political Thought*, Oxford: Polity Press.

Hartley, K. (1991) *The Political Economy of Defence Spending*, London: Brassey's.

Ingham, G. (1984) *Capitalism Divided: The City and Industry in British Social Development*, London: Macmillan.

Kaldor, M. (1990) *The Imaginary War: Understanding the East–West Conflict*, Oxford: Blackwell.

Kaldor, M., Sharp, M. and Walker, W. (1986) 'Industrial competitiveness and Britain's defence', *Lloyds Bank Review*, October, 31–49.

Kelly, G., Kelly, D. and Gamble, A. (eds) (1997) *Stakeholder Capitalism*, London: Macmillan.

Kidron, M. (1970) *Western Capitalism since the War*, Harmondsworth: Penguin.

Krugman, P. (1996) *Pop Internationalism*, Cambridge, Mass.: MIT Press.

Lee, S. (1996) 'Manufacturing', in D. Coates (ed.), *Industrial Policy in Britain*, London: Macmillan.

Lovering, J. (1993) 'Restructuring the British defence industrial base after the Cold War: institutional and geographical perspectives', *Defence Economics*, **4**, 123–39.

—— (1996) 'Mixed blessings: unmaking and remaking the British arms industry', in R. Turner (ed.), *From the Old to the New: The British Economy in Transition*, London: Routledge, 88–122.

—— (1998a) 'Labour and the defence industry: allies in "Globalisation"', *Capital and Class* (forthcoming).

—— (1998b) 'The European defence industry: economic governance without government?', *Journal of European Integration* (forthcoming).

Mayes, D. with Soteri, S. (1994) 'Does manufacturing matter?', in T. Buxton, P. Chapman and P. Temple (eds), *Britain's Economic Performance*, London: Routledge, pp. 373–96.

Morris, A.J.A. (1984) *The Scaremongers: The Advocacy of War and Rearmament 1896–1914*, London: Routledge and Kegan Paul.

NAO (1997) *1996 Major Project Report*, London: National Audit Office

Norton-Taylor, R., Lloyd, M. and Cook, S. (1996) *Knee Deep in Dishonour: The Scott Report and its Aftermath*, London: Gollancz.

OST (Office of Science and Technology) (1995) *Technology Foresight 12: Defence and Aerospace*, London: HMSO.

Samuels, R. (1994) *Rich Nation, Strong Army: National Security and the Technological Transformation of Japan*, Ithaca, NY: Cornell University Press.

Sandler, T. and Hartley, K. (1995) *Cambridge Surveys of Economic Literature: The Economics of Defense*, Cambridge: Cambridge University Press.

Shapinker, M. and Gray, B. (1997) 'BAe calls for headhunters to be used by Airbus', *Financial Times*, 27 February.

Storper, M. (1993) 'Regional "worlds" of production: learning and innovation in the technology districts of France, Italy and the USA', *Regional Studies*, 27, 433–55.

Taylor, T. and Hayward, K (1989) *The UK Defence Industrial Base*, London: Brassey's.

Tyson, L.D'A. (1992) *Who's Bashing Whom? Trade Conflict in High-Technology Industries*, Washington, DC: Institute for International Economics.

WDM (1995) *Gunrunners Gold*, World Development Movement, 25 Beehive Place, London SW9 7QR.

Weiner, M. (1981) *English Culture and the Decline of the Industrial Spirit, 1850–1980*, Cambridge: Cambridge University Press.

Wulf, H. (ed.) (1993) *Arms Industry Limited*, London: SIPRI/Oxford University Press.

10 The political economy of manufacturing change in the regions

Andy Pike and John Tomaney

INTRODUCTION[1]

'Deindustrialization', the growth of disparities between and within regions in the level and nature of manufacturing activity and jobs, and the geographically uneven shift towards a 'service economy', have been clearly evident within the UK and across the EU (CEC 1996). The manufacturing sector has been – and continues to be – reshaped by pressures including 'globalization', 'tertiarization', industrial reorganization, employment change, accelerated technical development, and shifting policy frameworks. At the heart of these issues is a regional dimension which often conditions the development of the manufacturing sector as a whole.

A recognition of the importance of manufacturing has a long tradition in regional economic development. Kaldor's 'flywheel of growth' (1972) captures the image of the sector as a motor of sustainable regional development through output, employment, trade, investment performance and the sector's potential for productivity growth and technical progress. As Coates (1994: 18) notes, 'it is still the competitive strength of UK-based manufacturing industry which holds the key to *local* prosperity, employment and growth both inside and beyond the manufacturing sector' (original emphasis). Recent debates concerning manufacturing more broadly have therefore had a bearing on regional economic development questions. The collapse in the importance of manufacturing to both employment and GDP in the UK compares badly with competitor nations. Between 1984 and 1994, the contribution of manufacturing to employment fell from 33 per cent to 26 per cent and to GDP declined from 35 per cent to 28 per cent (OECD 1996). Manufacturing in France and Germany have illustrated less steep declines, while the US and Japan have held their own. The balance of trade in manufactures has also worsened, and compares unfavourably with other industrialized countries. Despite rises in exports, imports have increased at faster rates (House of Commons 1994b).

A shift is discernible in more recent analyses of these dimensions of the UK's manufacturing problem from a picture of generalized 'decline' towards 'underperformance'. This angle is based on three premises: the decline in competitiveness of key manufacturing sectors; the 'negative deindustrialization' of falling contributions to output, exports (declining into deficit since 1983) and employment based on a lack of industrial dynamism and poor performance; and a general slowness to modernize (Coates 1994; Rowthorn and Wells 1987). This cocktail of maladies has had particular regional expressions, and, in turn, has been influenced by the uneven structure of manufacturing activity in the UK regions.

Our aim in this chapter is to illustrate how the broad transformations occurring in the manufacturing sector have been constituted geographically. We begin by painting a broad picture of the long-run evolution of manufacturing in the regions. Drawing on the pressures bearing on the manufacturing sector, we then go on to explore the regional experience of a historically significant manufacturing region, the Northeast of England, in relation to the nature and impact of inward and outward investment, tertiarization and the place of manufacturing in the regional and national economy, the structure of manufacturing industry and the role of Research and Development (R&D), entrepreneurship and finance. Finally, shifting policy priorities, including likely future directions, are examined.

MANUFACTURING IN THE REGIONS

The regional structure of manufacturing has evolved through historically accumulated rounds of investment which have created particular geographical – or spatial – divisions of labour over time (Massey 1995). From the industrial revolution, regions were often specialized in particular industries – textiles in Lancashire, coal, steel and shipbuilding in the Northeast – and grew rapidly, benefiting from the positive externalities of proximity. In the postwar period, rounds of investment overlaid a more pronounced specialization amongst regions based upon particular functions; assembly or manufacturing branch plants tended to be located in 'peripheral' or depressed regions far from 'core' regions endowed with headquarters and R&D facilities (Massey 1995). Regional convergence in output and employment marked this so-called Golden Age of growth in the 1950s and 1960s. Disparities and regional divergence characterized the fragmentation of economic growth trajectories, beginning in the early 1970s and intensifying in the 1980s, where the rationalization and closure associated with deindustrialization were pronounced in the manufacturing regions (Martin and Rowthorn 1986). In particular, inter-regional 'North–South' and intra-regional 'urban–rural' divides emerged in the location and growth of manufacturing industry (Martin and Tyler 1992). By 1986, the heartland manufacturing regions were the West Midlands, followed by the East Midlands, Northwest and the Northern region (Figure 10.1).

The mid- to late 1980s witnessed a revived interest in the agglomeration of manufacturing activities and the alleged return to regional industrial specialization in more localized 'districts' (Harrison 1994). By the early to mid-1990s, discussion of these localized structures were situated in the context of globalizing tendencies. An emphasis on mosaics of regionalized 'clusters' and 'learning regions', capable of innovative responses to heightened change and uncertainty, has been evident (Cooke 1995; Storper and Scott 1995).

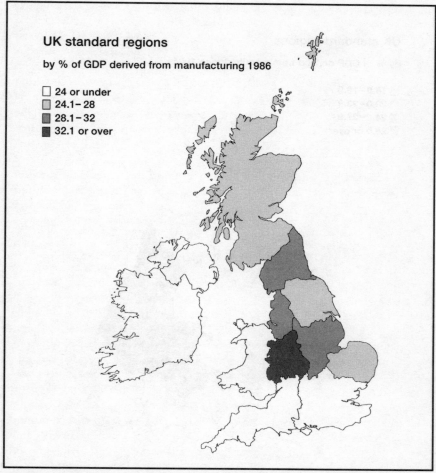

Figure 10.1 Percentage of gross domestic product derived from manufacturing (1986)
Source: CSO (1988: 133).
Note: Factor cost at current prices.

Against this backdrop of change, manufacturing activity in the UK remains regionally uneven, and the map of pronounced manufacturing regions has been redrawn. A careful comparison with 1986 reveals that, by 1994, the West Midlands had retained its heartland role, while manufacturing had increased in relative importance within the East Midlands and Northern region as well as, to a lesser extent, Yorkshire and Humberside and Wales (Figure 10.2). In addition, some evidence points to the emergence of localities within these regions that are specialized to an extent in particular sectors or contain related 'clusters' of firms sometimes overlapping traditional sectoral definitions. These include electronics in Scotland (Turok 1993) and electronics and automotive components in Wales

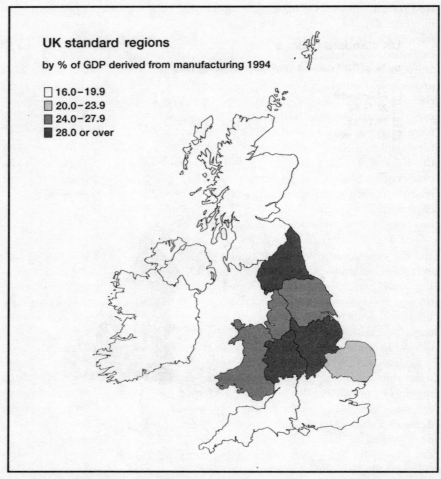

UK standard regions

by % of GDP derived from manufacturing 1994

☐ 16.0–19.9
▨ 20.0–23.9
▦ 24.0–27.9
■ 28.0 or over

Figure 10.2 Percentage of gross domestic product derived from manufacturing (1994)
Source: CSO (1996: 182).
Note: Factor cost at current prices.

(Cooke 1995). However, these localized manufacturing economies are often inserted into resilient hierarchical structures, more associated with traditional geographical functional divisions of labour, which are now often operating not only at the national level, but also increasingly at European and even global scales.

The trajectory of change in the Northeast of England

The broad transformations occurring within the economy and the manufacturing sector develop unevenly between and within regions. The manufacturing heartland regions have experienced great upheaval in their socio-economic structures in recent decades. The Northeast is a prime example. The condition of manufacturing within the region is bound up with national trends in the sector but also exhibits its own particularities accrued through its historical development.

By the mid to late nineteenth century the Northeast had emerged as a fast-growing and innovative region. This growth was stimulated by an interrelated complex of coal, steel, shipbuilding and engineering industries, with a strong export orientation (McCord 1979). These industries for the most of the nineteenth century were supported by a local financial system, although by the century's end, the Northeast's financial system was increasingly under the control of the Bank of England and the City of London. Moreover, by the end of the nineteenth century the region's main industries were beginning to underperform relative to their competitors in Germany and the US. This period, then, was characterized by falling investment, a failure to modernize and rationalize, and a loss of technological leadership in key sectors.

The period after the First World War saw the collapse of traditional industries and the emergence of mass unemployment. At the same time, the rise of new industries tended to occur elsewhere, such as the West Midlands or Southeast of England. Despite the scale of the crisis in the Northeast and other regions, conditions generated only a very limited policy response from government and the now London-dominated financial institutions. It was the Second World War and the concomitant increase in demand for the region's traditional products which led to renewed growth in the region's economy that continued into the 1950s.

Since the 1950s, though, it has been the decline of traditional industries – coal, steel, shipbuilding and heavy engineering – which has lain at the core of the region's employment problem. Most decline occurred under state ownership or following external acquisition, and reflected both shifts in the structure of the demand (for instance, the shift from a coal-based economy to an oil- and gas-based one, leading to falling employment in mining) and a 'competitive failure' in the face of foreign rivalry (for example, shipbuilding and heavy engineering) (Hudson 1989). Thus there was nothing 'inevitable' about the nature or pace of decline in the traditional industries.

The region saw two sharp falls in coal-mining employment, in the 1960s and again in the late 1980s and early 1990s. Shipbuilding and heavy engineering experienced an employment rundown which accelerated from the end of the 1970s, although, unlike coal-mining, these latter two industries still have a presence in the industrial structure. While in the 1970s the traditional sectors did benefit, to some degree, from national policy support, this all but disappeared in the 1980s (Hayward and Tomaney 1997). This legacy of decline is the background to the reformulation of manufacturing in the region.

FROM 'WORKSHOP OF THE WORLD' TO . . . ?

The condition of the manufacturing sector in the UK has often been taken as a bellwether of the position of the UK in the putative international economic order

(Coates 1994). An emergent 'globalization' thesis has received recent attention in this context. It seeks to describe the current situation of often unprecedented uncertainty, increasingly rapid and ongoing institutional and technological change, the apparent ease with which factors of production can be mobilized across national boundaries, and the heightened interdependency between economies (Allen 1995; Hirst and Thompson 1996). The thrust of this fashionable argument remains in question. Notwithstanding the often momentous changes, corporate forms remain divergent between nations, particularly with respect to internal governance and long-term financing (Pauly and Reich 1997). There is also much evidence to support the more qualified world-view of national political economies inserted into an international economy, increasingly structured into supra-national 'blocs', and marked by tensions concerning economic and political rivalry, dominance and leadership (Michie and Grieve Smith 1995; Zysman 1996).

It is in this context that we can question the situation of manufacturing within the UK and its regions within the emerging international division of labour. The historic openness of the UK economy and its place within the EU has made inward and outward investment in the manufacturing sector a key issue for the national economy. The UK is a globally significant destination and source of FDI flows. The gross figures for all sectors reveal that, between 1984 and 1994, inflows increased from −$241m (−0.06% of GDP) to $11,066m (1.1% of GDP) while outflows increased from $8,039m (1.86% of GDP) to $29,721m (2.93% of GDP) (current prices) (OECD 1996). The inward and outward balance shifts over time, and the most recent attention focused on manufacturing competitiveness and the import and export of jobs (House of Commons 1994a, 1994b). Clearly these issues have great bearing on the prospects for regional economic development.

Inward investment

Inward investment has risen to a primary significance in considering questions of regional manufacturing growth and the regeneration of declining economies (Hudson 1995). Debate has focused on the degree of 'embeddedness' within regional economies, in terms of acknowledging the social influence upon economic outcomes as well as the extent of economic and institutional linkages (Oinas 1997). Proponents of inward investment focus on the output, jobs and investment that new investors bring to regional economies within their factories and supplier networks. Benefits are seen through the application of 'greenfield' development strategies employing leading-edge technology, localized purchasing, links to indigenous sectors, often through technology transfer, and a 'demonstration effect' through the supply chain (Coopers and Lybrand Deloitte 1991). Sceptics point to renewed dependencies upon branch plant economies in a 'global' context where capital is increasingly mobile and 'footloose'. Other issues question the value-added content of output, the assembly of imported components, the quality of jobs, the limited and often bulky, low-value local sourcing, the modest technological development functions, and the problems of linkage and adjustment among indigenous firms and 'brownfield' sites (Pike 1996; see also Delbridge *et al.* in Chapter 12 in this volume). The influence of investors upon the agendas of local institutional structures and the context of intensified inter-regional competition for mobile investment, particularly at the expanding EU level, are also interpreted as significant (Pike and Tomaney 1996).

The Northern region (Northeast and Cumbria) has received a disproportion-ate share of inward investment among the English regions, reflected in the jobs created during the 1980s, although Northern Ireland, Scotland and Wales have a higher share of regional manufacturing employment accounted for by foreign firms (Table 10.1). Wage costs relative to value added per employee in manu-facturing have also become less 'competitive' than several other regions through-out the 1980s (Table 10.2). The UK's attractions to mobile capital have comprised relatively low labour and social costs, but also sufficient workforce skills and education to provide acceptable quality and productivity levels, as well as low corporate taxation, the deregulated environment, easy exit (particularly with regard to hiring and firing labour), and the English language. The Northeast in particular has supplemented these attractions with the infrastructure, sites, rela-tively flexible incentive regime, targeted marketing from dedicated investment promotion agencies (for example, Northern Development Company (NDC)), and labour surplus. Indeed, the abundant labour and regional support framework attracted an initial wave of inward investment from the US and relocations within the UK in the 1960s and 1970s, including household names, such as Caterpillar and Courtaulds. Many of these plants (including the two just mentioned) experi-enced retrenchment and closure in the early 1980s recession, although some have survived, including firms such as Black & Decker, which employs over 2,000 at its plant in the region. A second wave of investment from the Asia-Pacific bloc followed in the mid- to late 1980s and 1990s, including Fujitsu, Nissan, Komatsu (formerly the Caterpillar factory) and Samsung, which offset at least some of the losses associated with the earlier wave, and has been supplemented by European investment more recently, most notably Siemens. Entry mechanisms have included large 'greenfield' sites, which generate greatest publicity, but also important is acquisition, often incorporating takeovers of locally owned com-panies, and joint venture.

Direct employment in foreign-owned manufacturing (FOM) firms in the Northern region reached 55,700 in 1993, and its share of manufacturing employment rose from 12 per cent in 1979 to 23 per cent in 1993 (Stone 1993). However, net employment change in FOM firms was only 6,455 between 1979 and 1993. To some extent, this modest net employment growth reflects both the final assembly orientation of much of the investment and its linkage to the vagar-ies of trading conditions in export markets. Inward investors have tended to create full-time, male employment, although recently inward investment has come in the form of teleservice centres, and here, jobs are frequently more oriented to women and are more likely to be part-time. Within manufacturing, however, spillover effects are evident, often through the supply chain and labour market.

Table 10.1 New jobs promoted by foreign firms investing in the UK (1981–90)

| | Jobs promoted[1] | | Relative concentration index[3] (UK = 100) | Estimated jobs created[2] | |
	Total ('000)	Share of UK total (%)		Total of region's manufacturing employees ('000)	As %
The South of England					
Southeast and East Anglia	21.5	9.8	39.1	16.1	1.2
Southwest	11.2	5.1	69.4	8.6	2.1
The Midlands					
West Midlands	29.6	13.6	104.8	19.4	2.7
East Midlands	10.5	4.8	51.3	6.9	1.4
The North of England					
Yorks and Humberside	9.2	4.2	43.1	6.2	1.2
Northwest	15.5	7.1	57.6	10.6	1.6
North	23.5	10.8	205.1	17.0	5.9
The periphery					
Wales	30.1	13.8	298.5	22.2	8.8
Scotland	52.2	23.9	308.1	36.1	8.5
Northern Ireland	14.8	6.8	343.8	8.0	7.5
United Kingdom	218.7	100.0	100.0	151.4	2.9

Source: Department of Trade and Industry, cited in House of Commons (1995).

Notes:
[1] Jobs promoted are those promised by the firm. Normally, 100 per cent of jobs approved do not materialize as actual jobs. Also, those jobs that are created will not all appear in the same year as they are approved.
[2] Estimated jobs are computed by assuming that 75 per cent of approvals in each year convert to actual jobs over the following three-year period. The estimates use approvals data back to 1979. For Northern Ireland the conversion rate is 40 per cent.
[3] Estimated jobs are computed by assuming that 75 per cent of approvals in each year convert to actual jobs over the following three-year period. The estimates use approvals data back to 1979. For Northern Ireland the conversion rate is 40 per cent.

Table 10.2 Wage costs relative to value added per employee in manufacturing (UK = 100)

Region	1980	1986	1990
Southeast	99	101	101
East Anglia	102	96	100
Southwest	117	102	109
East Midlands	105	101	102
West Midlands	108	101	104
Yorkshire–Humberside	99	100	99
Northwest	98	98	95
North	97	104	102
Wales	106	92	92
Scotland	99	96	94
Northern Ireland	115 (110)	101 (97)	99 (92)
United Kingdom	100	100	100

Source: BSO Census of Production cited in House of Commons (1995: 155).
Note: Wages per employee divided by gross value added per employee adjusted for the composition of industry at four digit level of the SIC.
Low values indicate favourable cost competitiveness.
Northern Ireland figures in parentheses exclude state-owned companies.

Foreign-owned manufacturing firms have higher rates of productivity than UK-owned firms, but their utilization of manufacturing systems and working practices are only marginally more innovative than UK firms (Stone and Peck 1996). Local purchasing varies with sector, vintage of investment and regulatory context of 'local' (EU) content requirements as well as the extent to which assemblers are rationalizing their supply chains. Nissan, for example, makes significant purchases among its largely foreign-owned 'doorstep' suppliers due to the growth of outsourcing in the automotive sector and its synchronous production strategy, the 'localization' corporate strategy, the plant's history in the region, and the need to meet 80 per cent EU 'local' content regulations (Lagendijk *et al.* 1996). Elsewhere, allusions to 'global' sourcing have often been utilized as a threat designed to squeeze further cost reductions from existing suppliers under the threat of the business going offshore. Other investors, such as the wafer fab plants of Siemens and Fujitsu, have somewhat limited local purchasing of materials and tend to procure only lower-level services within the region.

Outward investment

Outward investment has been allied to a debate concerning the 'hollowing out' of manufacturing in the UK (Williams *et al.* 1990). As noted above, outward flows of investment have proceeded apace in recent years. In particular, investment has been shifted offshore by the increasingly concentrated UK-owned manufacturing sector, often including firms with substantial regionally concentrated operations from the past legacy of public ownership and/or regional policy assisted relocation. For the Northeast, ICI in Teesside is a case in point (see also Beynon *et al.* 1994). ICI's employment has shrunk significantly, reflecting shifts in the company's strategy. ICI has invested heavily overseas, especially in Southeast Asia where, unlike Europe, high levels of economic growth have sustained the demand for bulk chemicals. Within the UK, the company has tended to divest its low-margin, bulk and commodity chemicals and, instead, has invested in higher-margin, speciality chemicals and pharmaceuticals. Indeed, ICI placed most of its high-value activities into a separate company, Zeneca.

This strategy has not generally favoured Teesside which, historically, has been a site for bulk chemical production (Cleveland County Council 1994). In addition to running down its own operations, ICI has sold off parts of its massive Wilton complex to rival chemical firms such as BASF, Union Carbide and Du Pont, and disposed of its 300-strong maintenance division to Redpath Engineering, now part of Kvaerner. The disposal of these assets in each case was associated with significant job losses. At the same time, Zeneca has relatively few operations on Teesside. Here, regional manufacturing has been restructured through a complex and interlinked pattern of inward and outward investment.

'TERTIARIZATION' AND THE PLACE OF MANUFACTURING

> I think the manufacturing base is a critical part of the economy, but it is not the only part of the economy we are concerned with. We are concerned with all the wealth-creating aspects of the economy, and the manufacturing base will get a very proper share of our attention, but in many of the things we do we will be helping the service industries as much.
>
> (Rt. Hon. Michael Heseltine, former President of the Board of Trade, cited in House of Commons 1994c: 400)

The previous Government's ambivalence towards support for specific industrial sectors reflected its horizontal, supply-side approach to industrial policy. Significantly, this commitment to *laissez-faire* took a benign view of the structural shift in advanced economies towards services, or 'tertiarization' (Marshall 1992; Lawson 1992), which had gathered so much pace in recent years, particularly in the UK of the 1980s. While the contribution of manufacturing to employment and GDP has plummeted in the UK, services have grown from 64 per cent to 72 per cent and 63 per cent to 71 per cent respectively between 1984 and 1994 (OECD 1996). This is a comparable performance to the US and France, but it is greater than that of Germany's and Japan's relatively low-productivity service sectors. Debates concerning post-industrialism and the relative unimportance of manufacturing have, as a consequence, persisted. This traditional controversy stretches back to the Selective Employment Tax of the 1960s (Greenhalgh *et al.* 1989). In this chapter we agree with much of the 'manufacturing matters' argument (Cohen and Zysman 1987; see Chapter 1 in this volume); the debate should not be about manufacturing *or* services since at the heart of most dynamic modern economies is a strong manufacturing sector, capable of generating growth, and providing spin-off benefits to reinforce service growth. The problem in the UK is that the relative shrinkage and neglect of the manufacturing sector has raised questions of its viability and problems of capacity and balance of payments constraints (Michie and Kitson 1996). In addition, the nature of 'tertiarization', in terms of the level and type of jobs and their 'footloose' nature, and the links between the service and manufacturing sectors, remain key issues. It is these questions that have very real consequences for local employment and prosperity.

'Tertiarization' has been experienced unevenly across the UK regions (see

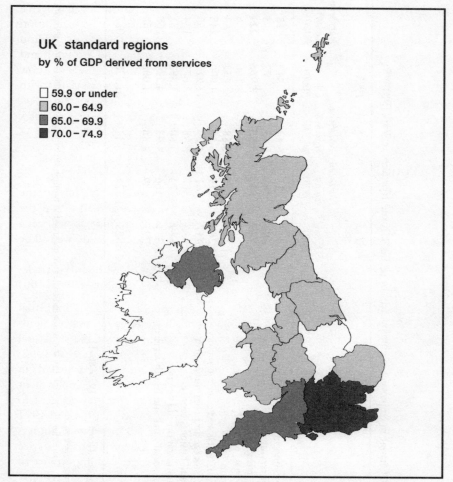

Figure 10.3 Percentage of gross domestic product derived from services (1994)
Source: CSO (1996: 182).
Note: Factor cost at current prices.

Table 10.3 Change in employees in employment by sector, UK and Northern region (1981–95)

Sector*	1981			1995			1981–95 (% change)	
	UK ('000)	Northern region ('000)	Northern region % of UK	UK ('000)	Northern region ('000)	Northern region % of UK	UK	Northern region
Agriculture, hunting, forestry and fishery	403	15	3.84	342	13	3.72	-15.04	-17.68
Mining, quarrying	684	65	9.45	77	3	4.32	-88.68	-94.82
Manufacturing	5,740	318	5.53	3,956	221	5.60	-31.08	-30.31
Electricity, gas, water**	0	0	–	166	6	3.67	–	–
Construction	1,143	67	5.88	852	63	7.43	-25.51	-5.89
Distribution, hotels and catering, repairs	4,288	219	5.10	4,906	245	5.00	14.42	12.02
Transport, storage and communication	1,417	61	4.29	1,279	53	4.14	-9.75	-12.89
Financial and business services	2,436	97	3.98	3,672	134	3.65	50.73	38.07
Public administration and defence	1,549	74	4.80	1,382	81	5.86	-10.77	8.88
Education, social work and health services	3,371	166	4.93	4,289	208	4.86	27.24	25.24
Other	797	39	4.86	1,008	58	5.74	26.42	49.22
Total	21,828	1,122	5.14	21,928	1,087	4.96	0.46	-3.12

Source: Calculated from CSO (1996: 80–1).
Notes:
* Figures are based on SIC92.
** For 1981, figures for electricity, gas and water industries are included in mining, quarrying (including oil and gas extraction).

Figure 10.3 and Table 10.3). For the Northern region relative to the UK, growth has been more modest and declines sharper in the mainly private service sectors while the public service sector has grown in importance, particularly for female employment (Table 10.4). The deregulation of financial services and expansion of consumer services in the 1980s benefited the City of London and the outer Southeast.

The marked difference in the relative contribution to GDP made by services and manufacturing in the Southeast and the Northern region is important in terms of national economic policy and therefore regional political priorities. As well as the high level of corporate, financial and research activity in the Southeast, the region also dominates in terms of the location of financial services. Over half (53 per cent) of UK financial services' GDP derives from the Southeast and 95 per cent of all pension fund assets (which now include one-third of the London stock market) are controlled from the Southeast (Martin and Minns 1995). The percentage employed in the Southeast in financial services (banking, finance, insurance, business services and leasing) grew during the 1980s and over half (52 per cent) of the sector's employees work in the Southeast, far exceeding any other region in the UK.

In the Northern region, the proportion of the workforce employed in manufacturing is higher than the national average and for financial services it is below. As a result of these different sectoral compositions of the areas and the different proportions of decision-making centres and control functions, the Northern region also has a lower-than-average representation of employers and managers compared to the rest of Great Britain and a lower-than-average representation of professional occupational groups. In contrast, the Southeast has the highest proportion of upper-income groups, accumulated financial assets, individual share owners, and so on (Minns and Tomaney 1995).

Earlier we noted the relative contributions of manufacturing and services to regional GDP (see Figures 10.1, 10.2 and 10.3). Although the largest contribution to total UK manufacturing GDP comes from the Southeast, and manufacturing GDP as a whole contributes more to national GDP than financial services, these facts must be seen in the context of the long-run decline in the contribution of manufacturing to national GDP relative to, in particular, financial services. Undoubtedly the Southeast has suffered from the decline in manufacturing industry, particularly in the electronics and R&D activities related to cutbacks in defence expenditure. But as the economy has become less dependent on manufacturing industry in general, and more dependent on financial services, the more reliant it has become on the financial and related services of the Southeast's economy, thus exacerbating a long-standing tendency (Lee 1984). As a result of this deepening alignment, the Southeast has become an increasingly integral object of policy makers' attention and broader political projects.

Meanwhile, the Northeast has experienced 'tertiarization' of a particular kind. Business services are weak, reflecting unsophisticated regional demand, and are often serviced by regional outposts of international operations or by smaller local players. Their future growth potential is limited due to the proliferation of

Table 10.4 Change in employees in employment by sector and gender, UK and Northern region (1981–95)

Sector *	1981			1995			1981–95 (% change)	
	UK ('000)	Northern region ('000)	Northern region % of UK	UK ('000)	Northern region ('000)	Northern region % of UK	UK	Northern region
Male								
Agriculture, hunting, forestry and fishery	300	13	4.37	255	11	4.15	−14.90	−19.19
Mining, quarrying	600	59	9.84	67	3	5.02	−88.90	−94.33
Manufacturing	**4,064**	**236**	**5.81**	**2,787**	**158**	**5.69**	**−31.42**	**−32.90**
Electricity, gas, water **	0	0	–	133	5	3.77	–	–
Construction	1,013	62	6.09	722	57	7.96	−28.74	−6.79
Distribution, hotels and catering, repairs	1,988	85	4.26	2,254	95	4.23	13.37	12.76
Transport, storage and communication	1,138	51	4.44	933	41	4.43	−18.03	−18.25
Financial and business services	1,301	52	3.98	1,832	74	4.02	40.88	42.13
Public administration and defence	850	39	4.63	711	40	5.65	−16.43	2.07
Education, social work and health services	913	43	4.74	966	49	5.02	5.83	12.13
Other	350	16	4.68	466	24	5.14	33.20	46.30
Subtotal	12,519	656		11,127	558		−11.11	−14.94

Female

Agriculture, hunting, forestry and fishery	102	2	2.28	87	2	2.44	−15.44	−9.18
Mining, quarrying	84	6	6.67	11		0.00	−87.08	−100.00
Manufacturing	**1,676**	**82**	**4.87**	**1,169**	**63**	**5.39**	**−30.24**	**−22.81**
Electricity, gas, water**	0	0	–	32	1	3.26	–	–
Construction	130	6	4.29	130	6	4.48	−0.35	4.06
Distribution, hotels and catering, repairs	2,299	134	5.84	2,652	150	5.65	15.32	11.55
Transport, storage and communication	279	10	3.67	346	12	3.36	24.01	13.52
Financial and business services	1,136	45	3.98	1,840	60	3.28	62.01	33.41
Public administration and defence	698	35	5.01	671	41	6.07	−3.89	16.55
Education, social work and health services	2,458	123	5.01	3,323	160	4.81	35.20	29.86
Other	447	22	5.01	541	34	6.26	21.11	51.36
Subtotal	9,309	465		10,801	528		16.03	13.52
Total	21,828	1,121		21,929	1,086		0.46	−3.13

Source: Calculated from CSO (1996: 80–1).

Notes:

* Figures are based on SIC92.

** For 1981, figures for electricity, gas and water industries are included in mining, quarrying (including oil and gas extraction).

intra-corporate delivery of services within much of the externally controlled regional manufacturing base. Recent rapid growth in teleservice activity has incorporated mainly relocations from relatively higher wage cost localities in the UK. These 'call centres' constitute 'footloose' activities which require little investment, incur low start-up costs, and create much needed employment, but provide limited spillovers to the regional economy (Richardson and Marshall 1996). Many of their activities provide back-up for service rather than manufacturing activities, including insurance, telecommunications and travel operations, and have little or no linkages to regional manufacturing. Moreover, the Northeast's relative dependence on public services, including both the civil service outposts (Marshall *et al.* 1997) and local government (Patterson and Pinch 1995), are facing further public expenditure squeezes leading to rationalization, and privatization through outsourcing. Retail services have remained dependent upon often sustained but ultimately cyclical consumer demand and have become marked by a somewhat variegated hierarchy of retail outlets across the region.

MANUFACTURING INDUSTRY STRUCTURE IN THE REGIONS

Concentration and centralization continue to characterize many manufacturing sectors. Indeed, the oligopolistic structure of UK manufacturing means that a relatively high proportion of UK firms are among the largest global players (e.g. Glaxo and Shell) (Institution of Electrical Engineers 1992). Scale, market power, and, increasingly, scope and flexibility, have come to characterize the dominant corporate form for manufacturing. Despite trends in vertical disintegration, which have seen the number of VAT-registered businesses in UK manufacturing rise from 144,000 to 170,000 between 1980 and 1990 (House of Commons 1994b), the emergent myriad of networks, outsourcing deals, subcontracting webs and strategic alliances often retain the control of large firms at their hub (Martinelli and Schoenberger 1991). Manufacturing SMEs tend to be brought into the locus of large-firm influence, often occupying prefigured roles in increasingly segmented supply chains, and/or exploiting market niches (whether locally oriented consumption or technological) (Semlinger 1992; cf. Bresnen and Fowler in Chapter 8 in this volume). The number of firms may be rising, therefore, but their prospects remain heavily influenced by the strategies of the largest players. Harrison (1994) describes this process as 'concentration without centralization', and emphasizes the need for multimarket presence, agility and responsiveness in driving corporate activity. A particular problem of the manufacturing sector in the UK is the lack of a strong '*Mittelstand*' , as in Germany, of medium-sized firms that make substantial contributions to value-added and employment creation in their own right and not just as dependants in relation to an internationalized large-firm sector (Institution of Electrical Engineers 1992; see also Jones and Tang in Chapter 7 in this volume). Medium-sized firms, employing between 100 and 499 people, accounted for 15.7 per cent of UK manufacturing employment in 1990, compared to 28.2 per cent elsewhere in Western Europe (Germany, France, Italy, the Netherlands and Belgium) (House of Commons 1994b).

The broader trends in manufacturing have fuelled, and, in turn, been reinforced by, the trend of corporate 're-engineering' which has been rife in the manufacturing sector (Aggarwal 1997). Mergers and acquisitions, joint ventures, disposals, buyouts and so on have created waves of reorganization of the industrial structures of manufacturing activities (Love 1994). The domicile of the ownership and control of capital, and the extent to which a 'home base' matters, have further complicated matters in the context of 'globalization' (Kozul-Wright 1995). Former US Labor Secretary Robert Reich's (1991) often quoted 'Who is us?' question draws attention to the complexity of internationalized ownership structures, and perhaps, if understating the enduring role of the territorially bounded nation state, has made it more problematic to talk about 'British manufacturing'. Indeed, the House of Commons (1994b: 32) noted that 'the size of the UK manufacturing sector now depends much less on the health of UK-owned manufacturing firms, and much more on the attractions of the UK as a location for manufacturing'.

For the UK regions, these issues are pertinent. While there is little difference in the firm size structure between the Northern region and the UK as a whole (measured by turnover of VAT-registered enterprises from figures for all sectors) (CSO 1996a), these data fail to capture the nature and dynamics of the interfirm relationships in the regional manufacturing sector. At the regional or more localized scale, whole local economies can be dependent upon large firms and/or webs of dependent subcontractors. The Northeast has been affected to an extent by the changing role of branch plants within this context of industrial reorganization and increasingly flattened corporate hierarchies (Amin *et al.* 1994). These putative 'performance plants' are said to offer enhanced potential for contributions to local economic development that include heightened autonomy, broadened functional responsibility, increased porosity and nodes capable of linkage with local institutional structures (Pike (forthcoming)). The reality of change is rather modest, however. Supply-chain reorganization has witnessed rationalization, and attempts to combine competition and collaboration within new 'partnership' sourcing agreements for an increasingly select band of favoured suppliers (Morgan *et al.* 1992). Ownership structures have experienced upheaval in the context of the UK's liberalized market in corporate control, with uneven regional implications (Ashcroft *et al.* 1994). Mergers and acquisitions have marked the regional manufacturing sector with their attendant problems of increased external control, reduction in the sophistication of operations, the fracturing of local supplier relations, and the downgrading of local labour-market skills (Love 1994). Traditional sectors have been targets, as well as indigenous companies with linkages into the recent inward investors, and the predators have been increasingly international. Examples include either outright acquisition and takeover, such as offshore fabrication yard McNulty's by Aker (Norway), automotive suppliers Elta Plastics by Nifco (Japan) and Tallent Engineering by Thyssen (Germany), or – commonly in the traditional sectors – corporate 'rescues' such as shipbuilder Swan Hunter by THC (Netherlands) and the power equipment firm Parsons by Siemens (Germany).

HOW MANY AND WHAT SORT OF MANUFACTURING JOBS?

The Northern region has seen a dramatic decline in the total number of manufacturing jobs, falling from 318,000 to 221,000 between 1981 and 1995, but
their marginal rise as a proportion of national manufacturing jobs (Table 10.3). In
particular, the Northeast's contraction of manufacturing employment was mainly
experienced by male, full-time employees in traditional skilled, often trades-
related, occupations bound by largely permanent employment contracts in union-
ized workplaces within the traditional sectors. Redundancies in the Northern
region as a whole remain high, relative to national levels, often due to the decline
associated with the last vestiges of the older industries, and unemployment, particularly long-term, persists at levels stubbornly above the national average (CSO
1996b). Rationalization and restructuring has dramatically reshaped the nature of
manufacturing jobs, challenging virtually every tenet of previously accepted practice. Conceptions of what constitutes paid work in the manufacturing sector have
been shaken.

Overall, the Northeast's manufacturing sector is smaller, employs considerably
less people than hitherto, and has experienced productivity growth without closely related gains in job generation. Sectoral composition has experienced a relative
shift towards lighter engineering and assembly activities. The gender composition
has changed in tandem, displaying a relative 'feminization' of the workforce.
While male manufacturing jobs have collapsed from 236,000 to 158,000
between 1981 and 1995 (nearly one-third), female manufacturing employment fell from 82,000 to 63,000 over the same period (just over one-fifth)
(Table 10.4).

Flexibility has become the guiding principle for manufacturing employment.
Insecurity and irregularity have increased in importance through the utilization of
part-time and temporary working. The proportion of part-time employment in
manual sectors increased from 4.7 per cent to 5.9 per cent for males and fell
marginally from 61.6 per cent to 61.5 per cent for females between 1991 and
1995 in the Northern region (CSO 1996b). Temporary contracts, often to meet
seasonal peaks in demand, are common among the larger employers such as
Flymo and Black & Decker in Sedgefield Borough. Such contracts have provided
both numerical flexibility as well as a screening device for future permanent
employees. Firms have also worked closely to dampen wage inflation, contain
poaching, and often co-operate in taking on those recently laid-off temporary
contracts (Pike and Tomaney 1996). Working hours have been extended, and the
employment relationship has become increasingly individualized, with wages tied
to performance, employing the common 'HRM' lexicon. Pay has become increasingly determined by labour-market segment and local rates, often depressed by
relatively high regional unemployment. In the traditional maritime engineering
sector, localized closure and the labour-market experiences of those made redun-
dant, such as at Swan Hunter prior to its recent resurrection, have contributed to
a reshaped employment relation and reinforced the contract-based, 'hire and fire'
culture among the offshore yards (Tomaney et al. 1997).

Manufacturing job content has been shaped by the current orthodoxy of new techniques contained in the 'best practice' rubric of 'lean production' (see Morgan *et al.* 1992). Nissan's 'flagship' investment has been emblematic in this regard. Reducing labour hours per unit of output and increasing job mobility and functional flexibility have been central. Intensification and transparency have resulted in these Japanese-inspired, highly cost-efficient productive techniques, which also embody their own '*kaizen*' (continuous improvement) dynamic within the factory and through the supply chain (Tomaney 1994). Occupational structures have been simplified and increasingly polarized, in the context of flatter organizational hierarchies and shorter lines of command, between an upper echelon or core of professional and technical grades, with fewer supervisory posts, and a lower mass or periphery of un-, semi- and skilled operatives subdivided into teams and regulated by team leaders. All of which groups are supported by a smaller band of increasingly 'multiskilled' support and maintenance technicians. Entry-level recruitment requirements have risen, with modularized apprenticeships tailored to company needs increasing in importance. Recurrent skills shortages, suggesting ingrained structural problems relating to incentives to train among employers, have emerged, particularly for engineers and supervisory grades, at the technician and craft levels. Training has been driven by needs analysis, and the resource expended has intensified through 'on-' and 'off-the-job' modes (Rutherford 1994), often including in-house company 'schools' facilities (e.g. Stadium, Siemens) and increasingly specialized, client-focused local providers (e.g. South West Durham Training).

Uncertainty regarding future skills requirements has often been met with strategies to implant a 'learning culture', or at least habit, on the shop floor. The industrial relations climate has been recast. Shifts are apparent away from the traditional multi-unionism present in the Northeast, due to the establishment of single (e.g. Nissan) or non-union (e.g. Fujitsu, Samsung, Siemens) plants among more recent inward investors. These factories have set the tone with 'Company Council' arrangements not necessarily including trade-union representation. This development appears to run counter to recent thinking about social partnership within Europe (House of Commons 1994d), and is pertinent since the Northern region retains high levels of trade-union membership in the national context (Martin *et al.* 1996).

R&D AND THE INNOVATION GAP

Intensified competition and the accelerated pace of technological change in product and process have required a step change in approaches to traditional R&D and broader innovation processes within manufacturing. Innovation is a key lever through which higher value-added manufactures can support upgrading activity and relieve the regressive pressures of price-based competition, as well as maintain the impetus in export markets. Techniques have emerged, such as 'simultaneous engineering', which (re)integrate design with manufacture to cut lead times, reduce costs, and devolve design responsibility down the supply chain. Such techniques often imply concentration in single, lead sites. Outsourcing of R&D has also increased due to escalating costs, rising technical complexity and skill requirements, with the attendant risks for organizations of becoming less sophisticated consumers and developers of technology. Underperformance is again evident in manufacturing R&D in the UK. Relatively low levels of investment, sluggish growth, and a marked dependency on defence-related spending vulnerable to 'Peace Dividend'-related rationalization are evident. R&D intensity in manufacturing has increased, but at lower rates than competitor nations (Cabinet Office 1994), and investment in medium-technology sectors is particularly laggard (House of Commons 1994b).

These problems have been compounded by the question of 'short-termism' and the high propensity of, particularly, UK-owned industry to boost profitability and shareholder dividends at the expense of longer-term investment, particularly in R&D (Walker 1993). Current investment in manufacturing R&D is concentrated in a few sectors (aerospace, electronics, computers and pharmaceuticals) which, while helping to promote specialization, are often dominated by UK and foreign-owned transnational firms conducting R&D globally. Indeed, 90–95 per cent of R&D in manufacturing is carried out in just 100 firms, which is a far higher degree of concentration than in the US and Germany (House of Commons 1994b: 46). In addition, the context of falling public support for R&D has made the contribution of the private sector critical and the legacy of its under-investment even more apparent.

The technological development activities present in manufacturing R&D activity are integral to regional economic development. The positive investment and employment impacts are supplemented by the strategic nature of R&D functions, technological spillovers to local firms, trading relations, demand for support services and the creation of a highly skilled local labour market (Howells 1992). Positive externalities accrue where regional concentrations of R&D activity exist, often fostering an innovative environment. In both the public and private sectors, R&D expenditure and employment is overwhelmingly concentrated in the Southeast region, and in several localities within the region, often linked to the major formerly public research establishments undergoing privatization (Pike and Tomaney 1994). Participation in national and European programmes, for example, is markedly higher in these regions, feeding a virtuous circle of linkages and investment, and, at least to some extent, limiting developments elsewhere (Charles and Howells 1991).

The disparity in R&D and innovation in manufacturing is acute for the Northern region. Recent figures from the DTI have shown the particularly poor performance of the Northeast region (along with Scotland, Wales and Northern Ireland) in relation to R&D in manufacturing (Table 10.5). This relatively poor R&D and innovation performance has reflected the rationalization associated with several reinforcing tendencies which have led to a spiralling decline and the loss of quality jobs and investment. In conjunction with the collapse of the traditional industries within the region has been the run down of their R&D and technological development capacity. For example, since becoming part of

Rolls-Royce's Industrial Power Group, IRD (International Research and Development) struggled to find a clear role within the organization working as a supplier to both in-house and external markets. It has been rationalized, and has lost highly qualified and experienced staff, despite its strategic importance within a power engineering specialization within Tyneside (Pike and Tomaney 1994). Privatization amongst the utilities has also led to rationalization and the concentration of activities in lead sites outside the region. The British Gas Engineering Research Station in Killingworth was closed and functions were relocated to a single site in Loughborough, despite having developed advanced technologies for pipeline inspection and repair. The dire prospect of losing 400 R&D jobs was likened by the then leader of North Tyneside council to 'closing a university'.

Such problems are reinforced by the tendency among new inward investors not to locate significant R&D functions within the region, although there are some pockets of technological development activity at dedicated sites, such as Procter & Gamble, and within some plants with product and process development briefs, such as Black & Decker and Thorn Lighting (Pike and Tomaney 1996). Overall, however, the net result is the loss of quality R&D jobs which are not being replaced with jobs at similar occupational levels or remuneration among recent inward investment. Some development has occurred due to the increasingly porous relations between the region's manufacturing sector, particularly inward investors, and external institutions within the local economy for technology support. These include the Regional Technology Centre (RTC) North, and the networks of support, such as the 'Knowledge House' 'one-stop-shop' initiative

Table 10.5 Business enterprise R&D for manufactured products as a percentage of gross value added

Region	%
UK	6.1
Northeast	2.1
Northwest and Merseyside	6.4
Northwest	6.4
Merseyside	6.5
Yorkshire and Humberside	2.5
East Midlands	5.5
West Midlands	3.7
Eastern	15.1
London	4.6
Southeast	13.1
Southwest	5.3
England	6.9
Wales	1.6
Scotland	2.0
Northern Ireland	2.1

Source: DTI (1997: 39).
Note: Table uses government office region/country definitions.

linking to the regional universities (Charles 1996). Even where clusters of expertise can be identified in particular sectors, however, the policy framework to
develop these is frequently lacking (Pike and Tomaney 1996).

'ENTERPRISE' AND THE ENTREPRENEURSHIP GAP

There was a rapid growth in new firm formation rates in the UK from the end of
the 1970s and this continued through the 1980s. To an extent, this process
reversed the trend of the twentieth century which had seen large firms accounting
for an increasing proportion of employment. The stock of VAT-registered firms
(all sectors) rose from 158,000 in 1980 to 235,000 in 1990, peaking in 1989,
before falling back to 190,000 by 1994 (CSO 1996b). Net VAT registrations
increased from 16,000 to 66,000 between 1980 and 1990 alone. There was also a
significant and related growth in self-employment. The number of self-employed
(all sectors) increased from 2.3 million in 1986 to 3.3 million in 1995 (CSO
1996b). The growth of new-firm formation was linked centrally to the growth of
the service sector, where the majority of new firms were established (Mason
1992). By contrast there were much lower rates of net growth in new-firm formation in the early 1990s as a result of the downturn in economic conditions
(Keeble 1993). However, even in the 1980s, research showed that only a
handful of small firms went on to become large employers (Storey 1994).

There were several reasons for the sharp growth in new-firm formation in the
1980s. First, redundancy forced some people to set up their own business. Second, large firms' increased use of subcontracting and externalization of service
activities created new opportunities for small firms. Third, structural economic
change and rising real incomes created new niche markets in the service sector.
Finally, ideological and policy support for the development of a small firms-based
economy played a part (Mason 1992; Storey 1994).

The growth of new-firm formation during the 1980s was distributed very
unevenly between regions and localities. There were two main dimensions to the
geography of new-firm formation. First, there was a clear *north–south divide*:
formation rates were highest in the Southeast, Southwest and East Anglia, and
were lowest in Scotland and the North. This pattern was linked to the rapid
growth of services – especially business services – in the South. Second, there was
a clear *urban–rural divide*: formation rates were highest in rural/semi-rural loca-
tions (e.g. rural Wales, the Southwest, outer Southeast) and lowest in urban/
industrial areas (e.g. Merseyside, South Yorkshire, Tyneside, Teesside and central
Scotland). Notably, rates in new-firm formation in manufacturing were highest in
rural areas and lowest in industrial areas (Mason 1992).

There are a number of explanations for these geographical variations. First,
industrial structure has meant that new-firm formation is low in sectors with high
barriers to entry and in economies dominated by large firms. Such sectors tend to
dominate regions such as the Northeast, in the spirit of Checkland's (1976) *The
Upas Tree*, and militate against high levels of new-firm formation rates. A second
and related factor concerns occupational structure: new firms tend to be formed

by those with managerial, professional or technical background. These groups are under-represented in the occupational structure of regions such as the Northeast. Third, broader economic conditions also influence new-firm formation rates. For instance, the size of market and levels of personal incomes will determine levels of demand, especially in the service sector. In regions such as the Northeast, where these are constrained, formation rates are low.

Finance

In many cases initial finance for new-firm formation is raised from internal sources. This generally disadvantages regions like the Northeast, where personal incomes, levels of savings and house prices (a key source of collateral) are generally low. Moreover, information concerning technologies, equipment, materials, and so on, are more abundant and more rapidly accessible in the South (Mason 1992), perhaps due to linkages to leading-edge developments and social networks in London and the Southeast.

The growth of small and medium-sized firms, especially the prospect of a UK *Mittelstand*, is critically dependent on the availability of external finance. Debates concerning the role of finance capital in explaining Britain's manufacturing performance have a long history (Lee 1996). There are distinct geographical biases in the operation of the financial system. For instance, 75 per cent of bank loans go to companies in the Southeast in the UK. By contrast, bank lending is more regionally diversified in other European countries (Ross Mackay and Molyneux 1996). Venture capital lending reveals a marked bias in favour of the Southeast and has remained little changed between 1984 and 1993 (Table 10.6) (Martin 1992; Holmes 1995). Moreover, pension fund investment, a major source of industrial investment, is heavily concentrated in the South (Martin and Minns 1995).

CHANGING POLICY REGIMES

In this chapter we have sought to insert the regional dimension into the centre of debates about the changing nature of manufacturing in the UK. To the extent that the UK's economic dynamism depends on its ability to trade successfully in international markets, so too is this a condition for regional prosperities. Yet the geographically imbalanced nature of economic development in the 1980s and 1990s led to a sharply contracting manufacturing base in the North and an 'over-heating' service-based growth in the South, which manifested itself in the much discussed 'North–South divide'.

Successive Conservative governments during the 1980s and 1990s rejected Kaldorian arguments about the importance of manufacturing industry (e.g. Lawson 1992). The Conservative political settlement contained an implicit 'anti-industrial' policy stance that privileged the interests of finance over industrial capital, and consumption over production, which together, as we have shown, had pronounced regional ramifications. Thus government policy during this

Table 10.6 Regional structure of venture capital activity

	BVCA full members (1993): office location		Venture capital investment (% of amount invested)	
	Head office (number)	All offices (number)	1984	1993
United Kingdom	117	178	100	100
North	1	4	2	2
Yorks/Humberside	7	15	0	3
East Midlands	1	3	5	4
East Anglia	3	4	6	4
Southeast (incl. London)	80	89	51	53
Southwest	1	3	4	3
West Midlands	3	7	5	6
Northwest	3	14	10	13
England	99	139	83	88
Wales	1	11	6	1
Scotland	13	24	11	10
Northern Ireland	4	4	0	1
Total amount invested (£m)			140	1,231

Source: Martin (1992).

period contributed to the accelerated growth of the Southeast and the widening of the North–South divide. Despite the attraction of inward investment, and government claims that the emphasis on 'local strengths' and 'free enterprise' had 'helped close the gap on the North–South divide and gained the [Northeast] region international recognition as a world class manufacturing centre' (Lang 1996), during this period the relative position of the Northeast deteriorated. The region's share of UK GDP fell (almost) year on year between 1984 and 1995 (CSO 1996b). Per capita GDP and average relative earnings declined sharply at the beginning of the 1980s and both have remained about 10 per cent below UK average since. In short, deindustrialization and the shift to a service economy have been associated with a widening of disparities in wellbeing between the Northeast and the Southeast. To the extent that government operated an industrial policy it was restricted to the attraction of investment based on the availability of financial incentives, a favourable tax regime and heavy marketing of the UK as a low-cost production base in the context of the EU. Policy was conceived nationally, with limited local discretion in execution, especially as far as the English regions were concerned.

Conservative government policy during the 1980s and 1990s contained sharp breaks, tempered by some notable continuities with past approaches to regional development. During the 1960s and 1970s, large expenditures were made on regional policy by both Conservative and Labour governments, although these began to be reduced under the Callaghan Labour Government after 1977. As well as providing investment incentives for designated assisted areas in the declining regions of the UK, governments also operated constraints in the faster-growing areas of the South. This 'carrot and stick' approach influenced the flow of investment during this period. Governments of both major parties accepted an 'economic' case for regional policy: that is, the decentralization of investment from fast-growing regions to slower-growing ones was to the advantage of the economy as a whole. It was during this period that the stock of externally controlled manufacturing activity was built up in regions like the Northeast.

On coming to office in 1979, the Conservative government continued to reduce levels of expenditure on regional policy. Moreover, the Conservatives explicitly rejected the 'economic' case for regional policy, arguing instead that the justification for policy was merely a 'social' one (Martin and Tyler 1992). However, one important area of continuity concerned the primacy attached to attracting mobile investment as the main means of restructuring regional economies. Levels of inward investment remained much lower than in the 1960s and 1970s, but their political importance was increased as they were seen as harbingers of new industrial practices. In addition, the Conservative Government was vigorous in its marketing of the UK – and its constituent regions – as primarily a low-cost and lightly regulated location for industrial activity.

There is evidence that this approach might be changing in subtle ways yet again. The election of a New Labour Government in 1997 may presage both a new attitude to inward investment and a new approach to regional development. One of the earliest statements by the new President of the Board of Trade, Margaret Beckett, was to signal a move away from an emphasis on the UK as a low-cost production base to a centre of 'quality, added-value, high technology and market leadership' (quoted in the *Financial Times*, 24 July 1997). In opposition, Labour had signalled its new approach to regional policy by establishing an independent Regional Policy Commission, chaired by the former EU Commissioner Bruce Millan. The Commission's report drew on previous critiques of regional policy (House of Commons 1995) and contained over one hundred recommendations (Regional Policy Commission 1996). Among this material was a call for a shift in emphasis from inward investment to indigenous development through the promotion of R&D and the development of new financial instruments. In this respect, the proposal mirrored developments occurring elsewhere in Europe (Tomaney 1995). The central recommendation of the Commission, however, was for the establishment of Regional Development Agencies (RDAs) in England to bring greater co-ordination to the development effort and to implement the new approach. These proposals contained only a reconfiguration of the priorities and mechanisms of existing funding and no commitment to additional resources.

This new approach is also linked to the new Government's wider agenda of devolution, signified by its early moves to establish a Scottish Parliament and a Welsh Assembly and the now somewhat muted proposals for assemblies in the English regions. This approach allows for greater customization of policy approaches at the regional level. However, as even its proponents note, the new approach contains the danger that regions will be left to their own devices. Martin (1992) has pointed out that central government activity has a great bearing on the development capacity of a region (see also Amin and Tomaney 1995). Locally conceived and executed development strategies are no panacea in the face of powerful international forces of restructuring, as Gertler's (1995) study of industrial decline and policy response in Ontario illustrates. A successful integrated regional industrial policy for the manufacturing sector in the UK would need to be accompanied by accountable regional level institutional capacity and capability with real democratic legitimacy and authority. This structure would have to be situated within the framework of appropriately defined national and European relations. In particular, safeguards would be needed to stem the interregional competition that might intensify as both less favoured *and* prosperous regions bolster the coherence of their institutional capacities. RDAs represent a modest step in the right direction, but as our analysis of the Northeast shows, they face a large task ahead.

NOTE

1 This chapter reports ongoing work conducted within the Centre for Urban and Regional Development Studies (CURDS), University of Newcastle. The research has been supported through various sources, including the European Commission, ESRC, CSEU, DTI, MSF, and Sedgefield Borough Council. Thanks are due to those who participated in the various research projects and colleagues in CURDS, especially David Charles, for their comments.

We also thank the organizers of the Employment Research Unit, Cardiff Business School, 'Manufacturing Matters' conference, 18–19 September 1996. Earlier versions of this paper were presented to the LATTS/DATAR seminar: 'The New Geography of Europe: Great Britain', Paris, 28–29 April 1997, and the International Seminar on Economic and Social Development in the Greater ABC Region, São Paulo, 8–9 May 1997. The usual disclaimers, as always, apply.

REFERENCES

Aggarwal, S. (1997) 'Re-engineering: a breakthrough or little new?', *International Journal of Technology Management*, **13** (3), 326–44.

Allen, J. (1995) 'Crossing borders: footloose multinationals?', in J. Allen and C. Hamnett (eds), *A Shrinking World? Global Unevenness and Inequality*, Oxford: Oxford University Press.

Amin, A., Bradley, D., Howells, J., Tomaney, J. and Gentle, C. (1994) 'Regional incentives and the quality of mobile investment in the less favoured regions of the EC', *Progress in Planning*, **41** (1).

Amin, A. and Tomaney, J. (eds) (1995) *Behind the Myth of the European Union: Prospects for Cohesion*, London: Routledge.

Ashcroft, B., Coppins, B. and Raeside, R. (1994) 'The regional dimension of takeover activity in the United Kingdom', *Scottish Journal of Political Economy*, **41** (2), 163–75.

Beynon, H., Hudson, R. and Sadler, D. (1994) *A Place Called Teesside: A Locality in the Global Economy*, Edinburgh: Edinburgh University Press.

CEC (1996) *First Report on Economic and Social Cohesion 1996*, Luxembourg: Office for the Official Publications of the European Community.

CSO (1996a) *Size Analysis of UK Business*, Business Monitor PA 1003, HMSO: London.

CSO (1996b) *Regional Trends*, HMSO: London.

Cabinet Office (1994) *Annual Review of Government Funded Research and Development*, London: HMSO.

Charles, D. (1996) 'Building Technology Networks in the Northeast', unpublished paper, Centre for Urban and Regional Development Studies, University of Newcastle.

Charles, D. and Howells, J. (1991) 'European innovation and regional policies: implications for the periphery of the UK', in R. Harrison and M. Hart (eds), *Spatial Policy in a Divided Nation*, London: Jessica Kingsley.

Checkland, S. (1976) *The Upas Tree*, Glasgow: Glasgow University Press.

Cleveland County Council (1994) *Changes in the Chemical Industry and the Impact on Cleveland in the 1990s*, Department of Environment, Development and Transportation, Middlesbrough: Cleveland County Council.

Coates, D. (1994) *The Question of UK Decline: The Economy, State and Society*, London: Harvester Wheatsheaf.

Cohen, S. and Zysman, J. (1987) *Manufacturing Matters: The Myth of the Post-Industrial Economy*, New York: Basic Books.

Cooke, P. (ed.) (1995) *The Rise of the Rustbelt*, London: UCL Press.

Coopers and Lybrand Deloitte (1991) *A Study into the Knock-On Effects of Inward Investment in the English Regions*, London: HMSO.

DTI (1997) *Regional Competitiveness Indicators*, London: Government Statistical Service for the DTI.

Gertler, M. (1995) 'Groping towards reflexivity: responding to industrial change in Ontario', in P. Cooke (ed.), *The Rise of the Rustbelt*, London: UCL Press.

Greenhalgh, C., Gregory, M. and Ray, A. (1989) 'Why manufacturing matters', *Employment Policy Institute Economic Report*, 4 (8).

Harrison, B. (1994) *Lean and Mean: The Changing Landscape of Corporate Power in the Age of Flexibility*, New York: Basic Books.

Hayward, S. and Tomaney, J. (1997) 'The Political Economy of Regional Change: The Case of North East England', Discussion Paper 96/2, Centre for Urban and Regional Development Studies, University of Newcastle.

Hirst, P. and Thompson, G. (1996) *Globalization in Question: The International Economy and the Possibilities of Governance*, Cambridge, Mass.: Blackwell.

Holmes, P. (1995) 'The provision of finance: is the North disadvantaged?', in R. Evans *et al.* (eds), *The Northern Region Economy*, London: Mansell.

House of Commons (1994a) *The Import and Export of Jobs: The Future for Manufacturing*, Trade and Industry Committee, Session 1993–94, HC 160-I, London: HMSO.

—— (1994b) *Competitiveness of UK Manufacturing Industry*, Trade and Industry Committee, Session 1993–94, HC 41-I, London: HMSO.

—— (1994c) *Competitiveness of UK Manufacturing Industry: Minutes of Evidence, Thursday 20 January*, Trade and Industry Committee, Session 1993–94, HC 41-VI, London: HMSO.

—— (1994d) *The Future of Trade Unions*, Employment Committee, Session 1993–94, HC 676–1, London: HMSO.

—— (1995) *Enquiry into Regional Policy*, Trade and Industry Committee, Session 1994–95, HC 356-I, HMSO: London.

Howells, J. (1992) 'Patterns of research and development', in P. Townroe and R. Martin (eds), *Regional Development in the 1990s*, London: Jessica Kingsley/ Regional Studies Association.

Hudson, R. (1989) *Wrecking a Region*, London: Pion.

—— (1995) 'The role of inward investment', in R. Evans *et al.* (eds), *The Northern Region Economy*, London: Mansell.

Institution of Electrical Engineers (1992) *UK Manufacturing*, London: Institution of Electrical Engineers.

Kaldor, N. (1972) 'The irrelevance of equilibrium economics', *Economic Journal*, **82**, December, 328.

Keeble, D. (1993) *New Firm Formation and Small Business Growth in the UK*, Research Series no. 15, London: Department of Employment.

Kozul-Wright, R. (1995) 'Transnational corporations and the nation state', in J. Michie and J. Grieve Smith (eds), *Managing the Global Economy*, Oxford: Oxford University Press.

Lagendijk, A., Laigle, L., Pike, A. and Vale, M. (1996) 'The Local Embedding of International Car Plants', paper for the EUNIT seminar on The Territorial Dimensions of Innovation, Dortmund, 22–24 May; mimeo available from Centre for Urban and Regional Development Studies, University of Newcastle.

Lang, I. (1996) 'Ian Lang praises the North East: the fastest changing region in Europe', DTI Press Release, p/95 /99 8, 8 February, http://www.open.gov.uk/

Lawson, N. (1992) *View from Number 11: Memoirs of a Tory Radical*, London: Bantam Press.

Lee, C.H. (1984) 'The service sector, regional specialisation and economic growth in the Victorian economy', *Journal of Historical Geography*, **10** (2).

Lee, S. (1996) 'Finance for industry', in J. Michie and M. Kitson (eds), *Creating Industrial Capacity*, Oxford: Oxford University Press.

Love, J. (1994) 'EC mergers regulation and regional economic cohesion', *Environment and Planning A*, **26**, 137–52.

McCord, N. (1979) *North East England: The Region's Development 1760–1960*, London: Batsford Academic.

Marshall, J.N. (1992) 'The growth of service activities and the evolution of spatial disparities', in P. Townroe and R. Martin (eds), *Regional Development in the 1990s*, London: Jessica Kingsley and Regional Studies Association.

Marshall, J.N., Hopkins, W.J., Richardson, R. and Coombes, M. (1997) 'The civil service and the regions: geographical perspectives on civil service restructuring', *Regional Studies*, **31** (6), 607–13.

Martin, R. (1992) 'Financing regional enterprise', in P. Townroe and R. Martin (eds), *Regional Development in the 1990s*, London: Jessica Kingsley and Regional Studies Association.

Martin, R. and Minns, R. (1995) 'Undermining the financial basis of regions: the spatial structure and implications of the UK pension fund system', *Regional Studies*, **29**, 25–44.

Martin, R. and Rowthorn, B. (1986) *The Geography of Deindustrialisation*, London: Macmillan.

Martin, R. and Tyler, P. (1992) 'The regional legacy', in J. Michie (ed.), *The Economic Legacy, 1979–92*, London: Academic Press.

Martin, R., Sunley, P. and Wills, J. (1996) *Union Retreat and the Regions: The Shrinking Landscape of Organized Labour*, London: Jessica Kingsley and Regional Studies Association.

Martinelli, F. and Schoenberger, E. (1991) 'Oligopoly is alive and well: notes for a broader discussion on flexible accumulation', in G. Benko and M. Dunford (eds), *Industrial Change and Regional Development*, London: Bellhaven Press.

Mason, C. (1992) 'New firm formation and growth', in P. Townroe and R. Martin (eds), *Regional Development in the 1990s*, London: Jessica Kingsley and Regional Studies Association.

Massey, D. (1995) *Spatial Divisions of Labour*, 2nd edn., New York: Routledge.

Michie, J. and Grieve Smith, J. (eds) (1995) *Managing the Global Economy*, Oxford: Blackwell.

Michie, J. and Kitson, M. (1996) *Creating Industrial Capacity*, Oxford: Oxford University Press.

Minns, R. and Tomaney, J. (1995) 'Regional government and local economic development: the realities of economic power in the UK', *Regional Studies*, 29 (2), 202–7.

Morgan, K., Cooke, P. and Price, A. (1992) 'The challenge of lean production for German industry', Regional Industrial Research Report no. 12, Department of City and Regional Planning, University of Wales College of Cardiff.

OECD (1996) *OECD in Figures: Statistics on the Member Countries*, Paris: OECD.

Oinas, P. (1997) 'On the socio-spatial embeddedness of business firms', *Erdkunde*, 51, 23–32.

Patterson, A. and Pinch, P.L. (1995) 'Hollowing out the local state: compulsory competitive tendering and the restructuring of British public sector services', *Environment and Planning A*, 27 (9), 1437–61.

Pauly, L.W. and Reich, S. (1997) 'National structures and multinational corporate behaviour: enduring differences in the age of globalization', *International Organization*, 51 (1), 1–30.

Pike, A. (1996) '"Greenfields", "brownfields" and industrial policy for the automobile industry in the UK', *Regional Studies*, 30 (1), 69–77.

—— (forthcoming) 'Making performance plants from branch plants? In-situ restructuring in the automobile industry in UK region', *Environment and Planning A*.

Pike, A. and Tomaney, J. (1994) *R&D in the North East: An Issue for Public Policy*, Gateshead: Trade Union Studies Information Unit (TUSIU).

—— (1996) 'The State of the Economy in Sedgefield Borough', report for Sedgefield Borough Council, Centre for Urban and Regional Development Studies, University of Newcastle.

Regional Policy Commission (1996) *Renewing the Regions*, Policy Research Centre, Sheffield: Sheffield Hallam University.

Reich, R. (1991) *The Work of Nations*, London: Simon & Schuster.

Richardson, R. and Marshall, J.N. (1996) 'The growth of telephone call centres in peripheral areas of Britain: evidence from Tyne and Wear', *Area*, 28 (3), 308–17.

Ross MacKay, R. and Molyneux, P. (1996) 'Bank credit and the regions: a comparison within Europe', *Regional Studies*, 30 (8), 757–63.

Rowthorn, R.E. and Wells, J.R. (1987) *De-industrialization and Foreign Trade*, Cambridge, New York: Cambridge University Press.

Rutherford, T.D. (1994) 'From "sitting by Nellie" to the classroom factory? The restructuring of skills, recruitment and training in a South Wales motor components plant' *International Journal of Urban and Regional Research*, 18 (3), 470–90.

Semlinger, K. (1992) 'Small firms in big subcontracting', in N. Altmann, C. Kohler and P. Meil (eds), *Technology and Work in German Industry*, London: Routledge.

Stone, I. (1993) 'Remaking it on Wearside: de-industrialisation and re-industrialisation', *Northern Economic Review*, 20, 6–22.

Stone, I. and Peck, F. (1996) 'The foreign-owned manufacturing sector in UK peripheral regions, 1978–1993: restructuring and comparative performance', *Regional Studies*, 30 (1), 55–68.

Storey, D.J. (1994) *Understanding the Small Firm Sector*, London: Routledge.

Storper, M. and Scott, A.J. (1995) 'The wealth of regions: market forces and policy imperatives in local and global context', *Futures*, 27 (5), 505–26.

Tomaney, J. (1994) 'A new paradigm of work organization and technology?', in A. Amin (ed.), *Post-Fordism: A Reader*, Oxford: Blackwell.

—— (1995) 'Recent developments in Irish industrial policy', *European Planning Studies*, **3** (1).

Tomaney, J., Cornford, J. and Pike, A. (1997) 'Plant closure and the local economy: the case of Swan Hunter on Tyneside', Discussion Paper no. 97/1, Centre for Urban and Regional Development Studies, University of Newcastle.

Turok, I. (1993) 'Inward investment and local linkages: how deeply embedded is Silicon Glen?', *Regional Studies*, **27** (5), 401–17.

Walker, W. (1993) 'National innovation systems: Britain', in R. Nelson (ed.), *National Innovation Systems: A Comparative Analysis*, Oxford: Blackwell.

Williams, K., Williams, J. and Haslam, C. (1990) 'The hollowing out of British manufacturing and its implications for policy', *Economy and Society*, **19** (4), 456–90.

Zysman, J. (1996) 'The myth of the "global" economy: enduring national foundations and emerging regional realities', *New Political Economy*, **1** (2), 157–84.

11 Engineering our future again

Towards a long-term strategy for manufacturing and management in the United Kingdom

Ian Glover, Paul Tracey and Wendy Currie

INTRODUCTION

Our aim is to discuss the character, competence and future of manufacturing and management in the UK. We hope to encourage a freeing up and broadening out of some of the more focused thinking on our topic. We concentrate on engineers to a significant extent as the most numerous and important occupational group in manufacturing management.

In the next section we emphasize the importance of manufacturing and engineers in advanced economies. We also offer a slightly novel interpretation of the UK's relative economic decline since mid-Victorian times. In our third section we consider the current position of manufacturing and management in the UK. We discuss the character and quality of management, and that of manufacturing and management performance. We present data from representatives of managements, managers and professionals, and from individual managers and professionals. We discuss these along with findings of other studies. In the last section we consider the future of manufacturing and its management in the UK. We do so by relating earlier points about them to relevant elements of tentative SWOT (strengths, weaknesses, opportunities and threats) and PEST (political, economic, social and technological features of the environment) analyses of the UK and its situation, and to other considerations.

MANUFACTURING, ENGINEERS AND RELATIVE DECLINE

In this book and elsewhere the continuing or growing importance of manufacturing has been attributed to several factors (see, for example, Gershuny and Miles 1983; Cohen and Zysman 1987; Porter 1990; Glover 1992). It is strange that so many question its economic and social importance. In 1962 Allan Bullock wrote of Hitler, '*Si monumentum requiris, circumspice*' (if you want to see his monument, look around you). Manufacturing has achieved levels of affluence and sophistication unimaginable even two centuries ago, but familiarity and luxury appear to have bred contempt. Its significance for employment can be gauged by randomly checking the entries in the Yellow Pages telephone directories. While about a quarter are for service sector or other organizations with *no* strong links to or dependence on manufactured goods, about a half do have such links or dependence, and the remaining quarter are manufacturing organizations as such. Manufacturing and services jobs are increasingly interdependent: abrasive 'either-or' questions about one *versus* the other are increasingly futile.

Engineers are central to and crucial for manufacturing. Physically, logically, definitionally and chronologically, engineering production is central to it (Lawrence 1980). Engineering is often ahead of the frontiers of scientific knowledge. Almost all technical change is technique- and market-led, not 'mere' applied science (Sorge and Warner 1986). Top and senior managers should be technically aware or knowledgeable and entrepreneurial, as has long been understood by the UK's major competitors (Swords-Isherwood 1979; Finniston 1980; Glover 1978, 1985; Johnson 1993; Meiksins and Smith 1996).

Policies for the long term should be informed by historical understanding. A variety of interpretations of the UK's relative economic decline since around 1860 must be permitted: interpretations of the performance of all countries and sectors being compared are inevitably evolving and subjective, with the effects of many relevant events not yet fully apparent. Sorge (1979) argued that 'the whole [UK] perception of the world of making useful artefacts' was the country's true economic problem, rather than symptoms or parts of it like bad industrial relations, poor management quality, lack of investment, and irrelevant education and inadequate training, and that to understand the causes one had to explore political and general history.

We agree and could add some further points in the case of the UK. We think that its problems were (and are) largely ones of confusion about identity and loss of will and purpose following three or four centuries of unprecedented and almost unbelievable success. While it had to cope with two world wars and much other dramatic change, the UK was also undergoing the slow culmination of a very remarkable era from the reign of its first Queen Elizabeth to that of its second. The notion that the UK underwent some kind of collective identity crisis and failure of will, as if a declaration had been made that (self-imposed) failure ought to be experienced after centuries of continuous development or success, is very compatible with the conclusions about educational and occupational choices (Coleman 1973) and social movements and ideological and organizational choices (Glover 1985, 1991), was long apparent in writings on the UK's relative economic decline.

Mid-Victorian and later confusion about the kinds of institution needed for a twentieth-century (and later) industrial society – seen partly in the rather celebratory nature of some of those set up in mid-Victorian times – is itself suggestive of a deeper confusion. International comparisons and, above all, historical awareness have produced powerful insights into UK decline (Barnett 1972, 1986, 1995; Fores 1971; Horne 1969; Locke 1984, 1989, 1996; Nairn 1977; Perkin 1969; and Wilkinson 1964). They focus on influential periods and events, accounting for unique and definitive features of national institutional arrangements by reference to specific 'political circumstances at crucial points in history' (Sorge and Warner 1986: 8) and they follow the 'societal effect' philosophy of much organizational analysis since the 1970s (Maurice *et al.* 1979; Maurice *et al.* 1980).

Major features of the confusion and uncertainty referred to include half-hearted, arm's-length approaches to core activities like production, and to wealth creation in general. Beliefs in generalism rather than in the sector-specific in higher vocational education and the notion of engineering as (mere) applied science have drawn on the Victorian assumption that hard work was unfit for a gentleman. More recently they have been associated with such displacement activities as human resource management, business process re-engineering and total quality management. Supposed short-termism in financing private and public sector activities has been a particularly complex and interesting aspect of the syndrome. Definitions of short-term and long-term vary across frontiers and over time. It is also possible to operate within a short-termist structure in a relatively long-term way, and vice versa. This was more than hinted at by UK engineers, accountants and marketing managers recently interviewed by Tracey (1997; also see Conyon and Mullin 1997; Eltis 1993; Kitson and Michie in Chapter 2 in this volume; and Labour Research 1991, on these issues).

Our interpretation is subjective, vague and psychologistic, but probably less one-sided than most previous ones. It includes the notion of a mid-Victorian 'gentlemanly settlement' whereby some middle- and lower-class dynamism was tamed by being co-opted and bought off by the upper classes (Glover 1977, 1985; Anderson and Blackburn 1965; Coleman 1973; Wilkinson 1964). This notion is accepted widely, but when some of the more prominent writers on the UK's difficulties have developed their own perspectives they have not always clarified matters. Thus Wiener's (1981) notion of an 'industrial society with an anti-industrial culture' almost certainly exaggerates the extent to which the (minority) 'culture' of arts and other sympathetic graduates, emphasizing their tendency to despise events in factories, infected most inhabitants of the UK. Edgerton's (1991) thesis of a 'militant and technological nation' probably overstates the opposite case. Barnett's (1972, 1986, 1995) focus is on the overly high-minded outlook and behaviour of the UK's governing classes and academics whom he blames for appeasing Hitler and for developing after the Second World War ended the 'New Jerusalem' of cradle-to-grave state welfare without first ensuring that industry would be strong enough to pay for it. As with Wiener there is much truth in his case but it is one-sided and very much focused on (some of) the higher ranks of society. He also exaggerates the weaknesses of UK manufacturing.

Rubinstein (1993) is (like Edgerton) another critic of Wiener and Barnett. He emphasizes the perennial importance and weight of commerce, finance and London in the UK's economy compared with manufacturing, and such economically and socially valuable national characteristics as empiricism and the absence of extremism. His fascinating and often persuasive account of the relationships between the UK's elites and its economy since the eighteenth century is convincing in some respects about 'the illusion of all recent governments . . . that Britain could be restored to the "workshop of the world" by intervention in manufacturing industry' (ibid. 156). Rubinstein is clearly unsympathetic to manufacturing, however, and apparently unable to see how pervasive it is within both employment and consumption.

All four writers help to explain why UK society has exhibited unusually complicated attitudes towards manufacturing and engineering. They help to leave an impression of a deeply conservative yet very resilient and sophisticated society which is capable of making itself dramatically open to experience. Its ongoing problems include tendencies to overvalue inspiration and to undervalue perspiration, to defer too much to commanding social presence (Hampden-Turner and Trompenaars 1994), and celebrity and heroism, and even heroic failure (Huntford 1984). Belief in biologically fixed levels of ability is also a factor here, and out of tune with Japanese and much Western European management practice (Albert 1993; Locke 1989). Nairn (1977) and Lawrence (1996) linked UK snobbery about expectations to archaic, undemocratic sentimentality about the past and its living embodiments like the monarchy.

Contemporary discussion of UK economic 'decline' must be tempered by reference to the country's economic performance of the mid-1990s. Growth of GNP and unemployment trends compare well with those of major competitors. Real after tax incomes in the UK are now on a par with those in Germany and Sweden, for example (see recent issues of the *National Economic Review*, and O'Mahony and Wagner 1995, and O'Mahony and Wagner with Paulson 1995). The last-named authors attribute relevant UK productivity gains to a mixture of the 1980 recession's shock effect on labour and product markets, and the subsequent associated organizational changes which facilitated improvements in output quality as well as volume.

However personal incomes in Japan and the US and in several other European and other countries remain higher than UK ones, and in general, manufacturing remains a source of relative weakness (Williams *et al.* 1990; Froud *et al.* 1997). These authors point to UK manufacturing companies increasingly investing abroad, with the manufacturing that remains in the UK tending to be technically unsophisticated. However, this view may be too pessimistic about endogenous growth in manufacturing in the UK, and it also tends to play down the long-term value of its foreign direct investments. Yet it also reinforces the impression of arm's-length, predatory, and, in the UK context, perversely anti-industrial elements in management, which can wilfully stifle innovation and encourage tails to wag dogs (see Lawrence and Locke 1997, for an extremely telling example of the syndrome in another sector, of 'the management of' scientific research).

What eventually emerges is an impression of an economy and society undergoing an immensely complex process of transition, from being the tough hub or core of a far-flung empire, through much change and uncertainty, to one which is very independent and subtly proactive within the much deregulated, partly global economy of the late twentieth and early twenty-first centuries. Finally in this section, we re-emphasize our view that the underlying reasons for the UK's difficulties have been less superficial and more general than is usually thought. See the volume edited by Coates and Hillard (1995), for example: thirty or so chapters discuss often contradictory reasons, but almost all are merely symptoms or parts of the problem.

THE CURRENT POSITION

Management quality

What of management and manufacturing now? There are good reasons for regarding UK management quality as improving fairly dramatically. Elsewhere, three main ways of producing, organizing and managing broadly defined technical knowledge, skill and work have been identified (Glover and Tracey 1997). First, with the *professional-managerial* approach of the English-speaking countries, expert labour is developed partly in full-time education, partly through on-the-job experience and post-experience training. Expert labour of this type is often subordinated to general management. Second, there is the *university-formed technocratic* approach of the Benelux and Scandinavian countries, Germany and France. Here, most or all expert labour is formed in full-time higher education, often with employer help. Management is part of technical expertise, not vice versa. Third, with the *company-centred technocratic* approach of Japan and other Far Eastern countries, expert labour is recruited from mainly specialist vocational higher education but trained and developed beyond its theoretical base by employers. Management tends to be part of, or subordinated to, technical expertise.

In the Anglo-Saxon countries, especially the UK, top and senior management jobs in commerce, industry and elsewhere tended to be staffed by gentlemanly liberal arts and pure science graduates, sometimes called 'philosopher-kings', 'amateurs', or *custodians* (Glover 1977). In many sectors their immediate subordinates, who tended to be 'on tap but not on top', were or are *professionals*. When these were salaried employees in the private or public sectors, and until the large-scale expansion and vocationalization of university-level education starting in the 1960s, they were generally products of part-time study and on-the-job training. Nowadays, they are generally graduates in relevant subjects, who either qualify for membership of their professional associations after suitable and accredited on-the-job learning and/or further study, or whose degrees are enough on their own for them to secure appropriate employment.

On the continent of Europe, and up to a point in Japan, *technocrats* have long dominated senior positions in most sectors. Originally such people were mainly broadly educated and high-powered engineers, but through most of the twentieth century they were joined by increasing numbers of broadly similar kinds of individual qualified in business economics. All such people were *both* generalists like Anglo-Saxon custodians *and* specialists like Anglo-Saxon professionals, although the construction of their specialisms tended, especially in the case of engineers, to be rather more sector-specific and to have less to do, than in the Anglo-Saxon case, with the vested interests and other non-task related priorities of professional-occupational groupings and associations. All of these three types of senior job holder existed in relatively large numbers in the nineteenth century. However, *managers* are mainly products of the twentieth century. A typical 'manager' would have a business studies or business administration degree or an MBA, and is typically Anglo-Saxon, although some continental Europeans and others have relevant backgrounds. He or she tends to be more mobile between sectors (and employers) than professionals and custodians and even technocrats. Apart from the unqualified 'practical man' (Barnett 1972; Locke 1984), managers, custodians, professionals and technocrats cover the whole range of backgrounds of top and senior job holders.

The categories are not mutually exclusive and many individuals combine the features of two or more of them. In the UK, management-level people 'tend [because they are increasingly professional specialists with business management kinds of qualification] to be professional-managerial but are evolving into a mixture of all three ways of producing people – they are becoming more technocratic – with elements of the custodian still around' (Glover and Tracey 1997). Because vocational (and academic) higher education in the UK has been expanded and developed since the 1960s to meet, anticipate or even create a wide range of market and other needs, often very imaginatively, because the traditionally open-ended approach to learning of the system has generally been maintained, and because the age participation rate is increasingly close to the average of other industrial countries, the prospect of the UK's approach to higher education leap-frogging those of its competitors has become genuinely possible (for a more detailed exposition, see Glover and Hughes 1996: 4–11). These changes are not merely products of UK responses to foreign competition and practice: many are largely or entirely domestic in origin (cf. Tiratsoo 1996).

Manufacturing performance

Our guarded optimism about the improving quality of UK managers is partly tempered and partly encouraged by our perceptions of the clearly varied quality of the outputs and performance of UK manufacturing and related industries. Relevant macro- and microeconomic data and management research offer evidence of consistently or recently very strong performance in several sectors, of considerable improvement in others, and in pockets across the whole system, of the persistence and even development of old bad habits of short-termist and arm's-length management. There is of course considerable evidence of foreign direct and portfolio investment, both abroad by UK-owned multinationals and in the UK by foreign-owned ones, giving UK manufacturing its very international and fragmented character. Labour productivity in UK manufacturing rose from about 40 per cent to about 60 per cent of US levels between 1973 and 1989, and Germany's level was 105 per cent of the UK's in 1989 compared with 119 per cent in 1973, although Japan's had risen from 95 per cent to 143 per cent in the same period (Williams *et al.* 1990).

In the 1980s and 1990s the UK overcame difficulties attributed to inadequate shopfloor control, to price fixing, government intervention in industry and overreliance on soft Commonwealth markets, but still needed to invest more in human and physical capital (Broadberry 1997; see Kitson and Michie in Chapter 2 in this volume). Some optimism is engendered by evidence of a persistent ability to innovate, often in the face of ongoing failure and considerable indifference. Also it is wrong to assume that the workers are largely unskilled and intractable. Given technically competent and committed management, they appear able and willing to perform well by most and sometimes any standard (Nicholls 1986).

Views from professions, management, industry and research

Some evidence concerning management, engineering and engineers in the UK appears to favour a relatively optimistic long-term scenario. In late 1995, 1996 and 1997 Glover and Tracey conducted twenty-five interviews with senior representatives of a number of the public bodies which represent organizational professions, managers and directors of companies, manufacturing and cognate employers, economic and political interests, and a small number of experienced individual academic researchers. One of the interviewers/authors of this chapter had enjoyed research contacts in the 1970s with several of the professional and management associations visited and was struck quite forcefully two decades later by their greater pragmatism, self-awareness and proactivity.

In early 1996 the Engineering Council, which previously manifested slightly autocratic and bureaucratic tendencies, was reformed to make it more democratic and representative. However, representation of industry on the Council had been reduced and this was a matter of some concern. On the other hand it was clear that it had done much to rationalize and clarify engineering qualifications, and to build and modernize engineering's image. By developing its routes to chartered engineer status the Engineering Council was trying to emphasize the centrality of engineering excellence to manufacturing success. Now that it was free of the government, the Engineering Council needed to achieve a single voice that included industry. It had to move beyond its involvement in education and qualifications and representing engineers and the engineering institutions.

The five engineering institutions that were visited offered a study in contrasts. However, they were generally agreed on a need for engineering education to attract people and to produce engineers with entrepreneurial flair, and they wanted their 'profession' to have a higher and more up-to-date profile. The important Institution of Electrical Engineers seemed to be a little more content with the general development of the Engineering Council than most of the other engineering institutions.

Among the smaller institutions, that of Marine Engineers exuded an air of constructive and quite energetic self-awareness, especially about the prospects for educating engineers to be entrepreneurial in the widest sense. Our main impression was one of quiet determination to achieve whatever was possible combined with a realistic awareness of the limitations of the profession and its members, and of society's perceptions of engineering. We also visited the Royal Academy of Engineering, which aimed to promote UK engineering by encouraging and publicizing best practice. Our discussion there was very wide-ranging, touching on public perceptions and media portrayals of engineering education from secondary to doctoral level, entrepreneurship, ethics, management, the environment and design.

A number of sometimes surprisingly disparate insights were presented during visits to the Chartered Institute of Management Accountants (CIMA), the Chartered Institute of Marketing (CIM) and the Institute of Personnel and Development (IPD). At the CIMA, differences between 'traditional' chartered and management accountants were depicted as ones between people who emphasize standards and focus on inputs to business, and people who are concerned with quality and business outcomes. Partly because of developments in their education and training, management accountants increasingly worked in close partnership with engineers and marketing people. Accountants were less often feared and mistrusted harbingers of doom than in the past.

The interviewee at the CIM was equally sanguine about its development. Its main concerns were with raising standards of practice, by improving skills on the one hand and education on the other. Despite recent growth, its membership still only included a small percentage of the UK's eligible or potentially eligible marketing managers and specialists. However, its growing and increasingly active links with employers, with government, and with the related bodies which have recently created the Marketing Council appeared to make it punch considerably above its superficially apparent weight.

The themes of widening concerns, and of greater proactivity and practicality, were also evident at the IPD. The IPD had not bought into the human resource management movement although it did believe strongly in efficiency, competitiveness and in employers investing in people. Its relationships with employers and government and other public bodies were generally cooperative. Yet they did tend to be focused on employment and personnel matters like health and safety rather than on more general issues of competitiveness and efficiency which might have been pursued through interprofessional collaboration.

The interviews held with representatives of management institutes and employers' associations were significant, as might be expected, in different ways from those with the professional associations and the Engineering Council. The (formerly British) Institute of Management (IM) had quite wide interests and concerns and it had a very public and sometimes influential role. The IM was increasingly tailoring its management development efforts to particular companies and individuals. It had excluded supervisors from most of its courses but it now no longer did so: 'of course they are managers'. Rising standards of education and skill, organizational delayering, teamworking, empowerment and the notion of the learning organization were being combined in many organizations to involve high proportions of employees in management. However, the IM was neither the voice nor the servant of management. It represented managers and sought to improve and promote the standing and standards of management. Most of the IM's members had management as their second skill. Many engineers and many other kinds of specialists used the IM for management training.

A rather similar tale of humble moderation and pragmatism was heard in the course of the interviews at the Institute of Directors (IOD). It was more concerned than hitherto about improving the performance of company directors. The IOD was concerned with three relatively controversial issues. One was its desire for cuts in capital gains and inheritance taxes which would help directors to take money out of their businesses when they retired or left to join other companies. Another was directors' pay, which had been a subject of concern in the media. Third, it was increasingly involved in engineering education. It was also much concerned with public perceptions of business in general and those of its members in particular.

At the Engineers' Employers Federation (EEF) it was suggested that the Engineering Council's changes had not gone far enough. History was a barrier to true unification. One major engineering institution was particularly, and in some respects damagingly, independent. Most 'professional' engineers did not see the Engineering Council as their main or primary focus of loyalty. However, unification was only one way to deal with engineering's image problems. Engineering's problems began when girls were given dolls and boys cars and train sets to play with. The education system badly needed a period of stability. The baccalaureate and (even) the Scottish Highers systems were superior to A-levels which forced pupils into early and narrow specialization. The title 'engineer' needed to be restricted to graduates to stop engineers being confused with technicians. But engineers complained too much: they were reasonably paid, and some were extremely well paid. Many doctors and lawyers had to work cruelly long hours for only a little more money than top engineers. The media were unhelpful to engineers and the 'chattering classes certainly don't want their kids to go into engineering'. There were plenty of jobs for graduate engineers. However, there was a severe lack of applicants for engineering apprenticeships because secondary schools needed to keep their numbers and would not release their pupils.

The average education level of UK managers was still low by international standards. Engineers were not generally discriminated against in the workplace, yet promotion without training was still widespread. Interfunctional segmentation was still a problem in many companies, although manufacturing industry was much improved compared with twenty years ago. Short-termism was still a valid notion, however: companies were driven towards shareholders, not capital reinvestment. There *were* plenty of engineers in top jobs in manufacturing, but many still needed to be more assertive and entrepreneurial. However, some technical engineers did make poor managers.

At the CBI, assurances about the organization's non-political stance were given, and about its strongly practical orientation. The CBI campaigned actively, and lobbied government with the aim of improving the UK's competitiveness. Many UK manufacturers were 'world class', but there was a lack of up-and-coming companies and a long tail of weaker ones. In 1979, manufacturing produced a third of the UK's total output. Now the proportion was a fifth, and the country's capital stock had been diminished. Nevertheless, the story was not all bad: some productivity gains of the 1980s had been genuine. Manufacturing exported nearly 70 per cent of its output, it earned most of the UK's foreign exchange, and many services fed into and off it. These views were coming back into fashion. Inward foreign direct investment was helping to improve the public's perception of manufacturing and to lift UK standards of knowledge and skill.

One of the more surprising interviews was conducted at the right-wing Institute of Economic Affairs, the Conservative equivalent of the Fabian Society. It was felt that business people still enjoyed less respect in the UK than elsewhere. However, the UK's relative economic decline was over and the economy was now quite competitive with those of the EU and Japan, although not with those of the newer Pacific Rim countries. It was wrong to argue that the UK should focus on manufacturing as if it was something special or that it needed a manufacturing 'base' of a particular size. Yet it was an important element of the economy. The UK did need to invest more in it, both physically and in terms of skills. This stance towards manufacturing was not very different from the others that we heard and was, indeed, quite similar to that expressed in conversations with staff of the Labour-supporting Institute of Public Policy Research.

The small and fairly disparate group of academic experts whom we interviewed only had an interest in manufacturing of some kind in common. One said that UK living standards had been much higher since 1870 relative to those of the country's major competitors than is commonly assumed, and that there was little evidence of serious anti-industrial prejudice in the UK, now or in the past. Another, an expert on careers, criticized the anarchic and laissez-faire stance towards employee development taken by most employers. There was more evidence for deterioration in employment practices since the 1970s than improvement. However, better-managed companies did tend both to retain able staff and to be more unified and focused in senior management on their core tasks than previously. Another academic argued that UK management quality had been improving quite quickly in recent decades, with qualifications being increasingly relevant and levels of individual commitment and intellectual roundedness and international awareness being much higher. Many companies had been learning a great deal from abroad.

Another was very keen to point out how engineers had long been the numerically dominant occupational group at all levels of the managements of manufacturing companies in the UK. Engineers made very competent functional and middle managers but tended to lack divergent thinking skills needed for top management. Engineers did not really lack status, and there was no major 'cultural problem' regarding industry in the UK. Poor indigenous manufacturing performance was partly a product of lack of investment, which was due to poor returns. Manufacturing in the UK did not attract enough of the most able people. They did have a genuine failing, too: they tended to persist in searching for right or wrong answers in genuinely ambiguous and politicized situations where there were none. Nevertheless, many were very able and had excellent and well-rewarded jobs and enviably interesting careers (Barry *et al.* 1997).

Views from professionals and managers in industry

One of us (Tracey) also interviewed eighty-five engineers, accountants and marketing specialists, managers and directors, employed in chemicals, construction and mechanical (and electro-mechanical) engineering. In semi-structured interviews of between one and two hours they were asked about the employment and work, the influence and power, the abilities and the public perceptions and general position in society of engineers, and about the prospects for constructive change. The sample consisted of fifty-three engineers, eleven accountants, ten marketing and sales specialists, all of whom had engineering backgrounds, two personnel managers, six quantity surveyors and three architects. The average age was 41. Four respondents were female. All were graduates or professionally qualified and held management positions of some kind.

On the influence and power of engineers, respondents said that there was little conflict and competition between them and other specialists, that cooperation tended to prevail and that multifunctional teams, very often led by engineers, were common. Both engineers and accountants were seen as powerful in management, with the former much more numerous, and slightly more valued. Engineers were often found to be at the top in marketing, and even personnel and managing directors were more likely to be engineers than accountants. Three-fifths of the engineers were not overtly concerned with issues of power and status. They felt that they had enough, and they also believed that the engineers, accountants, marketing and sales, and personnel specialists and managers in their companies were equally well or badly paid. Engineering was a rewarding career, in general offering high job satisfaction, autonomy, responsibility, influence and opportunity.

About three-quarters of respondents seemed to believe that the position of engineers in their companies was more than adequate or better, but that there was still a problem in weaker companies and elsewhere in society. They tended to think that to restrict the title 'engineer' to graduate or equivalent engineers by law would be a helpful step, but noted, also, that in (most of) their companies this was done already.

The respondents' comments on the abilities of engineers were as follows. Detailed marketing knowledge was considered unnecessary unless an engineer was employed in marketing. The financial skills needed by engineers were very basic and quickly grasped: engineers were numerate people. Knowledge of human resource management was generally unnecessary, but person management was very important. Other functions needed some kind or level of technical awareness, but technical knowledge was unnecessary. Senior managers needed some technical awareness, and technical knowledge was considered to be an advantage for promotion to senior posts. Engineers were generally neither inferior nor superior to financial, marketing and sales, HRM and other counterparts in terms of the ability to work well with others, leadership and motivation skills, or as young graduates.

About four-fifths of engineers complained about their social standing, although a small number felt that the 'status' of engineers was not much different to most other graduates or professionals. UK people were not generally perceived as anti-industrial. However, there was a feeling that the society had somehow 'given up' on manufacturing. The UK's financial system seemed to generate polarized responses, with a third of respondents believing that it allowed companies to be flexible and responsive to external factors and new technologies, while another third believed that the threat of possible hostile takeovers and apparent difficulties in obtaining long-term finance kept companies more focused on financial than production performance and led to underinvestment in equipment, technical development and training.

Real improvements had, it was felt, been made to engineering education. About four-fifths of the engineer respondents felt that the introduction of management subjects in degree courses in the 1970s and 1980s had been long over-due, although a very small number were concerned that some of the technical aspects of engineering degrees, particularly the mathematics content, had been diluted. About three-fifths of the engineers believed that the practical element of degrees should be increased by introducing a compulsory one-year placement. Four-fifths argued that the practical parts of an engineer's formation should remain the responsibility of employers and that universities should continue to focus on producing theoretically competent graduates, which most of them had been doing very successfully. It was also suggested that, contrary to popular belief, there was not a shortage of engineering graduates in the UK, and that the opposite was the case.

The engineering institutions were criticized heavily. Half of the engineers thought of them as 'old boys' clubs' which did little to serve their members' needs. Some engineer respondents had left them in protest. The Engineering Council was seen as being more effective than its constituent institutions and there was widespread approval of the changes which it had helped to make to engineering education. Its fostering of and support for chartered engineer status was generally popular. However, it was thought that it should do more to promote engineering in society. Trade unions were seen as largely irrelevant by and for virtually all of the engineers in the study: only three respondents were in the public sector.

Three-quarters of the respondents were unconvinced about the extent to which the standing of engineers, engineering and manufacturing should or could be improved in the eyes of an apparently sceptical public. Concern was expressed about the 'non-portrayal' of engineers in the media. It was felt that schools should do more to encourage brighter pupils to study engineering.

Overall these findings and the evidence marshalled by Barry *et al.* (1997) on the backgrounds of managers in manufacturing certainly shed considerable doubt on the notion of the powerless engineer. Barry *et al.* concluded that an able person wanting to get to the top in manufacturing stood the best chance if he or she was an engineer, after analysing data from their own and numerous official, private and professional association surveys. Engineers outnumbered accountants by at least three to one among graduate or equivalent top executives.

Our view of the situation of UK engineers in general is that it is very varied and dangerous to generalize about, except to say that it is nothing like as unfortunate as conventional thinking suggests. We now look at a number of other fairly recent studies to consider whether or not they contradict or support these perceptions.

Further evidence on engineers in management

Much of the literature on engineers is confused by a tendency among writers to separate engineering and management conceptually. We regard graduate or professional and otherwise equivalent engineers as part of society's managerial stratum, as being among those who are engaged in the broadly defined tasks of planning, organizing and supervising the work of others, or who contribute advice, ideas and information to their performance while receiving similar levels of material reward (Glover 1977: chapter 1). To exclude engineers from management in the way referred to is divisive and incompetent, and of course often symptomatic and part of the 'problem' in question.

Canainn (1995) reports data obtained from electrical and electronic engineers in electricity supply in Ulster and Eire, and in manufacturing in Eire. She found that many of the engineers in Ulster were effectively ghettoized into technical work and careers by the privatization and commercialization of their organization in the early 1990s and by their own 'traditional' self-perceptions as 'improved tradesmen'. They had been unable and unwilling, unlike their counterparts in Eire, to recognize how, in order to progress in their organizations, they needed to engage and involve themselves enthusiastically with non-technical work.

This evidence of varied possibilities and realities in the experiences of engineers was also demonstrated by Causer and Jones (1993). They found that electronics engineers in southern England, in spite of their scarce and important skills, were by no means always treated as long-term resources by their employers. This was due to the volatile character of markets in electronics, the considerable dependence of firms on external funding of research and development work, the highly varied and specialized backgrounds of the engineers involved, and the prevalence of 'poaching' highly qualified and skilled employees in the industry. McGovern's (1995) study of Irish engineers contains a discussion of ways in which relatively enlightened employers can and sometimes do help to make labour markets for engineers more stable and supportive by sponsoring university engineering students, offering superior pay and promotion prospects and so on. In a later study Causer and Jones (1996) demonstrate and emphasize the ambiguous, diffuse and varied character of authority in technical work in electronics work in England. Individual experiences of employment were often much more varied than the fairly homogeneous social, educational and occupational backgrounds of engineers might indicate.

Jones *et al.* (1996; see also Jones *et al.* 1994) discussed evidence from a wide-ranging study of young graduate engineers to explain how restricted jobs and careers in engineering in the UK are sectoral rather than general problems. The authors studied the employment of young engineers in electronics, aerospace, chemical engineering, mechanical engineering, power engineering and electricity supply. Poor use of graduate engineers was most common in electronics and aerospace, because employment was continually affected by market changes, leading to continual 'off-the-shelf' graduate recruitment. Lam (1994, 1996) made use of Japanese evidence in comparing the work roles and relationships between technical and managerial functions in the UK and Japan. She suggests that the (assumed) poor representation of engineers in top management in the UK, which we do not accept (see above), is only a symptom, not at the root of the problem, 'which lies in the split between technical and managerial expertise at the enterprise level' (Lam 1996: 183).

The above papers are generally not focused on the higher levels of competence in UK industry. Given the fact that the research on which they report was directed at the study of problems, this is reasonable. However, there is much within them, too, to suggest that UK engineers do experience very varied forms of employment, with at least some of them positive. They contained little to contradict Barry *et al.*'s points about the prevalence of engineers in top management. Even so, a recent paper by Carter and Crowther (1997) on the privatization of an electricity supply in 1990 showed how, in exceptional circumstances, engineers could be systematically stripped of much, even most, of their power by their employers.

A possibly more positive tone was struck by Newton and Keenan (1990) in a study of young graduates in civil, electrical and electronic, mechanical and chemical engineering and in the offshore oil and gas industry. Respondents who moved from one employer to another early in their careers generally experienced the move as 'proactive growth' rather than as 'stress-coping'. Although principally concerned with scientists, Randle (1996) explains how reducing demand for expert labour can lead to the systematic reduction of 'professional' autonomy, opportunities to be creative, and promotion opportunities. A more general, comparative and historical, account of changing industrial relations practices in the UK and Japan is that of McCormick and McCormick (1996), which considers such factors as the effects of Japanese transplants in UK labour markets and changes in the economic and strategic priorities of both countries. The chapter by Smith and Whalley (1996) in the volume on engineers in six major industrial countries edited by Meiksins and Smith (1996) is misleading in some respects (Glover and Tracey 1997), but it does nonetheless contain much useful information regarding the employment of UK engineers. Smith and Whalley exaggerate several features of the 'low status' and the sometimes uncertain career prospects of UK engineers. Yet in spite of this and the chapter's overly historical emphasis, it does contain points relevant to the present. So does Rubery's paper (1994) on the strong free market emphasis of the UK's 'production regime'. Rubery analyses links between the UK's employment, family and distribution systems and the institutions of its labour markets and of production in the context of the evolving world economy and 'the international transmission of ideas, ideologies and modes of operation' (ibid. 349). Her analysis of connections between many UK and other economic and social institutions is very suggestive about the specific reasons why engineers experience very varied employment situations and prospects.

In this section of the chapter we have suggested that while manufacturing performance and the employment of engineers in the UK exhibit many strengths and weaknesses, there are clear signs of improvement away from the broadly negative patterns of a generation ago. Significantly, better-qualified management and more cooperative behaviour within management teams appear to be two important contributions to a tendency for the competent segments of manufacturing and construction to be increasingly capable of performing well against foreign competition. Jones *et al.* (1994) also hinted at this sort of conclusion in their paper on the long-term employment prospects of UK engineers.

THE FUTURE

To consider the prospects for the UK's engineers, engineering and industry it is necessary to consider them in the context of a broader examination of the UK's economy and society. We now do this by subjecting the country to a (somewhat subjective) SWOT analysis, of its strengths and weaknesses, and of the opportunities and threats which face it.

Such an analysis might look like this. The strengths would include long traditions of pragmatism and innovation, weakened by diffidence and complacency over the last century or so, but still very strong by international standards; world-class science; very strong engineering education, which is not always taken advantage of by UK as opposed to overseas students; since the 1970s, and increasingly so, very strong business, management and professional education, which does tend, however, to neglect production and manufacturing; improving management quality, as defined in terms of motivation, self-awareness and qualifications; high standards of health care; very efficient agriculture; humility and openness to foreign experience after a century of tending to assume that God is English; rediscovered concern for detail and hard work, which is sometimes taken too far; long experience of international finance and overseas trading and of overseas contact in general; political experience and sophistication of quite a high order; experience of complex project management and of developing and managing multinational companies; a deeply conservative attitude towards institutions and to social arrangements in general – a strength in seriously changing times insofar as there is a willingness to make fundamental changes wholeheartedly, provided that they are seen as being really needed, and because once the UK becomes good at something, it seems to stay good at it; and a great deal of oil and natural gas.

The weaknesses would include social, economic and educational polarization; uncertain and varied status and power of technical experts; weak performance of much manufacturing industry and lack of manufacturing capacity in several sectors which a country with the UK's population arguably ought to have capacity in; poorly qualified management, in spite of the fact that it is improving quickly, and a tendency to dispense too readily with the services of older managers simply because they are older and to promote younger ones before they are experienced enough simply because they are younger; a poorly qualified and trained labour force, although one that has often shown, and often under overseas managers, that it is much more capable than it looks on paper; rather chaotic and overcomplicated work organization: much evidence in the last fifteen years or so of flatter, leaner organization structures and more flexible and unified management, but underlying problems of too many types of specialist, with line management tending to be underpowered in spite of top management attempts to give it more power, remain; tendencies to hark back to past glories; continuing power of institutions like the civil service and the education system which have routinely encouraged arm's-length attitudes towards detail; a society in transition, under strain, with confused moral and other values (fashion, image, possessions, confused with integrity, ability, achievement and so on), with lack of understanding and respect for other people's complex skills, much interprofessional and interoccupational conflict, and much stereotyping; a conformist and fearful tendency to pursue the 'excellent' at the expense of both the outstanding and the good or very good, high-flier worship in human resource management and in general, at the expense of the rest, involving waste of experienced people, rampant ageism, elitism based on stereotyping and the construction of self-fulfilling prophecies rather than on true potential, ability and effort; and of arguably major significance, short-termism on the part of some financial and other institutions which has long affected decision making, often to bad effect, in industry, commerce and the public sector.

The opportunities might include: superior experience of international trading and diplomacy in the EU and wider contexts; opportunities for expanding strategic alliances between companies from different countries and developing already considerable experience of complex project management in engineering construction, civil engineering, energy, aerospace, chemicals, and so on; for building on and exploiting superior experience and knowledge of international finance in a context in which international finance is increasingly in need of supranational monitoring and control; and for continuing to build on recent and current important developments in education to help build a society without old-style deference, but one with efficiency, respect and democracy designed into all of its institutions.

The threats would include a perception, still with at least a little basis in reality, that the UK is a declining middle power on the fringe of the EU, a sort of dreary offshore Italy, with delusions about the strengths of a rather weak 'special relationship' with the US (itself a nation with problems), and with a seat on the UN Security Council increasingly hard to justify; the national love of generalism and of mobility between jobs and sectors of activity, which works to the detriment of specialist skill and achievement of the kind which Germans embody in the anything-but-narrow notion of flexible specialization; the manufacturing strengths and technical expertise of competitor countries and the rapidly growing financial power of the Far East; the growth of China into an economic superpower, which may also be turned into an opportunity; the possibility of widely harmful instability in the former Soviet bloc parts of Europe; and the relative weakness of the UK's ties with countries with which it once enjoyed very close relationships, such as Australia and India.

We might also usefully ask what the 'organizational environment' of UK plc looks like. Here is a tentative outline of a PEST (political, economic, social, technological) environmental analysis.

Political situation. The country remains politically stable, perhaps a little worryingly so insofar as one political party was in power for so long until last year. The UK's scepticism regarding proposals from the EU seems a healthy if occasionally eccentric phenomenon. The country is still influential in the world given its size, and this is probably more of an asset than a liability, because an enhanced ability to affect one's own destiny outweighs the effects of remaining confusion associated with past grandeur.

Economic situation. Deregulation at the national level and a mixture of it with some protectionism at the regional trading bloc level seems likely to continue in a world context in which deregulation continues to be more politically correct than the alternatives. The former Soviet bloc and the newly industrializing and developing countries should provide the UK, along with its EC partners and rivals, with many opportunities for quite a long time to come. A 'fire at will' approach to opportunities there and elsewhere in the world, especially those in the 'developing' parts of the Far and Near East, should prevail. In the UK the growth of a complex and sophisticated professional-managerial class is a strong plus point. There is still, however, an urgent need to ensure that the whole labour force is well educated and trained, with varied and flexible skills helping to breed varied and flexible opportunities.

Social situation. Individualism on its own or taken too far seems inadequate; responsibility needs to be both individual and collective. Confusion about private and public boundaries appears to be endemic and often the subject of exploitation. We believe strongly in free markets, but as servants of the human race. Encouragement of pride in useful and excellent work may be a key to a situation in which people are much clearer about their roles and, in particular, about their responsibilities to learn, to produce and to pass knowledge and skills on to less experienced people.

Technical situation. More consistent and long-term finance is needed to support innovativeness on the part of engineers, scientists and entrepreneurs of all kinds in most sectors and types of employment. Technical education below graduate level needs comprehensive overhaul and development. Education and training policy needs to become less ad hoc, and informed by a much broader long-term vision.

The mixtures of fact, hypothesis and speculation just presented and the somewhat if not, we hope, overly optimistic views that we derive from them are not incompatible with those of McRae (1994). He lists the UK's relatively young population (in a European context), the speed of its 'adjustment out of midtechnology industry' compared with the rest of Europe, and its 'closer relationship with both North America and the Far East than those of its continental partners' (ibid. 231) as some of its main advantages. Its education system's relative neglect of the less academic, its valorization of creativity and individuality, and associated regional disparities of achievement, wealth and power are listed as some of its main problems.

Regarding attitudes and aspirations for work of different kinds in different economic sectors, there appear to be some grounds for cautious optimism about the adjustment from manual, 'industrial' jobs to a situation in which seven more people work in services. The fact that it is not necessary to make a tangible product (artefact) in order to experience job satisfaction and that there is nothing specially morally superior about physical labour, appear to be increasingly appreciated (Allen and Du Gay 1994). Much of so-called 'new' (Webb 1996) or 'new wave' (Wood 1990) thinking has been criticized for superficiality, faddishness and materialism (Du Gay and Salaman 1992). Yet while it is easy enough to have some sympathy with such criticisms, a balanced view of the ideas often associated, and with some kind of elective affinity with, the rise of service-sector employment in the 1980s should admit that aspects of human resource management, concern for service quality and customer care, and even business process re-engineering, are probably very useful in making work in services of virtually all kinds more effective and satisfying for all involved (Wentworth and Glover 1998).

On the technical resourcefulness (or otherwise) of UK managements and employees we believe that it has long been underrated. Thus it has not been lack of technical ingenuity that has caused the UK to lose industrial employment and which has seen powerful sectors become moribund or die. It has been the half-hearted attitude of both institutions and individuals (discussed in the section on relative decline above), who should have ensured that relevant support systems – including tough-minded expectations and aspirations – were kept in place. As old prejudices against dark Satanic factories fade away, encouraged by their virtual absence, so should those which do no favours to the technically ingenious.

On the general kind of approach that is needed to encourage economic and social dynamism, the choice between top-down institutional change and a mixture of friendly persuasion and tacit and national support is obvious, given our nation's history. The former, if at all heavy-handed, tends to provoke negative reactions from below. To develop education, knowledge, training and skills to superior levels across the whole UK economy will almost certainly require a flexible mixture of state support and encouragement and dynamic private action in and around internal labour markets (see Henderson 1993; Delbridge and Lowe 1996).

On the more specifically social influences, some of the main ones to be considered include affluence, age, the decline of bureaucratic careers, and deference, social mobility and social status. The UK is clearly a much wealthier and socially fluid society even if the idea that 'the class paradigm is intellectually and morally bankrupt' (Pakulski and Waters 1995: 26; see Scott 1996 for more balanced views) is almost ridiculous when one thinks of contemporary income and power disparities. Age is important because life expectancy is now so great in a context in which machines are substituted for much labour, meaning that the possibility of fulfilling 90-year lives consisting of one-third learning, one-third working and one-third principally engaged in leisure, social and civic activities becomes feasible (Branine and Glover 1997). The decline of bureaucratic careers and of associated behaviour patterns of control and deference are all associated with the foregoing developments. So too are high and varied rates of social mobility and the problem of affluence helping to create a capitalism driven by naked self-interest and an associated 'post-modern' culture of extreme moral relativism (Saunders 1995).

Finally, on the UK's economy and on the role of manufacturing in it we would re-emphasize an important point both hinted and sometimes more than hinted at several times in this chapter. This is that because manufacturing and services are so interdependent, with manufacturing, production and development increasingly transnational phenomena, the UK's talent for innovation and its traditional creativity in complex project management put it in a favourable position as regards contemporary economic development (cf. Ackroyd 1995; see also Conti and Warner 1997). We do not think that shortfalls in the provision of technical education in the UK need necessarily be much of a handicap in this context. As Meiksins and Smith (1996) have explained most effectively, there are many ways of producing a competent engineer, and university education can be an extremely valuable and a sufficient part of that process but it is not a necessary one (also see Ackroyd and Lawrenson 1996). Encouraging vibrations about UK policy making concerning technical innovation can be derived readily from a reading of a paper on the UK's Technology Foresight exercise by Elliot (1996). Current policy thinking in this area appears to embody proactive and sceptical optimism, with the grandiose and portentous elements of past decades seemingly absent.

Also, and although we have long been among admirers of the attitudes, aspirations, habits and institutions associated with the German word *Technik*, it is possible to embrace all of its positive features selectively and judiciously without having to learn German. Thus Leadbeater (1997) argued that contemporary California is a more relevant and impressive economic model for the UK than Asia or Germany. California was at the forefront of manufacturing and other economic development, and had strong cultural similarities with the UK. Germany was more corporatist and Asia too cavalier with civil liberties to be as easy to follow as California.

California was strong, like the UK, in soft assets like knowledge, ideas and creativity. It was an entrepreneurial culture, with mutually supportive networks of companies and their suppliers and backers, a creative cultural environment and an ethical approach to business with high standards of corporate responsibility. It was a fertile climate of knowledge-intensive high-growth technology and enterprise, full of 'diversity, tolerance and experimentation' – 'traditional' UK virtues. Yet all of this is totally compatible with the essence of *Technik*: unpredictable ingenuity and technical excellence.

We could write more, about environmental, political and social considerations creating pressures for the pace of economic and technical change to slow down, and for serious compromises between the different social arrangements associated with each of the 'two capitalisms' (Albert 1993) – the abrasive, fast-moving neo-American model and the more staid, cooperative yet at least equally effective

Rhine one – to be worked out (also see Kenworthy 1995, and Littek and Charles 1995, for more judicious perspectives). We could refer to cautionary tales about the extent, speed and relevance of globalization (Hirst and Thompson 1995, 1996). Finally, we could refer to the ways in which the possibility, implicit in some of the arguments just referred to, that the pace of economic change may be slowing, is reflected in the interesting discussion of contemporary management thinking by Tsoukas and Cummings (1997).

CONCLUSIONS

We have argued that manufacturing is of growing importance to the UK, that the country's relative economic decline was partly inevitable, partly a problem of success, more than a mere blip in the country's story, but from any rational standpoint not much more, and that management quality and industrial perform-ance are showing strong signs of long-term improvement. We have already writ-ten much on both general and specific aspects of policy. Given the apparent affinity between many of the UK's national characteristics and the 'disorganized', flexible and international character of contemporary capitalism, it might be enough simply to advocate a policy of going with the flow. We could be more active and list specific policies under the headings of manufacturing, management and engineers, with such (valid) old chestnuts as more training, stable long-term finance, broader secondary education, more assertiveness on the part of engin-eers, more language learning, more technicians, and so on and so forth. However, three things strike us as particularly important. One is the value of the increasingly lively activities of the more go-ahead professional and management associations. For example, it is good that the Engineering Council acts in creative and positive ways and that it is working to become a national advocate of technical excellence. Second, the positive aspects of manufacturing's role badly need explaining. These include its innovative power, affecting consumption and the development of ser-vices and new forms and patterns of employment and living. Engineering career prospects should also be spelt out powerfully.

This leads to our third and final point. Manufacturing only attracts about 4 per cent of non-engineering graduates. This is almost tragic in view of its potential. Business and management and arts and natural and social science graduates all need to be informed forcefully of the nature of manufacturing's role in con-temporary economic life, of its interdependence with services, of its substantial creative and material rewards, and of the even greater potential which might be realized with their help.

REFERENCES

Ackroyd, S. (1995) 'On the structure and dynamics of some small, UK-based informa-tion technology firms', *Journal of Management Studies*, **32** (2), 141–61.
Ackroyd, S. and Lawrenson, D. (1996) 'Manufacturing decline and the division of labour in Britain: the case of vehicles', in I.A. Glover and M. Hughes (eds), *The*

Professional-Managerial Class: Contemporary British Management in the Pursuer Mode, Aldershot: Avebury, 171–93.

Albert, M. (1993) *Capitalism against Capitalism*, London: Whurr.

Allen, J. and Du Gay, P. (1994) 'Industry and the rest: the economic identity of services', *Work, Employment and Society*, 8 (9), 225–71.

Anderson, P. and Blackburn, R. (eds) (1965) *Towards Socialism*, London: Fontana.

Ashton, D. and Green, F. (1996) *Education, Training and the Global Economy*, Cheltenham: Edward Elgar.

Barnett, C. (1972) *The Collapse of British Power*, London: Eyre Methuen.

—— (1986) *The Audit of War: The Illusion and Reality of Britain as a Great Nation*, London: Macmillan.

—— (1995) *The Lost Victory: British Dreams, British Realities, 1945–1950*, London: Macmillan.

Barry, R., Bosworth, D. and Wilson, R. (1997) *Engineers in Top Management*, Warwick: Institute for Employment Research.

Branine, M. and Glover, I. (1997) 'Ageism, work and employment: thinking about connections', *Personnel Review*, 26 (4), 233–44.

Broadberry, S.N. (1997) 'The long run growth and productivity performance of the United Kingdom', *Scottish Journal of Political Economy*, 44 (4), 403–24.

Bullock, A. ([1952]1962) *Hitler: A Study in Tyranny*, 2nd edn, Harmondsworth: Penguin.

Canainn, A.O. (1995) 'Herr Ingenieur or the grease-monkey? How the managerial prospects of engineers are perceived', *Human Resource Management Journal*, 5 (4), 74–92.

Carter, C. and Crowther, D. (1997) 'Unravelling a profession: the case of engineers in a British regional electricity company', paper presented to the conference on the Labour Process, Edinburgh; available in mimeo at the University of Aston.

Causer, G. and Jones, C. (1993) 'Responding to "skill shortages": recruitment and retention in a high technology labour market', *Human Resource Management Journal*, 3 (3), 1–20.

—— (1996) 'Management and the control of technical labour', *Work, Employment and Society*, 10 (1), 105–23.

Child, J., Fores, M., Glover, I. and Lawrence, P. (1983) 'A price to pay? Professionalism and work organisation in Britain and West Germany', *Sociology*, 17 (1), 63–78.

Coates, D. and Hillard, J. (eds) (1995) *UK Economic Decline: Key Texts*, London: Prentice-Hall.

Cohen, S.S. and Zysman, J. (1987) *Manufacturing Matters: The Myth of the Post-Industrial Economy*, New York: Basic Books.

Coleman, D.C. (1973) 'Gentlemen and players', *Economic History Review*, 26 (1), 92–116.

Conti, R.F. and Warner, M. (1997) 'Technology, culture and craft: job tasks and quality realities', *New Technology, Work and Employment*, 12 (2), 123–35.

Conyon, M.J. and Mullin, C.A. (1997) 'A review of compliance with Cadbury', *Journal of General Management*, 2 (3), 24–37.

Dahrendorf, R. (1982) *On Britain*, London: BBC.

Delbridge, R. and Lowe, J. (1996) 'It hurt, but it didn't work', paper presented at conference on Manufacturing Matters: Organization and Employee Relations in Modern Manufacturing, Employment Research Unit, Cardiff Business School, Cardiff, 18–19 September.

Du Gay, P. and Salaman, G. (1992) 'The cult(ure) of the customer', *Journal of Management Studies*, 29 (5), 615–33.

Edgerton, D. (1991) *England and the Aeroplane*, London: Macmillan.

Elliot, D. (1996) 'Technology foresight: an interim review of the UK exercise', *Technology Analysis and Strategic Management*, 8 (2), 191–9.

Eltis, W. (1993) 'The financial foundations of industrial success', *International Journal of Management*, **14** (6), 3–22.

Finniston, H.M. (Chairman) (1980) *Engineering Our Future: Report of the Committee of Inquiry into the Engineering Profession*, Cmnd. 7794, London: HMSO.

Fores, M. (1971) 'Britain's economic growth and the 1870 watershed', *Lloyd's Bank Review*, January, 27–41.

Froud, J., Haslam, C., Johal, S., Williams, J. and Williams, K. (1997) 'From social settlement to household lottery', *Economy and Society*, **26** (3), 340–72.

Gershuny, J.I. and Miles, I.D. (1983) *The New Service Economy*, London: Frances Pinter.

Glover, I.A. (1977) *Managerial Work: A Review of the Evidence*, London: Department of Industry/The City University.

—— (1978) 'Executive career patterns: Britain, France, Germany and Sweden', in M. Fores and I.A. Glover (eds), *Manufacturing and Management*, London: HMSO.

—— (1985) 'How the West was lost? Decline in engineering and manufacturing in Britain and the United States', *Higher Education Review*, **17** (3), 3–34.

—— (1991) 'The Hobsbawm–Wiener conundrum: economics, history and sociology in the study of British decline', *International Journal of Sociology and Social Policy*, **11** (5), 1–17.

—— (1992) 'Wheels within wheels: predicting and accounting for fashionable alternatives to engineering', in G. Lee and C. Smith (eds), *Engineers in Management: International Comparisons*, London: Routledge.

—— (1994) 'Problem child or prototype? Thoughts on the United Kingdom's options and prospects', Working Paper, University of Stirling.

Glover, I.A. and Hallier, J. (1996) 'Can there be a valid future for human resource management?', in I.A. Glover and M. Hughes (eds), *The Professional-Managerial Class: Contemporary British Management in the Pursuer Mode*, Aldershot: Avebury, 217–44.

Glover, I.A. and Hughes, M. (1996) 'British management in the pursuer mode', in I.A. Glover and M. Hughes (eds), *The Professional-Managerial Class: Contemporary British Management in the Pursuer Mode*, Aldershot: Avebury, 3–33.

Glover, I.A. and Tracey, P. (1997) 'In search of *Technik*: can engineering outgrow management?', *Work, Employment and Society*, **11** (4), 759–76.

Grupp, H. (1994) 'Technology at the beginning of the 21st century', *Technology and Strategic Management*, **6** (4), 379–409.

Hampden-Turner, C. and Trompenaars, A. (1994) *The Seven Cultures of Capitalism*, London: Piatkus.

Henderson, J. (1993) 'Against the economic orthodoxy: on the making of the East Asian miracle', *Economy and Society*, **22** (2), 200–17.

Hirst, P. (1996) 'Globaloney', *Prospect*, February, 29–33.

Hirst, P. and Thompson, G. (1995) 'Globalization and the future of the nation state', *Economy and Society*, **24** (3), 408–42.

—— (1996) *Globalization in Question: The International Economy and the Possibilities of Governance*, Cambridge: Polity.

Horne, D. (1969) *God is an Englishman*, Harmondsworth: Penguin.

Huntford, R. (1984) *The Last Place on Earth*, London: Pan.

Johnson, N.A. (1993) 'The future of UK competitiveness', *Policy Studies*, **14** (1), 21–6.

Jones, B., Scott, P., Bolton, B. and Bramley, A. (1994) 'Graduate engineers and the British trans-national business: elite human resource or technical labourers?', *Human Resource Management Journal*, **4** (1), 34–48.

Jones, B., Scott, P., Bolton, B., Bramley, A. and Manske, F. (1996) 'Under-education, under-utilisation or under-professionalisation? Redefining the "British Engineer Problem"', paper presented at conference on Occupations and Professions, Nottingham, 11–13 September.

Kay, J. (1997) 'A stakeholder society: what does it mean for business?', *Scottish Journal of Political Economy*, **44** (4), 425–36.

Kenworthy, L. (1995) *In Search of National Economic Success: Balancing Competition and Cooperation*, London: Sage.

Labour Research (1991) 'Who's to blame for industry's flops?', *Labour Research*, November, 11, 12.

Lam, A. (1994) 'The utilisation of human resources: a comparative study of British and Japanese engineers in electronics industries', *Human Resource Management Journal*, **4** (3), 22–40.

—— (1996) 'Engineers, management and work organization: a comparative analysis of engineers' work roles in British and Japanese firms', *Journal of Management Studies*, **33** (2), 183–212.

Lane, C. and Bachmann, R. (1997) 'Co-operation in inter-firm relations in Britain and Germany: the role of social institutions', *British Journal of Sociology*, **48** (2), 226–54.

Lawrence, P.A. (1980) *Managers and Management in West Germany*, London: Croom Helm.

—— (1996) 'Through a glass darkly: towards a characterization of British management', in I.A. Glover and M. Hughes (eds), *The Professional-Managerial Class: Contemporary British Management in the Pursuer Mode*, Aldershot: Avebury, 49–88.

Lawrence, P.A. and Locke, M. (1997) 'A man for our season', *Nature*, **389**, 24 April, 757, 758.

Leadbeater, C. (1997) *Britain: The California of Europe? What the UK can Learn from the West Coast*, London: Demos.

Leggatt, T. (1980) 'The status ranking of industries', *Journal of Management Studies*, **17** (1), 56–67.

Littek, W. and Charles, T. (eds) (1995) *The New Division of Labour: Emerging Forms of Work Organization in International Perspective*, Berlin: Walter de Gruyter.

Locke, R. (1984) *The End of the Practical Man: Entrepreneurship and Higher Education in Germany, France and Great Britain, 1880–1940*, Greenwich, Conn.: JAI.

—— (1989) *Management and Higher Education since 1940: The Influence of America and Japan on West Germany, Great Britain and France*, Cambridge: Cambridge University Press.

—— (1996) *The Collapse of the American Management Mystique*, Oxford: Oxford University Press.

McCormick, B. and McCormick, K. (1996) *Japanese Companies – British Factories*, Aldershot: Avebury.

McCormick, K., Cairncross, D., Hanstock, Y. McCormick, B. and Turner, A. (1996) 'Engineering, careers and technology transfer: Japanese companies in the UK', *New Technology, Work and Employment*, **11** (2), 96–106.

McGovern, P. (1995) 'To retain or not to retain? Multinational firms and technical labour', *Human Resource Management Journal*, **5** (4), 7–23.

McRae, H. (1994) *The World in 2020: Power, Culture and Prosperity*, Boston: Harvard Business School Press.

Marginson, P. (1993/94) 'Multinational Britain: employment and work in an internationalised economy', *Human Resource Management Journal*, **4** (4), 63–79.

Maurice, M., Sellier, F. and Silvestre, J. (1979) 'La Production de la hiérarchie dans l'entreprise: recherche d'un effet sociétal', *Revue française de sociologie*, **20**, 331–65.

Maurice, M., Sorge, A. and Warner, M. (1980) 'Societal differences in organising manufacturing units: a comparison of France, West Germany and Great Britain', *Organization Studies*, **1**, 59–86.

Meiksins, P. and Smith, C. (eds) (1996) *Engineering Labour: Technical Workers in Comparative Perspective*, London: Verso.

Millman, T. (forthcoming) 'Restructuring and repositioning of the UK engineering profession', in I.A. Glover and M. Hughes (eds), *Professions at Bay: Control and Encouragement of Ingenuity in British Management*, Aldershot: Avebury.

Mintzberg, H. (1978) 'Patterns in strategy formation', *Management Science*, **24**, 934–48.

Nairn, T. (1977) *The Break-Up of Britain: Crisis and Neo-Nationalism*, London: New Left Books.

Newton, T.J. and Keenan, A. (1990) 'Consequences of changing employers amongst young engineers', *Journal of Occupational Psychology*, **63**, 113–27.

Nicholls, W.A.T. (1986) *The British Worker Question*, London: Allen & Unwin.

Nossiter, B.D. (1978) *Britain: A Future that Works*, London: The Trinity Press.

O'Mahony, M. and Wagner, K. (1995) 'Relative productivity levels: UK and German manufacturing industry, 1979 and 1989', *International Journal of Manpower*, **16** (1), 5–21.

O'Mahony, M. and Wagner, K. with Paulson, M. (1995) *Changing Fortunes: An Industry Study of British and German Productivity Growth Over Three Decades*, Report Series no. 7, London: National Institute of Economic and Social Research.

Pakulski, J. and Waters, M. (1995) *The Death of Class*, London: Sage.

Perkin, H. (1969) *The Origins of Modern English Society 1780–1880*, London: Routledge & Kegan Paul.

Porter, M. (1990) *The Competitive Advantage of Nations*, New York: Free Press.

Randle, K. (1996) 'The white-coated worker: professional autonomy in a period of change', *Work, Employment and Society*, **10** (4), 737–53.

Reed, M.I. (1995) 'Experts, professionals and organizations in late modernity: the dynamics of institutional, occupational and organizational changes in advanced industrial societies', *Organization Studies*, **16** (2), 401–28.

Reid, S. and Garnsey, E. (1997) 'The growth of small high-tech firms: destinies and destinations of innovation centre "graduates"', *New Technology, Work and Employment*, **12** (2), 84–90.

Roberts, K. and Biddle, J. (1994) 'The transition into management by scientists and engineers: a misallocation or efficient use of human resources?', *Human Resource Management*, **33** (4), 561–78.

Rubery, J. (1994) 'The British production regime: a societal-specific system?', *Economy and Society*, **23** (3), 337–54.

Rubinstein, W.D. (1993) *Capitalism, Culture and Decline in Britain, 1750–1990*, London: Routledge.

Saunders, P. (1995) *Capitalism: A Social Audit*, Buckingham: Open University Press.

Scott, J. (1996) *Stratification and Power*, Cambridge: Polity.

Smith, C. and Whalley, P. (1996) 'Engineers in Britain: a study in persistence', in P. Meiksins and C. Smith (eds), *Engineering Labour: Technical Workers in Comparative Perspective*, London: Verso, ch. 2.

Sorge, A. (1979) 'Engineers in management: a study of the British, German and French traditions', *Journal of General Management*, **5**, 46–67.

Sorge, A. and Warner, M. (1986) *Comparative Factory Organization: An Anglo-German Comparison of Management and Manpower in Manufacturing*, Aldershot: Gower.

Swords-Isherwood, N. (1979) 'British management compared', in K. Pavitt (ed.), *Technical Innovation and British Economic Performance*, London: Science Policy Research Unit, University of Sussex/Macmillan.

Tiratsoo, N. (1996) 'British management 1945–1964: reforms and the struggle to improve standards', mimeo, London School of Economics.

Tracey, P.J. (1997) 'Engineers and the financial system', paper presented to the British Academy of Management Annual Conference, London Business School, London;

available in mimeo from Department of Management and Organization, University of Stirling.

Tsoukas, K. and Cummings, S. (1997) 'Marginalization and recovery: the emergence of Aristotelian themes in organization studies', *Organization Studies*, **18** (4), 655–83.

Watson, T.J. (1994) *In Search of Management: Culture, Chaos and Control in Managerial Work*, London: Routledge.

Webb, J. (1996) 'Vocabularies of motive and the "new" management', *Work, Employment and Society*, **10** (2), 251–71.

Wentworth, D.S. and Glover, I.A. (1998) 'Small business success: the sectoral and the dialectical', in M.G. Scott, P. Rosa and H. Klandt (eds), *Educating Entrepreneurs for Wealth Creation*, Aldershot: Avebury.

Wiener, M. (1981) *English Culture and the Decline of the Industrial Spirit 1850–1980*, Cambridge: Cambridge University Press.

Wilkinson, R. (1964) *The Prefects: British Leadership and the Public School Tradition*, Oxford: Oxford University Press.

Williams, K., Haslam, C., Williams, J. and Cutler, T. with Adcroft, A. and Johal, S. (1992) 'Against lean production', *Economy and Society*, **21** (3), 321–54.

Williams, K., Williams, J. and Haslam, C. (1990) 'The hollowing-out of British manufacturing and its implications for policy', *Economy and Society*, **19** (4), 456–90.

Wood, S.J. (1990) 'New wave management', *Work, Employment and Society*, **4** (3), 379–402.

12 UK manufacturing in the twenty-first century
Learning factories and knowledge workers?

Rick Delbridge, Martin Kenney and James Lowe

INTRODUCTION

In this chapter we reflect on current trends in contemporary manufacturing, particularly with regard to the development of large global corporations. Commentators have recognized certain tendencies in this development, including the increasing emphasis on innovation of both product and process technology and the role of both employees and external institutions in the solving of problems and creation of knowledge. These trends have been characterized as leading to 'learning factories' in which knowledge creation and application is the key 'product'.

The primary influence shaping this picture of the factory of the future has been Japanese manufacturing industry, principally the automotive and consumer electronics sectors, but, more recently, a number of western factories are moving in this direction. Fruin (1992) used the term 'learning factories' in describing Japanese manufacturers, Womack *et al.* (1990) derived lean production from their understanding of the Toyota production system, while other studies have identified the approach of certain major Japanese corporations as that of 'innovation-mediated production' under which the central feature is the integration of production and innovation (Kenney and Florida 1993). The success of the Japanese has led many commentators to promote the emulation of such practices by western manufacturers (Pascale and Athos 1982; Schonberger 1986; Womack *et al.* 1990; see also Oliver and Hunter in Chapter 5 in this volume).

The influence of the Japanese model has not been restricted to emulation, however, since Japanese capital has become increasingly international over the last twenty years. Both North America and Europe (in particular the UK) have been the recipients of very significant Japanese direct investment in manufacturing operations (see Munday and Peel in Chapter 4 in this volume). Thus the influence of Japanese manufacturers has been both direct and indirect. A major debate has developed among industrialists and academics regarding the transfer of Japanese manufacturing techniques and the so-called Japanization of western industry (Oliver and Wilkinson 1992; Elger and Smith 1994). Some have argued that the Japanese model will be efficient anywhere and that western firms should adopt it as quickly and completely as they are able (e.g. Womack *et al.* 1990) while others have reported research indicating that adoption is mediated by factors such as local institutional context and strategic choice (Abo 1994). In Chapter 5, Oliver and Hunter further question the benefits of adopting 'Japanese' methods, at least with regard to financial performance. In this chapter we report on evidence regarding the management practices of Japanese television assembly operations in Japan and their transplants in Mexico and the UK. In particular, we are interested to explore the extent to which the Japanese transplants exhibit the characteristics associated with the learning factories of their origin.

Our concerns in this chapter are, first, to articulate the learning factory concept epitomized by these large Japanese firms, before turning our attention to the evidence regarding the transfer of the learning factory outside Japan. As we will see, this evidence is mixed, with the transplant operations in Mexico and the UK displaying many similarities to each other but rather fewer of the characteristics of learning and knowledge creation associated with their parent organizations. This leads to a discussion of the reasons for the nature of Japanese transplant operations. In particular, we discuss the nature of the process technology, the international division of labour in the television production value chain, the resultant role of workers, and the issues of education, training and skill formation in contemporary manufacturing. Following this, we reflect upon the implications for the UK if it is to attract and support investment that engenders the development of learning factories. In particular, the role of the state and its various agencies in attracting investment is considered. It seems apparent that the requirement is to attract *the right sort of investment* into the UK manufacturing sector. In turn, the UK workforce must have the skills and education to fulfil the role of labour in the learning factory. Without significant change in the role of the state to encourage better quality manufacturing investment and in the provision of training and education, the fear is that UK manufacturing will wither, unable to compete on cost with newly industrializing countries and unable to sustain high value-added, knowledge-based manufacturing activity.

EMERGENT TENDENCIES IN MANUFACTURING

Cooke and Morgan (1998) identify four 'emergent tendencies' in the activities of the large-firm sector of manufacturing industry as these organizations seek to develop deeper and more durable forms of cooperation and expand their innovative capacity. Cooke and Morgan argue that leading firms have embarked upon a process of 'experimentation' in the areas of: corporate governance; research and development (R&D); manufacturing operations; and supply chain management.

In the sphere of corporate governance many firms are trying to strike a better balance between the interests of shareholders and stakeholders on the one hand, and between their central and peripheral organizations on the other. In the R&D sphere all firms are coming under intense pressure to forge better links between their labs and their factories, so much so that some technologists feel that their laboratories are being turned into factories. In the production sphere the more innovative firms are trying to devolve responsibility to work teams who are supposedly empowered to use their local knowledge in the name of continuous improvement, with the result that the factory becomes more like a laboratory. The advent of more integrated supply chains suggests that innovative capacity rests not so much with the firm *per se* as with a network of firms in which formally independent firms become ever more functionally integrated (Cooke and Morgan 1998).

For Cooke and Morgan these developments are linked in important ways. They characterize these developments as central features of a 'semi-permanent process of organizational innovation' whose common thread is 'the attempt to create a more collaborative corporate culture, both within the firm and between the firm and its principal suppliers' (ibid.). This collaboration is not an end in itself, but rather the means by which large manufacturing firms are seeking to meet the challenges of the twenty-first century and become more productive, more innovative and more profitable.

These emergent tendencies are indicative of a discontinuous shift in the organization and management of large manufacturing firms. If the developments anticipated by Cooke and Morgan are realized, then manufacturing in the twenty-first century will look very different from that which has characterized this century. Our particular concern in this chapter is to reflect upon the implications that these developments will have for factories and factory workers. In the following section we outline the 'learning factory' model and identify the role of labour under this form of organization.

The learning factory

A central premise of contemporary manufacturing 'best practice' is that the Tayloristic separation of task design from task execution must be reversed (Kenney and Florida 1993; Delbridge 1998; Cooke and Morgan 1998). Within the manufacturing corporation this demands a greater integration across functions, and closer links between the R&D laboratories and manufacturing plants in particular. Recent studies in new product development show that closer cross-functional links between design and production can result in products that are easier to manufacture and with quicker times to the marketplace (Clark and Fujimoto 1991). This intra-organizational relationship has been recognized as centrally important (and problematic) for many years (Burns and Stalker 1961). As Cooke and Morgan (1998) note, the approach of Japanese corporations to new product development has had a great deal of influence on changes taking place in firms around the world. Here, the emphasis has been on knowledge-creation, with a high premium on the acquisition of tacit knowledge which is recognized as context-specific and embedded (Nonaka and Takeuchi 1995).

Increasingly, the factory floor is being seen as a place where knowledge can be created as well as applied, where production workers think as well as do (Kenney and Florida 1993; Fruin 1992; Cooke and Morgan 1998). Hence the strictly routinized division of labour which has been the central tenet of factory work under the principles of 'scientific management' is under threat. Authors anticipating a 'post-Taylorist' or 'post-Fordist' era in manufacturing have outlined a new set of principles that will represent what Smith and Meiksins (1995) call the 'system-in-dominance' for the twenty-first century.

Perhaps the most influential of these models has been 'lean production', first summarized in Womack *et al.* (1990) and subsequently refined and further supported by MacDuffie (1995). The manufacturing and logistics principles of lean production have been well rehearsed, and what interests us here is the role of labour. Under the lean production model, multiskilled workers operate flexibly in teams with little indirect staff support. Additionally, all shop-floor workers actively engage in root cause problem solving in order to eradicate 'waste': that is, workers contribute their tacit knowledge and experience in order to improve productivity and quality. The 'lean production' model is a distillation of the practices of Toyota, Japan's largest carmaker. Kenney and Florida (1993) have also studied the 'Japanese model' of manufacturing and have conceptualized the approach of the most successful Japanese corporations as one of 'innovation-mediated production'. The central feature of this is the integration of innovation and production and of intellectual and physical labour. Kenney and Florida report five dimensions of the 'Japanese model': a transition from physical skill and manual labour to intellectual capabilities or 'mental labour'; the increasing importance of social or collective intelligence as opposed to individual knowledge or skill; an acceleration of the pace of technological innovation; the increasing importance of continuous process improvement on the factory floor; and the 'blurring of the lines between the R&D laboratory and the plant'. The identification of these features in the Japanese manufacturing sector has led to discussion of the 'learning factory' or what Fruin (1997) termed a 'knowledge works'.

Following this research, we may recognize various attributes as characteristic of the learning factory. First, innovation is the central motif of the learning factory. The learning factory generates, codifies and applies knowledge to improve its various products, structures and processes. Second, learning factories are host to continuous improvement activities that are driven by internal sources of information such as the tacit knowledge of shop-floor workers, the 'contextual' knowledge of technicians, and the 'formal' knowledge of professionals and craft workers (Barley 1996). Thus these factories are increasingly populated by problem-solving workers for whom, in addition to the traditional application of manual labour, the contribution of ideas on improving the production process is considered central (Kenney and Florida 1993). Third, the learning factory also benefits from improvement derived from external sources of information, such as 'problem-solving' suppliers (Kaufman *et al.* 1996) and the supplier development programmes of customers. Fourth, the learning factory is embedded in an innovation network of collaborators with whom there is information exchange and shared learning (Powell *et al.* 1996). These ties and alliances may be with a variety of organizations including technology specialists and research laboratories, training specialists, consultants, venture capitalists, trade associations, universities and government agencies.

EVIDENCE OF THE TRANSFER OF THE LEARNING FACTORY

The evidence on the transfer of the learning factory is mixed and the issue of transfer from Japan is now considered more problematic than was initially the case. There are three major factors that explain this. First, the simple conceptualization of a single, universal 'Japanese' model has proven ill-founded. Thus it is important to be clear of the characteristics of a particular production process in Japan. This is not as unproblematic as it might first seem. Though the macrosocial and political variables are similar for all the large Japanese corporations across Japan, there are clearly differences by firm and industrial sector. There can be little doubt that there are significant differences between, for example, Sony, Matsushita, Sanyo and Toshiba, though all are Japanese and compete in the television business, and between car assemblers such as Nissan, Toyota and Honda. These differences are also identifiable between the transplants of Japanese corporations, even those in the same group. Adler (1996), for example, argues that the Toyota factory in Kentucky and the Toyota–GM joint venture (NUMMI) in Fremont, California, differ on a number of dimensions and actually use different organizational models. Some differences might even be attributable to the different Toyota 'sister' factory responsible for overseeing each US plant.

A second and related issue is that of the industry sector and the nature of process and product technology. Aspects of management practice such as the nature of a team and teamwork can differ dramatically between, say, electronics and automotive industries. The greater complexity and variety of tasks on the shop floor in automotive assembly increases the interdependence of workers and places greater emphasis on coordinating activities among and between groups. For instance, workers must cooperate physically to place a bumper on a vehicle, work directly across from each other in carrying out a fairly complex set of movements, and conduct activities that may work away from the assembly line. In contrast, on a panel line in a CTV plant each person sits at a given work station and inserts a specified number of small parts; their task is self-contained and does not involve working with other line workers. Workers are lined up side by side and there is little opportunity to communicate with other workers about tasks. There is little activity which involves groups of workers collaborating in production. In this environment the team has far less meaning and significance (see Delbridge 1998).

Thirdly, there is a considerable literature arguing that the level of transfer differs by host country (Abo 1992; 1994; Hiramoto 1995). Nomura (1992) found, for example, that in the same Japanese television assembly company, the wage systems, industrial relations, recruitment, and employment adjustment systems differed between Taiwan and Malaysia. This is not surprising as different countries have varying legal and social environments that constrain an investor's ability to reproduce home country patterns. Thus the host country's environment has an impact on the nature and level of transfer.

A fourth factor that is important is the investing firm's strategy towards its factory. For example, for a highly routinized segment of a value chain there may be less incentive to invest in creating a learning factory (Kenney 1998). The potential gain might be rather minimal. An excellent example of such a situation is a factory assembling knockdown kits for a protected market – worker involvement in continuous improvement is of far less significance for such simplified assembly. So, corporate strategy can have a significant impact on the transfer process; moreover, the strategy may change overtime .

In order to consider the evidence of transfer of the learning factory in more depth we examine the case for a specific industry sector, television assembly. This allows us to compare plants that share relatively similar product and process technologies. In this section we report research conducted by the authors in Japan, Mexico and the UK (see Delbridge 1998; Kenney and Florida 1994; Kenney *et al.* 1998; Lowe *et al.* 1997).

Japanese-operated television assembly factories in Japan, UK and Mexico

This section summarizes our findings on the transfer of Japanese television assembly factory practices to transplants in the UK and Mexico. A brief discussion of the context for the two sets of transplants is necessary. The UK factories began production in the late 1970s and the early 1980s and have operated continuously since then. The reason Japanese firms established these plants was to circumvent European protectionism and that has persisted into the 1990s. The first Japanese transplants in Mexico were established in 1982 and in the intervening years these operations have expanded dramatically. The largest investments, such as those of Sony, Matsushita, Sanyo and Hitachi, now include multiple factories and employ up to 8,000 persons in all facets of television assembly. The Mexican factories were established to take advantage of the Mexican government's in-bond manufacturing programme and the inexpensive Mexican workforce.

Our research finds remarkably few differences between Japanese television transplants in the UK and Mexico. This suggests that in certain critical ways the context and organization of television assembly operations in the UK and Mexico are similar, an issue to which we shall return later. Tables 12.1 and 12.2 compare the practices of Japanese-owned television assembly plants in Japan, Mexico and the UK. From these tables we can see that the Japanese transplant operations are more like their sister plants in Mexico than they are like the parent plants in Japan. Generally speaking, the newest televisions with the most sophisticated technology are produced in Japan, though this is not always the case. In contrast, the UK factories tend to use older and less sophisticated process technology to make products that are often obsolete in Japan. Standard machinery for component insertion on printed circuit boards may be newer in Mexico than in Japan; the advances in automation, however, come from the Japanese factory. This is especially the case for proprietary machinery developed by the production engineers at the mother factory. In some areas, automation may be as advanced or even more advanced in the Mexican factories that tend to produce large batches of standardized televisions, whereas the Japanese factory produces a much greater

Table 12.1 The Japanese system transplanted: production aspects

Japan	Mexico	UK
Latest high-technology, complex products	Advanced printed circuit assembly, simpler products, generally less automated [1]	Lower-level process and product technology
PCB production outsourced	PCBs produced in-house, formerly imported from SE Asia	PCBs produced in-house
Quality control as part of labour process	Yes	Yes
Operators' work self-checked, little further inspection	Separate quality inspection	Separate quality inspection
Work quality is important in operator evaluation	Yes	Yes
High operator involvement in improvement activity	Little operator involvement in improvement activity	Little operator involvement in improvement activity

Sources: Kenney and Florida (1994), Kenney *et al.* (1998), Lowe *et al.* (1997), Delbridge (1998) and various secondary sources.
Note:
[1] In some cases, especially where quality is critical, the process used in Mexico may be more automated than in Japan. For example, in removing parts from plastic insertion machines, automation was used sooner in Mexico. The reason was that Japanese workers understood the care needed, whereas Mexican workers were inexperienced.

diversity of television sets in smaller batches, making automation with its inherent rigidities less economical.

In Japan, low value-added operations such as PCB production are outsourced because subcontractors have less overheads and pay lower wages. In contrast, in the UK and Mexico, PCB production is undertaken in-house and can absorb a large percentage of the transplants' total employees – typically most of these workers are female.

We are particularly interested in the extent to which the plants may be considered 'learning factories' and how the role of labour compares to that of the rhetorical 'knowledge worker'. There are some aspects of the labour process that are consistent across Japan, Mexico and the UK, in particular the responsibility of workers in monitoring and maintaining quality. However, it is noticeable that Mexican and UK workers' quality is further monitored by using a greater number of dedicated inspectors. In Japan there is a minimal number of formal inspectors; for the most part, Japanese workers are expected to verify their own work, but even more important, to be cognizant of the work done by others and to flag errors. So, a significant difference between the Japanese factories and the transplants is the larger number of inspections and inspectors per worker.

The most important difference between the transplants and the parent plants is in the area of innovation and improvement. As is consistent with the learning

Table 12.2 The Japanese system transplanted: organization and HRM aspects

Japan	Mexico	UK
Low turnover (3% per year)	Extremely high turnover (5–10% per month)	High initial turnover during probation, average thereafter
Strict hierarchy	Yes	Yes
Internal job ladder	Yes, but mitigated by extremely high turnover	Yes
Stratification of employment by gender	Yes	Yes
Some use of contract workers	No contract workers	Use of temporary contracts
Company union	No union	No union or single union agreement
Extensive screening of new recruits	Little screening	Some screening and testing
High initial training for new recruits	Little or no initial training	Little or no initial training
Significant off-the-job training for operators (not temps.)	Very little off-the-job training for operators	Very little off-the-job training for operators
Off-the-job training for off-line workers	Yes	Yes
All operators make suggestions for improvement	Very few operators make suggestions for improvement	Very few operators make suggestions for improvement
No separate technician classification	Technician classification	Technician classification

Sources: Kenney and Florida (1994), Kenney *et al.* (1998), Lowe *et al.* (1997), Delbridge (1998) and various secondary sources.

factory model, Japanese operators contribute their tacit knowledge towards process improvement in the form of suggestions and through their participation in problem-solving activities. In Mexico and the UK there is little or no operator involvement in improvement reported and few operators contribute formal suggestions. This is consistent with the findings of Delbridge (1998: 204) when he conducted participant observer research in a Japanese television manufacturer in the UK:

> there is little or no evidence of systematic and regular job rotation, multi-skilling, small group problem solving, decentralized decision-making and employee participation, or 'team' working . . . the research evidence . . . suggests that workers are 'a pair of hands' and little more to management who

appear to hold minimal expectations of the input of the workforce to 'discretionary activities' beyond the Taylorist notions of task execution and compliance to managerial prerogative.

These results are quite similar to Kenney and Florida's (1994) findings from interviews with Japanese managers in the Mexican transplants. There managers reported highly circumscribed innovation and improvement activity. One executive described his factory's continuous improvement activities as limited to each department's Mexican manager holding an occasional meeting and sometimes setting up a project for improvement (ibid. 33). In this company the regular workers were not expected to make important quality control improvement suggestions. However, a later study by Kenney et al. (1998) found that a significant number of Mexican transplant workers interviewed were asked for suggestions. Of course, the manager found that few suggestions were contributed.

Recent literature on Japanese consumer electronics factories has pointed out the critical importance of senior operators and, especially, supervisory personnel in the operation of the factory. Lowe et al. (1997) found that the roles of supervisory-level personnel were more similar at the Japanese and Mexican plants than either plant was to the UK factory. At the Mexican plant, the supervisors and group leaders were able to 'evaluate the industrial engineering implications' of a new product (Lowe et al. 1997), whereas in the UK they were merely required to supervise the work. A seniority form of payment was used in the Mexican factories in an effort to reduce turnover. In the non-union Mexican environment, the Japanese had found it much easier to transfer their supervisory system.

At this time there is mixed evidence about whether Mexican factory operators can be promoted to group leader and supervisor positions. Lowe et al. (1997) found that only rarely were operators promoted to higher levels. In contrast, Kenney et al. (1998) found that of twenty-four employees above operator level interviewed, 80 per cent began their work in the Mexican factory as an operator. This suggests that these Japanese firms predominantly fill higher-level, shop-floor positions through internal promotion, rather than recruiting outsiders to fill these positions. This would closely resemble the case of Japan and differ significantly from the case in some UK transplants.

One area in which the transplants and the parent factory did not differ greatly, but where television assembly factories differ significantly from the Japanese model as described by Womack et al. (1990), is in the structure and use of teams. As Tables 12.1 and 12.2 show factories in all three countries use teams, but these are rather large groups consisting of thirty or more members. There is not the intense interaction that characterizes the descriptions of teams in the auto industry. Also, in television assembly, there is little short-term rotation except in physically and mentally demanding areas such as picture adjustment. The fundamental difference is that in the Japanese factories every worker belongs to at least one small group meant to undertake various off-line improvement activities. These small group activities are not common in the Mexican and UK factories.

EXPLAINING THE NATURE OF TRANSPLANT OPERATIONS

There are various characteristics of the television sector that must be considered when one reflects upon the nature of the transplant operations found in the UK and Mexico. First, the process technology: television assembly has become a routinized and increasingly automated production process. Many assembly activities are now highly routinized, requiring diligence and attention but little intellectual input. Even in Japanese television assembly plants, at the junior operator level the intellectual component of work is more likely to occur in small group activities (SGAs) or when models are changed. Another method of contributing is the suggestion programme, to which all regular employees are expected to contribute a certain number of suggestions per month. An important role of the supervisors is to assist operators in developing suggestions and to monitor their performance in so doing. It is these intellectual contributions that make the Japanese factories more like learning organizations.

While much production is highly formalized and routinized in television manufacture, certain groups of shop-floor employees in particular play a significant role in learning and improvement activity. In Japan – and this is also the case in Mexico – the critical category of workers are the more senior operators who have much more experience (in Mexico these are often formally called 'technicians' or 'assistants to the line chief'). These employees undertake routine on-the-job (OTJ) activities and provide the on-the-job training for new employees. Moreover, they are involved in the constant routine problem solving that occurs within any complex production process. Though much of the work is routinized, the production machinery needs to be constantly tended to ensure its proper functioning.[1] This is what Barley (1996) called 'managing the empirical interface' in his study of technicians.

The western concept of the technician as a separate category of workers does not have a place in Japanese factories. The workers that perform the technician function in Japan are simply senior workers. Moreover, all of these workers have an important role in training other workers in machinery operations – something a western technician is not expected to do. The creation of a separate category of technicians in overseas operations, even though they are often recruited internally, underlies an important difference in the organization of the transplants and the home plants. Put another way, overseas it is necessary to divide the workers into operators and technicians.

A second and related factor is the role of television assembly facilities in the value chain. This is fundamental to our understanding of the nature of the transfer of management systems. A television production value chain contains the following steps: tube production, integrated circuit fabrication, chassis (printed circuit board) insertion, cabinet manufacture, and final assembly. The highest value-added components, and most capital-intensive segments, are tube and integrated circuit fabrication. These are costly and have important effects on the quality of the television and its picture, but these are done in separate factories and often in entirely different corporate divisions. Chassis production is increasingly a high-technology, high-speed operation, but it continues to require a significant number of employees. Cabinet production is usually outsourced in Japan, whereas overseas it is often done internally.

The final assembly operation has undergone a steady routinization, and significant effort has been expended to engineer televisions for manufacturability. Japanese firms were leaders in introducing integrated circuits because of their high reliability, low cost, and ability to simplify assembly procedures (Sugata and Namekawa 1969). In an effort to increase manufacturability, the parts count for a Panasonic colour television model went from 1,023 in 1972 to 488 in 1976 (OTA 1983: 223). Similarly, Baranson (1980: 103) found that Sanyo's Gifu factory decreased the parts count for its 20-inch televisions from 2,334 in 1970 to 1,006 in 1976 through an increasing use of large-scale integrated circuits. This is also expressed in a fivefold decrease from the early 1970s to the early 1980s in the number of processes Japanese manufacturers required to produce a television. The use of integrated circuitry accounted for over 50 per cent of this reduction in processes (Baba 1985). In other words, engineering changes dramatically simplified television assembly and have led to assembly becoming a relatively less important link in the value chain.

Assembly is only one segment in what has become an international division of labour. The different segments of the value chain can be situated in different countries. So, for example, printed circuit boards are often imported from low-cost regions of the world to be used in factories in developed countries. Television tubes are either made close to the assembly factory or they are imported from other countries. In the case of the UK television factories (as is also the case in the US) the decision to locate production in the UK was made specifically to circumvent national/regional protectionism. This implied that these factories were never meant to be more than assembly sites and were not expected to be competitive in the world market. To compete they needed only to perform as well as indigenous European factories. This is an important factor in determining whether the UK has been able, for whatever reason, to attract the right quality of investment.

The US situation was different because its market protection schemes did not exclude imports from other developing countries nor did they include strict local content laws. As a result, Japanese firms assembling in the US found themselves competing with low-price Korean and Taiwanese imports. Thus the US market never provided the same protection as did the European market. The result was that the Japanese began to produce parts and ultimately moved most television assembly in unit terms to Mexico, though larger screen sizes continue to be assembled in the US.

There is another generalized division of labour practised by Japanese firms which also contributes to our understanding of the characteristics of transplant operations. Still today, the design and prototype production of new models is usually undertaken in Japan, where the companies have excellent access to parts suppliers and their tube production operations and various other complementary assets such as integrated circuit design, designers for parts, tube designers, along with a very sophisticated market. Thus most of these activities, and the jobs associated with them, remain in Japan. This is gradually changing as Japanese television manufacturing firms have opened R&D and design facilities in other countries but today research, development and design, for the most part, are retained in Japan. In some measure, whether conscious or not, there has been a centralization of the greatest portion of learning in Japan. Recently, some firms like Sony and Mitsubishi are transferring more of the television design to the US; picture tube development and chassis layout, however, are largely retained in Japan.

This global value chain means that overseas factories have little linkage to R&D. In other words, there is little opportunity to integrate the factory with the other parts of the firm responsible for innovation. This means that there is less circulation of personnel from the R&D staff to the factory and thus less transfer of the newest ideas and innovations. This contrasts markedly with some of the auto transplants that have built relatively large R&D and process-engineering departments, particularly in the US, which interact closely with the transplant factories. In television assembly this linkage is limited.

The culmination of these various factors is that, instead of the overseas factories evolving into learning factories, they have usually stagnated or progressed relatively slowly. Given their role in the international division of labour, it might be more appropriate to call them 'reproduction factories'. Generally speaking, their role is to reproduce the best practice in the home or 'mother' factory, rather than contribute to the corporation's innovation and improvement activities. This means that they provide little value added beyond the physical labour of their employees. As a result, their position within the company's international value chain is rather perilous. In the last twenty-five years, fourteen Japanese television assembly plants have been opened in the US, of which, six have been closed completely (four moved production to Mexico) while eight factories continue production in the US. Of these eight, two are minor producers (Pioneer and Orion), three have experienced significant downsizing (Sanyo, Mitsubishi, and Sony San Diego) and are assembling only a few televisions (with the rest of the production now in Mexico), and three others are stable (Toshiba, Sharp and Sony Pittsburgh). However, with the exception of Sharp, all the Japanese firms have plants in Mexico.

Even in Japan, television assembly is moving off-shore. In 1995, for the first time, in quantity terms, more televisions were imported than domestic televisions purchased in Japan (Berggren and Nomura 1997). Japanese television assembly factories were able to continue production only by moving into large-screen, feature-rich televisions. This was possible because of the tight linkage between R&D and the factory, the ability of the factory to generate continuous improvements, and the Japanese factories' role in moving quickly down the learning curve with new product introductions. The point being that it is difficult for any television assembly plants to produce economically in the current environment of competition from developing countries.

OPPORTUNITIES AND REQUIREMENTS FOR UK MANUFACTURING

There has clearly been a greater effort to transfer the Japanese management system in autos than in television assembly, and the reasons for this are, at least partially, technical. Simply put, television assembly is highly standardized and simplified. There are not nearly as many opportunities for worker input that can create significant incremental improvements. This is especially true in cases where the production process consists of long runs of highly standardized televisions, as is the tendency in overseas factories. There is more need for worker input and improvement when there are constant changes of television models – a time when routines are disrupted and worker knowledge can be deployed. At these times workers can assist in standardizing and stabilizing the process. In contrast, auto production is far more complicated, providing greater opportunity for worker improvement and team-based learning coordination (Kenney 1998). Thus, in autos there are concrete reasons for pursuing a more active strategy of transfer of the learning factory model.

There seem to be two dimensions to the lack of transfer. First, some factories such as the UK Toshiba factory were brownfield plants in which it may have been difficult to change the organization of the factory. Second, in other factories it does not appear as though the Japanese firms invested great effort in transferring their factory organization and management system. The lack of transfer is probably also rooted in history, as the Japanese electronics firms relocated to the UK during a period when there was little recognition by Japanese managers of their system's strengths. Also, initially most factories were screwdriver facilities concentrating on assembling imported parts. Though this changed through time, as UK content increased there may have been no urgency or crisis that provoked a massive attempt to overhaul the system in use. In Mexico, the reason for limited transfer seems to be a combination of an ability to inspect in quality and such high turnover that firm-specific worker learning is quite limited.

High-quality investment

Protecting television assembly from displacement by production in lower labour-cost countries will be difficult. It seems particularly important for the UK to be able to attract the large-scale capital investments in television tubes and monitors, as these production processes require more skilled workers and provide opportunities for operator-level value added. Reproduction or screwdriver facilities are relatively easier to attract to a low-wage, low-skill economy because set-up and coordination costs are lower. However, for the very same reasons, this allows the Japanese parent to switch capacity and employment to another, lower-wage economy with relative ease. A future for UK manufacturing based on the low road of low wages and low skills is not therefore a sustainable strategy – reproduction factories compete largely on labour cost, and investment and employment will simply migrate to this lowest of common denominators.

A particular danger for the UK arises not from the lower-wage factories of Mexico which serve the North American market, but from the recent establishment of plants by the Japanese parents in more stable parts of eastern Europe. For example, Panasonic (Matsushita) recently established a plant in the Czech Republic which its sister plant in the UK has a key responsibility to assist and develop. The current expectation is that the eastern European market will be a source of rapid growth in the next few years, but the proximate location to a wider European market, combined with a reasonably skilled and educated workforce, means that it is entirely possible that the plant's expansion could threaten the medium-term future of the UK factory based in Cardiff. The impact of Panasonic's Czech-based plant could be felt more widely in UK television manufacturing if eastern European customers were to switch from other UK-based Japanese transplants that currently export there. Toshiba's Plymouth plant, for example, sells CTVs into eastern Europe.

Given these issues, therefore, it becomes vital for the state to create the conditions that attract the right kind of investment. Thus, if learning factories and knowledge workers are the future of manufacturing, then governments must consider far more consciously the *types* of production that are being transplanted. In the case of the television sector, this could come from attracting key components makers such as integrated circuit fabrication and more of the value-added activities that go into CTV manufacture. For instance, it seems particularly important for the UK to be able to attract large-scale capital investments in television tubes and monitors, as these production processes require more skilled workers and provide opportunities for operator-level value added. Indeed, this sort of investment in high value-added suppliers to final assembly is critical for the development of learning factories and networks of innovation, so that assemblers can start to benefit from day-to-day dialogue, information exchange and problem-solving activities that encourage and harness knowledge transfer through the value chain.

A high-quality workforce

In order for the UK to be able to attract 'quality' investment that leads to the development of learning factories, it must provide better education and training for its workforce. This has been a long-standing weakness of British manufacturing (see Chapter 1) and it is certainly a problem for this sector in the UK. Lowe *et al.* (1997), for instance, in their matched comparison of Japanese, Mexican and British factories, found particular weaknesses at operator and intermediate skills levels. Supervisors and senior operators in Mexico were far better trained and skilled than their equivalents in the UK. These personnel were skilled to the level that they could offer problem-solving solutions to organizational problems. In one instance, a Mexican supervisor had devised some air bags which modified the temperature fluctuation on a printed circuit board following a solder bath process. The fluctuation was causing a large number of defects. The initial idea had been modified by the supervisor five times before being perfected, and the final version brought about a 70 per cent reduction in the defects attributable to this fault. At both the Mexican and Japanese plants of this Japanese-owned electronics company there were several such examples publicly and graphically displayed in colour photographs, with such ideas being put forward and/or coordinated by senior operators. A manager at the Mexican plant explained the responsibility for innovation simply: 'The group leader's job is to see the process and how to make it better.' At the British plant such a role tended to be the preserve of skilled trades personnel and engineers, and workers were not involved.

In the study by Lowe et al. (1997), the crucial differences between the British plant and the Japanese plant were the higher educational attainments of new recruits, and the systematic measurement and provision of training at the Japanese plant. Although the Japanese education system has been criticized for its reliance on rote learning methods, it produces students with high levels of numeracy and literacy as evidenced by various international tests (The Economist 1997). The operators at the Japanese plant are high-school graduates and were relatively highly qualified when compared to their equivalents at the British plant (many of whom do not hold any formal qualifications). Thus Japanese managers were often startled at the lack of basic skills of some of their British workers. One manager interviewed in Japan said: 'When I was at the British plant I had difficulties with inventory. I discussed this with my managers. Their explanation was that some workers couldn't count to 100.' The difficulties created by poor basic skills at the British plant were corroborated by the authors' own shop-floor observations where one supervisor had to correct the production figures of her senior operator who apparently had not grasped the difference between cumulative and hourly production totals.

Developing indigenous manufacturers

For the UK manufacturing sector to develop sustainable growth potential, therefore, the attraction of high-quality investment must be matched by the development of indigenous manufacturers as part of a highly capable 'infrastructure' for manufacturing. The problems for the UK at this level have been summarized by Scott and Cockrill's (1997) study of multiskilling in the broader engineering sector. They report a historic overreliance on an apprenticeship system that produced an inadequate supply of skilled labour and, furthermore, that neither the traditional apprenticeship schemes, nor the firm- or college-based schemes that have replaced them, prepare workers adequately for the new organizational demands of the learning factory. Scott and Cockrill find that broad multiskilling, of a functionally flexible form, is occurring only in large firms and among craft workers; this is partly due to increased downtime and technical change, rather than to any deliberate training strategy pursued by these firms. Below the craft level, flexibility is more restricted, with an emphasis on the delegation of some quality control functions (see Table 12.1; for a discussion of flexibility in UK manufacturing, see Ackroyd and Procter in Chapter 3 in this volume). Nevertheless, British engineering firms seem 'ahead' of German counterparts in the social enskilling which is a necessary component of the learning factory agenda: that is, UK firms have concentrated on developing new 'core' skills such as communication, interpersonal skills and aspects of the social abilities of their workforce. This is to be applauded, yet in the future these firms will have to improve their technical training in order to ensure that they can sufficiently upgrade their skills.

The UK cannot expect to replicate the high value-added activities of Japan's learning factories unless its education and training provision bears comparison with those in Japan. There, the training and skills progression of workers and supervisors are much more extensive (Lowe *et al.* 1997). The individual's practical and technical capabilities are exhaustively tested and these determine future career progression. There is also much more off-the-job training and 'divisional training', which may take several months and is often completed in overtime or after work. Furthermore, a key difference between supervisors in Japan and the UK is that supervisors are trained, assessed and deployed on the basis of having high technical and people skills, with much of their training being company-specific and with an industrial engineering orientation.

These comparisons suggest that while opportunities do exist for British factories to become learning factories, government intervention to improve the education system so that basic skills are more thoroughly dispersed among the workforce will prove an absolute necessity. At the same time, British companies can also be more proactive and attempt to solve some of their own workforce skill deficiencies through better initial induction and training and by providing ongoing training to supplement workers' basic skills. It is likely that companies will need to orientate their efforts around both basic and company-specific technical training and that this should be ongoing, given the dynamic organizational changes that now dominate leading-edge manufacturing operations as we approach the twenty-first century.

NOTE

1 The automation of television assembly has simplified the assembly process. This has meant that more capabilities are required to service, adjust, and repair the automated machinery. For these tasks more capable workers are required.

REFERENCES

Abo, T. (1992) 'Toshiba's overseas production activities: seven large plants in the USA, Mexico, the UK, Germany, and France', paper prepared for the Symposium of the Euro-Asia Management Studies Association, Management Centre, University of Bradford, 27–29 November.
—— (1994) 'Sanyo's overseas production activities: seven large plants in US, Mexico, UK, Germany, Spain and China', in Helmut Schutte (ed.), *The Global Competitiveness of the Asian Firm*, New York: St Martin's Press, 179–202.
Adler, P. (1996) 'Hybridization: human resource management at two Toyota transplants', paper presented at the conference on Remade in America: Japanese Manufacturing Transformed, at Ann Arbor, Michigan, 6–8 September.
Baba, Y. (1985) 'Japanese colour television firms' decision-making from the 1950s to

the 1980s: oligopolistic corporate strategy in the age of microelectronics', Ph.D. dissertation, University of Sussex.

Baranson, J. (1980) *Sources of Japan's International Competitiveness in the Consumer Electronics Industry*, Washington, DC: Developing World Industry & Technology, Inc.

Barley, S. (1996) 'Technicians in the workplace: ethnographic evidence for bringing work into organization studies', *Administrative Science Quarterly*, 41 (3), 401–41.

Berggren, C. and Nomura, M. (1997) *The Resilience of Corporate Japan*, London: Paul Chapman.

Burns, T. and Stalker, G. (1961) *The Management of Innovation*, London: Tavistock Institute.

Clark, K. and Fujimoto, T. (1991) *Product Development Performance: Strategy, Organization, and Management in the World Auto Industry*, Boston: Harvard Business School Press.

Cooke, P. and Morgan, K. (1998) *The Associational Economy: Firms, Regions, and Innovation*, Oxford: Oxford University Press.

Delbridge, R. (1998) *Life on the Line in Contemporary Manufacturing*, Oxford: Oxford University Press.

The Economist (1997) 'World education league', 29 March, 25–7.

Elger, T. and Smith, C. (eds) (1994) *Global Japanization? The Transnational Transformation of the Labour Process*, London: Routledge.

Fruin, M. (1992) *The Japanese Enterprise System*, Oxford: Oxford University Press.

—— (1997) *Knowledge Works: Managing Intellectual Capital at Toshiba*, Oxford: Oxford University Press.

Hiramoto, A. (1995) 'Overseas Japanese plants under global strategies: TV transplants in Asia', in S. Frenkel and J. Harrod (eds), *Industrialization and Labor Relations: Contemporary Research in Seven Countries*, Ithaca, NY: ILR Press.

Kaufman, A., Merenda, M. and Wood, C. (1996) 'Corporate downsizing and the rise of "problem-solving" suppliers: the case of Hadco Corporation', *Industrial and Corporate Change*, 5, 723–59.

Kenney, M. (1998) 'Transplantation? Comparing Japanese television assembly plants in Japan and the US', in P. Adler, M. Fruin and J. Liker (eds), *Remade in America*, New York: Oxford University Press.

Kenney, M. and Florida, R. (1993) *Beyond Mass Production: The Japanese System and Its Transfer to the United States*, New York: Oxford University Press.

—— (1994) 'Japanese maquiladoras: production organization and global commodity chains', *World Development*, 22 (1), 27–44.

Kenney, M., Goe, W. R., Contreras, O., Romero, J. and Bustos, M. (1998) 'Learning factories or reproduction factories? Labor–management relations in the Japanese consumer electronics maquiladoras in Mexico', *Work and Occupations*.

Lowe, J., Morris, J. and Wilkinson, B. (1997) 'Hanchos, floats and team leaders: a comparative study of supervisors in Japan, Mexico and the UK, mimeo.

MacDuffie, J. (1995) 'Human resource bundles and manufacturing performance: organizational logic and flexible production systems in the world auto industry', *Industrial and Labor Relations Review*, 48 (2), 197–221.

Nomura, M. (1992) 'Japanese personnel management transferred', in S. Tokunaga, N. Altmann and H. Demes (eds), *Internationalization and Changing Corporate Strategies*, Munich: Iudicum Verlag, 117–32.

Nonaka, I. and Takeuchi, H. (1995) *The Knowledge-Creating Company*, Oxford: Oxford University Press.

Office of Technology Assessment (OTA) (1983) *International Competitiveness in Electronics*, Washington, DC: OTA.

Oliver, N. and Wilkinson, B. (1992) *The Japanization of British Industry*, Oxford: Blackwell.

Pascale, R. and Athos, A. (1982) *The Art of Japanese Management*, Harmondsworth: Penguin.

Powell, W., Koput, K. and Smith-Doerr, L. (1996) 'Interorganizational collaboration and the locus of innovation: networks of learning in biotechnology', *Administrative Science Quarterly*, **41** (1), 116–45.

Schonberger, R. (1986) *World Class Manufacturing*, New York: Free Press.

Scott, P. and Cockrill, A. (1997) 'Multiskilling in small- and medium-sized engineering firms: evidence from Wales and Germany', *International Journal of Human Resource Management*, **8** (6), 807–24.

Smith, C. and Meiksins, P. (1995) 'System, society and dominance effects in cross-national organisational analysis', *Work, Employment and Society*, **9** (2), 241–67.

Sugata, E. and Namekawa, T. (1969) 'Integrated circuits for television receivers', *IEEE Spectrum*, May, 64–74.

Womack, J., Jones, D. and Roos, D. (1990) *The Machine that Changed the World*, New York: Rawson Associates.

13 Towards an agenda for manufacturing renewal

Rick Delbridge and James Lowe

In the introduction to this book we identified certain themes that recur through discussion of the UK's relative decline in manufacturing and in appraisal of the current situation. In particular, there have been questions raised over the macro-economic policies of government, the quality of foreign direct investment, the availability of capital for investment and the role of financial institutions, the competence and vision of British management, and the education and skills of the workforce. However, as we have seen, some of our contributors are more sanguine than others about the future, at least in the short to medium term. Certainly the chapters here tell a story of transition, partial success and opportunity as well as one of ossification, defensiveness and failure. The future of UK manufacturing is not lost – but neither is it assured.

It is firmly our belief that fundamental reform is required if UK manufacturing is to look to the future with any great optimism. In this final chapter we identify briefly a number of issues and areas that we would like to see considered as part of a major and inclusive review of the UK's manufacturing sector and the options for renewal. As we have said in Chapter 1, we view government as the catalyst for, and facilitator of, this regeneration, and as will become clear in this chapter, we believe that the agenda for renewal must be wide-ranging, deep-seated, holistic and founded on institutional change. In particular, we advocate better *quality* of investment and education provision, closer collaboration between the state and the various institutions of business, greater regional awareness in economic policy, more extensive partnership between capital, industry and labour, and greater evidence of collective decision making reflecting local interests. The end goal is a competitive and innovative economy founded on manufacturing *and* services that offers the prospect of economic growth and prosperity. These ideas and ideals are not new, but we feel they are well worth repeating.

THE CASE FOR INSTITUTIONAL CHANGE

It is increasingly evident that an understanding of economic organization and national economies must proceed from a realization of multiple interacting factors. Institutional analysis broadens the partial perspectives provided by political science (emphasis on the state), economics (emphasis on markets) or anthropology (emphasis on culture and values) in considering the interaction of economic and political structures and incorporating several organizational dimensions and their interrelations (Orrù 1997a). Thus societal context and modes of economic action significantly affect the political sphere, which in turn affects the emergence of distinct economic structures. Advocates stress a concern with both structure and action (and their interrelation) and that 'institutional analysis is multilevel analysis' (Biggart 1997: 29); 'unidirectional causal explanations' of economic structures are abandoned, as 'the contextual, interactive production and reproduction of complex economic systems' is emphasized (Orrù 1997a: 298). Under institutional theory, modern industrial economies do not exist *apart* from the political system that supports them. This realization underpins our concern for a broad conception of UK manufacturing's future needs. It also emphasizes the significance of the various institutions involved in industry, and underscores that the key in embarking upon reform and renewal is their interrelationship.

From his comparative research into business networks in different countries, Orrù (1997a) argues that three major types of political structure – 'corporatist', 'statist' and 'segmental' – are identifiable. These political structures combine with different organizational patterns of economic action and each may be associated with a different 'capitalist typology' – 'alliance', 'dirigiste' and 'familial', respectively. Some of the characteristics of each typology are represented in Table 13.1.

Orrù makes clear that these typologies are abstractions of the distinctive features that characterize different capitalist economies, and we are not interested so much in how the current UK situation maps onto these typologies, but rather how the UK might learn from the 'general logic that guides social and economic action' within different contexts (Orrù 1997a: 310). It should be clear, for instance, that Orrù's 'alliance capitalism' has many of the attributes we would like to see in the UK. Our essential point is that the institutional analyses of Orrù and others indicate an agenda for change in recognizing the interconnectedness of institutions of business, finance, education, etc., and the potential role as facilitator for the state.

Table 13.1 Three typologies of capitalism

	Alliance	*Dirigiste*	*Familial*
Political structure	Corporatist	Statist	Segmental
Systematic relations	State with society	State above society	State outside society
State	Facilitative	Orchestrating	Weak
Institutional relations	Horizontal and vertical, collaborative	Vertical, hierarchical	Horizontal, fragmented
Industrial relations	Partnership	Strong management	Paternalistic

Source: Adapted from Orrù (1997a: 304–10).

CHANGE IN THE UK

Notions of alliance capitalism are commonly associated with Japan (Gerlach 1992) and also Germany (Orrù 1997b), and it is no surprise that a number of the contributors in this volume have considered the extent to which the UK might learn lessons from these two successful modern economies. Orrù's exposition of Japanese and German capitalism identifies a common overarching characteristic: 'institutional cooperation', that is, the formulation of economic strategies and the practice of production based on the emergence of collectively shared responsibilities (Orrù 1997b: 325). Moreover, this cooperation functions at three levels of analysis: industrial relations within firms; relations between institutions relevant to economic action; and between the state and the private sector. We now consider briefly some of the implications for change in the UK at each of these levels. We do not advocate attempts to become 'more like' the Japanese or Germans, but rather we recommend that such lessons as may be learned are considered in respect to the specifics of the UK context.

Employer–employee relations

While the nature of employment relations in Japan has been the subject of some debate (see, for example, Cole 1971; Gordon 1985; Kamata 1973), Orrù argues that 'cooperation within firms is significantly amplified and strengthened by the larger framework of cooperation among the major institutional actors in the capitalist economies of both Japan and Germany' (Orrù 1997b: 328). Certainly 'cooperative' or 'partnership' based trade unionism has been widely debated within a UK context in recent years, with proponents advocating a 'shared objective' between management and unions (Bacon and Storey 1996) and the Trades Union Congress itself advancing the case for social partnership. However, it should be noted that this position has been strongly criticized for, *inter alia*, weakening union autonomy and power, eroding members' capacity to challenge priorities, and underestimating employer antagonism to workplace trade unionism (see Kelly 1996). This debate reinforces the significance of the political and economic climate of workplace relations.

Institutional collaboration over industrial relations suggests a greater and more central role for individual trade unions and their national body, a move away from individualized bargaining relationships, and a greater onus on communication and collaboration between employer and employee representatives. However, as Taylor has correctly noted, the prospects for this in the UK are undermined by

> the absence of deeply rooted, strong and effective institutions ... either at national or perhaps even more importantly in local labour markets that can enable employers and trade unions to work together harmoniously for their mutual self-interest in a practical, stable and long-term way.
>
> (Taylor 1996: 212)

Therefore a substantial item for any agenda for renewal must be the consideration of bi- and tri-partite institutions that convene in support of discussion between employers and employees. The truncated remit of the bodies currently in existence, such as the Advisory, Conciliation and Arbitration Service (ACAS), reflects the need for further institutional change. The Low Pay Commission of trade union and employer representatives (and academic advisers) is a welcome development in encouraging common purpose between employer and employee. However, this must be one of a number of institutional changes in this direction. For instance, at firm level, the European works council Directive must be given the backing necessary to make it viable and meaningful. On the positive side, recent developments at the TUC and within key individual trade unions suggest a willingness to engage with this agenda for change (Monks 1993; Fisher 1997). The Government may find greater resistance among employers, and the role of bodies such as the Confederation of British Industry (CBI) and Engineering Employers' Federation may prove critical in addressing this.

Relations between institutions

Gerlach's (1992) view of alliance capitalism emphasizes the profound difference in the nature of corporate ownership and control between Japan and the US. Gerlach shares with Orrù the view that the financial system is closely related to other aspects of a national economic system. Specifically, Gerlach sees the financial system of Japan supporting greater stability and predictability of business relations, which, in turn, makes it possible for managers to focus on investment opportunities, product development and growth. This and Japan's system of corporate cross-ownership, argues Gerlach, contributes to the stable internal labour markets, lifetime employment commitments and long-term career orientations found in large Japanese corporations. In a similar vein, Hardach (1980) argued that the cartel-like level of cooperation between German firms allowed trade unions to expect better job security and helped to avoid 'destructive' competition.

Orrù (1997b) makes it clear that the banking system in both Japan and Germany plays a 'tutelary' role and cites the system as the cornerstone of the formation of long-term corporatist relations. Berggren and Nomura (1997: 17), in their analysis of the resilience and revival of corporate Japan, reflect that the 'role of equity in Japan's system of relational corporate governance is to act as a financial glue that holds various parties together in long-term trading relationships'. The other key point that they make is that capital is both relatively immobile and under the control of management under this system, whereas in a system of shareholder control such as that in the UK, capital is much more mobile and the fear of divestment is pervasive.

As we have reflected in Chapter 1, Britain's financial system has been debated endlessly and 'solutions' to the 'problem' are not straightforward. However, as Hutton (1995) makes clear in his sweeping critique of key UK institutions, fundamental change is required. In his version of the future the UK needs – 'stakeholder capitalism' – this change would include 'a republican-style central bank which understood that its role was to recast the financial system as a servant of business rather than its master' (ibid. 298) – sentiments with which we concur. Of equal importance is his concern that the bank's structure should meet the needs for regional development. Hutton's outline of regional banks echoes the concerns and meets the requirements of contributors in this book. Other considerations we share with Hutton are less readily tackled, but addressed they must be. They include lowering the cost and increasing the provision of capital, and addressing (and lowering) short-term shareholder expectations. The Labour Government has made some changes in the financial system and its regulation during its first months of office, but a more fundamental review is required.

Relations between the state and industry

It is perhaps with regard to education and training that the significance and responsibility of the state may be most clearly drawn. As Ashton and Green (1996) make clear in their examination of education and training, businesses aiming to maximize profits may not favour the 'high skills, high value-added' route, and hence the leading role of government is clear. Nonetheless, our institutional approach demonstrates the significance of other actors, something which Ashton and Green (1996: 177) also recognize: 'It will not . . . be possible to sustain policies for high levels of good quality training if a large proportion of employers is unwilling to cooperate with the policy.' Again it is the *relationship* between institutions which emerges as key.

Ashton and Green identify certain institutional requirements that policies for high skill formation must reinforce: an education system that at minimum inculcates the large majority of children with intermediate-level academic skills in core subjects; a system of regulatory practices which underpin the provision of good quality workplace training by employers; a means by which individuals of all levels and backgrounds have incentives to participate in skill formation; and an institutional means of allowing workplace skill formation to be complemented by periods of off-the-job training (ibid. 178). These are the objectives against which the UK's current systems must be judged and that evaluation must be at the heart of our agenda for renewal (to the benefit of the economy in general, not just manufacturing industry).

It is clear that considerable change will be necessary. However, there are individual examples that may offer some encouragement, and some guidance for wider developments: for instance, the recently established Waterton Technology Centre in Bridgend, South Wales. The Centre is a joint venture between Ford Motor Company, the Welsh Development Agency (WDA) and Mid and South Glamorgan Training and Enterprise Councils specifically designed to provide manufacturing training, particularly to local small and medium-sized enterprises. In addition, the Centre will provide training to unemployed people in the area. The Centre has been developed and funded jointly by Ford and the other institutions involved and is a prime example of state–industry collaboration in training provision.

According to Morgan (1997) we may be even more optimistic about the extent of institutional collaboration. In his recent paper on the 'learning region', Morgan considers recent EU regional policy measures and the WDA's innovation strategy in Wales and concludes that these are 'promoting the principle of innovating-by-networking and by exploring the potential of social capital (including trust and reciprocity) at the regional level' (ibid. 500). Morgan describes how the WDA has shifted from concentrating on attracting FDI in quantity to seeking to improve the quality and growth prospects of that investment through developing local supplier networks, the provision of 'aftercare' to new investors, the support of technology transfer, and by encouraging skills formation in initiatives such as that with Ford reported above. In his localized version of the state as facilitator, Morgan identifies the development agency as *'animateur'* in moves towards a 'learning economy in Wales'.

At a more general level there are also significant opportunities to promote collaboration to good purpose. For instance, in attempting to support and educate UK management as it attempts to innovate and develop industry we recommend a rather more decisive role for the Department of Trade and Industry in gathering intelligence on 'best practice' and in effectively determining the value of that information for UK manufacturing. The world is awash with 'big ideas' and various types of consultant ready to push them; we would like to see a rather more coordinated effort in distinguishing those practices that may offer tangible benefit *and* in determining what that benefit may be and how it might be attained. It is possible that this activity might be funded and conducted in partnership with the CBI, and it should involve academia, where much of the more innovative and critical research is conducted. A review body specifically tasked with researching and evaluating developments in manufacturing would go some way to improving the current situation where businesses are swamped with the latest fads and fashions and those most likely to be adopted are those supported by the biggest budgets and the loudest voices.

CONCLUDING REMARKS

In this final chapter we have reflected briefly upon future developments in support of UK manufacturing and the economy in general. As our contributors have made clear in various ways, UK manufacturers are in a period of transition, and we have added our voice to those who have looked to the state to catalyse and support this development. A failure to do so may leave the longer-term prospects of UK manufacturing extremely bleak. We have identified key issues that must be addressed as part of a holistic agenda for reform and renewal and stressed our belief in the need for institutional change – change in institutions and change in the functioning of institutions.

Specifically, we have advocated a review of the UK's institutions with particular regard to employment relations, interfirm and institutional collaboration, and an emphasis on the role of the state in facilitating change. We see the state's responsibility in establishing the context and infrastructure for economic growth, driven by an innovative and strong manufacturing sector. In our opinion, this will require careful attention to: the quality of education and investment ('more' is not necessarily 'good'); the role and provision of finance; the education and competence of management; and macroeconomic policies which support indigenous manufacturers.

Moves towards institutional collaboration are consistent with the espoused goals of Tony Blair prior to the election win of 1997. Blair outlined his (pre-election) 'vision for Britain' in his introduction to a recent publication entitled *What Needs to Change* (Radice 1996). The thrust of his argument, oft-repeated, is that of a 'strong and active community' in which the individual has both a stake and a set of responsibilities, that is, a 'stakeholder society'. With regard to the economy, Blair advocates 'a culture of respect, trust, cooperation and team-working' and he also recognizes the value of 'partnership' that stretches 'to cooperation between government and business in regional development, infrastructure, science and innovation and technology' (Blair 1996: 12). Worthy words; we await the necessary action.

REFERENCES

Ashton, D. and Green, F. (1996) *Education, Training and the Global Economy*, Cheltenham: Edward Elgar.

Bacon, N. and Storey, J. (1996) 'Individualism and collectivism and the changing role of trade unions', in P. Ackers, C. Smith and P. Smith (eds), *The New Workplace and Trade Unionism*, London: Routledge.

Berggren, C. and Nomura, M. (1997) *The Resilience of Corporate Japan*, London: Paul Chapman.

Biggart, N.W. (1997) 'Explaining Asian economic organization: toward a Weberian institutional perspective', in M. Orrù, N.W. Biggart and G. Hamilton (eds), *The Economic Organization of East Asian Capitalism*, Thousand Oaks, Calif.: Sage.

Blair, T. (1996) 'My vision for Britain', in G. Radice (ed.), *What Needs to Change*, London: HarperCollins.

Cole, R. (1971) *Japanese Blue Collar*, Berkeley: University of California Press.

Fisher, J. (1997) 'The challenge of change', *International Journal of Human Resource Management*, **8** (6), 797–806.

Gerlach, M. (1992) *Alliance Capitalism: The Social Organization of Japanese Business*, Berkeley: University of California Press.

Gordon, A. (1985) *The Evolution of Labor Relations: Heavy Industry, 1853–1945*, Boston: Harvard University Press.

Hardach, K. (1980) *The Political Economy of Germany in the Twentieth Century*, Berkeley: University of California Press.

Hutton, W. (1995) *The State We're In*, London: Jonathan Cape.

Kamata, S. (1973) *Japan in the Passing Lane*, New York: Random House.

Kelly, J. (1996) 'Union militancy and social partnership', in P. Ackers, C. Smith and P. Smith (eds), *The New Workplace and Trade Unionism*, London: Routledge.

Monks, J. (1993) 'A trade union view of WIRS3', *British Journal of Industrial Relations*, **31** (2), 227–33.

Morgan, K. (1997) 'The learning region: institutions, innovation and regional renewal', *Regional Studies*, **31** (5), 491–503.

Orrù, M. (1997a) 'The institutional analysis of capitalist economies', in M. Orrù,

N.W. Biggart and G. Hamilton (eds), *The Economic Organization of East Asian Capitalism*, Thousand Oaks, Calif.: Sage.

—— (1997b) 'Institutional cooperation in Japanese and German capitalism', in M. Orrù, N.W. Biggart and G. Hamilton (eds), *The Economic Organization of East Asian Capitalism*, Thousand Oaks, Calif.: Sage.

Radice, G. (ed.) (1996) *What Needs to Change*, London: HarperCollins.

Taylor, R. (1996) 'Democracy in the workplace', in G. Radice (ed.), *What Needs to Change*, London: HarperCollins.

Index